THE CURIOUS
ENLIGHTENMENT
OF
PROFESSOR CARITAT

A COMEDY OF IDEAS

BY

STEVEN LUKES

VERSO

London · New York

First published by Verso 1995
© Steven Lukes 1995
All rights reserved
Paperback edition published by Verso 1996

Verso
UK: 6 Meard Street, London W1V 3HR
USA: 180 Varick Street, New York NY 10014–4606

Verso is the imprint of New Left Books

ISBN 1–85984–073–6

British Library Cataloguing in Publication Data
A catalogue record for this book is available from the British Library

Library of Congress Cataloging-in-Publication Data
Lukes, Steven.
The curious enlightenment of Professor Caritat : a comedy of ideas
/ by Steven Lukes.
p. cm.
ISBN 1–85984–073–6 (hbk)
1. Political science—Philosophy—Fiction. 2. Political
scientists—Fiction. 3. Social values—Fiction. 4. Philosophers—Fiction.
I. Title.
PR6062.U43C87 1995
8238.914—dc20 95–31457
CIP

Typeset by Keystroke, Jacaranda Lodge, Wolverhampton
Printed and bound in Great Britain by
Biddles Ltd, Guildford and King's Lynn

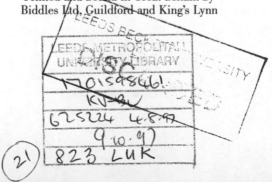

The Curious Enlightenment of

Professor Caritat

; L

Contents

The Curious Enlightenment of
Professor Caritat

·1·

Arrest

*T*he worst thing about Professor Nicholas Caritat's arrest was that they smashed his spectacles. It was the thing he most feared and least expected. They strengthened their control over reality by weakening his control over appearances.

Nicholas had been reading peacefully in his study, wrapped in the black velvet cloak lined and edged with silver-white fur that he always wore during his nightly debates with the thinkers of the Enlightenment. He had gone to bed late and was sleeping fitfully, uneasily aware that, judging by the fate of many of his friends, his days of freedom were numbered. Yet he had not gone into hiding. He had always avoided compromising political involvements. He was a scholar, a historian of ideas and a philosopher – and thus a person, he hoped, of no significance.

There was a sudden sharp rap at the front door. He sat up in bed and listened. There was certainly no hope of escape: they would have surrounded the building and would shoot him on sight. He could see flashing lights outside the window. There was more violent knocking on the door. He rose from his bed, put on his spectacles and silk dressing gown, and walked in measured steps in the darkness towards it along the

narrow carpeted hall. Before he could reach the door, he heard a loud crash and the splintering of the wood of the door frame. Another crash, the lock gave way and before him in the dim light of the hallway stood what were plainly four silent soldiers in plain clothes. They entered the flat and, without speaking, switched on the lights and marched forward to his study at the far end of the hall. Nicholas followed them into the room. Their boyish leader, the youngest of the lot, looked at him with menacing indifference.

'Go and get dressed!' he ordered.

Then came the gratuitous assault on his spectacles. As he turned to go into the bedroom, one of the soldiers, burly, sweating and snorting, came close to him, ripped them from his face, flung them on the carpet and crushed them with both feet. Nicholas found the crunching of the glass and the indistinct sight of the twisted frames peculiarly distressing.

Without them the world was a shimmering blur. He recalled James Thurber's encouraging thoughts about the strange pleasure of going blind. As one's eyesight fails, the role of the external world in fixing what one sees declines while that of interpretation increases, so you only have to be optimistic for women to be attractive, buildings to be elegant, the sun to shine. Yet there was scant reason to be optimistic about his present situation or, indeed, about the state of things in Militaria.

The latest coup had been the worst. The new Junta had unleashed a new terror campaign. Their declared aim was to exterminate the guerrilla movement the Visible Hand, whatever the cost. You never knew who was responsible for which outrage, guerrillas or government *agents provocateurs*. Until recently, the Hand had been divided into two factions: the Left Visible Hand and the Right Visible Hand. Invariably, each blamed the other for the killings and the bombings. All that seemed certain was that neither Hand knew what the other was doing, and that there was blood on both. Railway stations

were bombed; bank raids were daily occurrences. Two months ago the Central Police Station in the Capital had been set ablaze. The guerrillas were kidnapping businessmen; the military were killing lawyers. Thousands of people had 'disappeared', some of them thrown out of helicopters into the sea. Most of his friends and former students were in hiding. Grey Ford Falcon cars without number plates roamed the streets. Hit men and death squads ranged freely. Different elements of the army, the navy, the air force and the military police pursued different strategies and different enemies. In short, the various arms of the military were as out of control as the Hands of the guerrillas.

But now the new Junta's terror was more systematic and the guerrillas united. Both supporters and opponents of the regime were in danger. He had long feared that, if seized, his absence would go wholly unnoticed, especially in the outside world. His own academic contacts had long since faded, ever since his colleagues abroad had, out of solidarity, declared an academic boycott. As for his son and daughter, they were both unavailable to help. Marcus was in some guerrilla camp fighting for the Hand, and doubtless one of the reasons, or excuses, for his arrest. Eliza was also beyond reach, working underground as a human rights activist. She would certainly contact foreign governments and journalists once she heard of his seizure and campaign for his release, but, with so many arrests, disappearances and tortures, who would listen?

The order to get dressed came from the young, baby-faced officer with the commanding presence. His three oversized companions were clearly in awe of him and stood, twitching and quivering like nervous bulldogs with suppressed and menacing energy under the control of their Trainer. All four intruders followed Nicholas into his bedroom. As he slowly dressed in front of them, he decided to ask the Trainer the obvious question.

'Why are you arresting me?'

Without expression, the Trainer said, 'Why are we arresting you?'

Was this question an answer? Or was he repeating it the better to understand it? Or to make it clear to his bulldogs? Or was the answer a question? Was he to answer his own question? Or was the Trainer mocking the question? After all, why should he *not* be arrested? And why should there be a *reason* for his arrest? In Militaria, these days, the military did not need reasons.

He continued to dress, as elegantly as he could (the chance was not likely to recur soon) and waited to see what else might be said.

The Trainer replied, 'We are not arresting you.'

This was not much help. Of course they had no warrant for his arrest, but such warrants were meaningless, since the courts had ceased to function. He, Nicholas Caritat, was about to disappear into some black hole, unnoticed and unlamented, his life unfulfilled, his life's work incomplete.

His work had, so far, been what sustained him. The study of eighteenth-century ideas of progress had been, for three decades, the focus of his research and his teaching. He was obsessed with the study of past ideas about the future to the exclusion of a close interest in the present. What had it been like to have convincing reasons for hope about the future of mankind? Were any of these reasons still valid? Could one any longer have such hopes after all the horrors of this century? Were his favourite thinkers just purveyors of dangerous illusions that blinded true believers and armed cynical manipulators with rationalist dogmas that had, ever since the Jacobin Terror, wreaked havoc upon mankind? Optimism, in short, was both his subject and his object.

At his captors' insistence, Nicholas started to pack a travelling bag. He neatly folded his cloak, for future evening discussions with Diderot and d'Alembert, Leibniz and Kant, Helvétius and Voltaire, and the others. He also packed a

shaving bag, two pairs of trousers, a jacket, some shirts and ties and, optimistically, his empty spectacles case.

As the Trainer led him down the hall, Nicholas took a long last look into his study, the framework and cocoon of his daily researches and his nightly conversations, storing in his memory a final blurred image: the large deep red oriental carpet that almost covered the entire floor, the bay window overlooking his well-cultivated garden, the book-lined walls, his rolltop desk and cane rocking chair, the mahogany bookcase with its rows of mottled brown eighteenth-century volumes behind protective criss-crossed wire netting.

The Trainer pointed to the open doorway. Once outside, he heard the sound of three bulldogs, now unleashed, as they carried out the order to search and destroy his inner sanctum.

·2·

Prison

*T*he Trainer took hold of him by the shoulders and threw him into the back seat of a car and two more soldiers moved in on either side of him. As the Trainer joined the driver in the front and the car moved off, he was blindfolded and handcuffed. The blindfold was something of a relief, sparing him the strain of trying to see through a dark, myopic fog. The handcuffs marked the beginning of his physical confinement and were doubtless only a mild inconvenience in comparison with what he was about to suffer.

The car sped on for something like an hour. It finally stopped at what Nicholas imagined to be a military prison. He could hear muffled voices and clanking doors and even, though he could not be sure, a distant cry of pain, or was it despair, or anger? He was hustled out of the car and pushed down two flights of stone steps and then along a long passage. Then, without warning, he was thrust into what was obviously a cell. The door slammed closed with a metallic clang that echoed down the corridor as the clumping of footsteps receded. Nicholas sat in total darkness and silence on a hard, narrow bunk with his hands between his knees. With every movement the handcuffs became tighter and his claustrophobia more intense. He had read of this moment in countless novels

and prison memoirs but never imagined its chilling sense of finality or that he might himself experience it. No longer able to protect himself from immediate physical danger, he thought of poor Condorcet, the finest and the noblest philosopher of the Enlightenment, captured and imprisoned while on the run from the Revolutionary Terror, disguised as a worker on his own estate. No longer the Marquis Jean-Marie-Antoine-Nicolas Caritat de Condorcet, he died two days later in prison as plain 'Pierre Simon'. Had he really died from 'natural causes' or had he taken poison from his aristocrat's ring?

Suddenly the door clanked open, and his handcuffs were brusquely removed and his blindfold ripped off. As his eyes adjusted to the thin electric light, he could see that he had joined the Prisoners of Conscience club.

For a crazy moment, it even occurred to him to thank the remover of his blindfold and handcuffs. A closer look instantly dissuaded him from such misplaced courtesy, for he could see that the person he would have thanked was exceptionally unpleasant to behold. His jailer bore the standard marks of villainy – a tattoo on the arm, a scar on the cheek, a leer on the lips and a bald bullet head – and was clearly a specialist in intimidation. Brandishing a pistol near Nicholas's face, he set forth the basic rules of the establishment: no reading, no writing, no talking.

What about thinking? the scholar wanted to ask, but then thought better of it.

'You're some kind of a professor, aren't you?' said Bullet Head. He spat out the words in a rough, loud, hoarse voice, as though describing something truly nauseating. 'Well, don't think you can outsmart us!' he bellowed, slamming the cell door behind him.

Now, Nicholas realized, it was not only possible to think, it was necessary. Two lines of thought stretched indefinitely before him. One concerned the Great Question: how to conceive the future of Humankind? The other was no less urgent: how to preserve the future of Nicholas Caritat?

He started to plot these two itineraries of reflection. Yet, as he did so, he was overcome by an overwhelming feeling of loneliness. He had lost most of the social relations that had made him a person. He was a displaced unperson, a disengaged particle, a moleculeless atom. Not only had the military terror robbed him of the sustaining company and comfort of friends and colleagues, it had also split apart the protective nucleus of his family, whose bonds had become all the tighter after his wife Susanna's death in childbirth. All of them, Susanna, Marcus, Eliza and Nicholas himself, had always tried to be reasonable, and all had reasonably insisted that they knew what was reasonable in the most unreasonable of situations.

When Susanna died, because of medical neglect in a hospital against which all complaints were unavailing, the arbitrariness and terrorism of the regime were still at an early stage. Nicholas still often visualized her pallid, troubled, tight-lipped face, her soft brown eyes admonishing him for his scholarly escapism, her tiny, tense body always elegantly clothed with a shawl round her shoulders. It was her fierce passions, and indeed their very ferocity, that had first drawn him to her: for painting, music, literature, friends, travel, having and enjoying children. Yet even before Eliza's birth the darkening political situation had begun to make intimidation and insecurity a reality in their lives, and her passions had coalesced into one overriding superpassion: that of caring for her own, like an anxious bird cowering over her nest. By the time of her death her reason had become the slave of that passion. She would do anything that would protect them from the threatening world of military policemen, informers and suspect friends. For Susanna to be reasonable was to be prudent.

For Marcus to be reasonable was to solve problems. From his earliest years he had exhibited a marked impatience with the world's complexities. If a problem looked soluble, he would quickly seize its essentials; if it did not, he would avoid

or ignore it. As a child, he loved to take things apart to repair them, but he always found social relations more baffling and therefore tended to shun them. Throughout his adolescence, he was on the lookout for a map that might reduce the world's complexity to some manageable order and, after the briefest of temptations, decided that religion did not offer it. From that experience and a summary perusal of the alternatives, he soon concluded that the point of religion was to make difficult questions seem impossible by offering unintelligible or paradoxical or contradictory mysteries instead of explanations, objects of faith instead of reasons for belief. Marcus hated mysteries, which, being neither true nor false, did not even qualify as illusions, which were at least false. Nicholas recalled his fond pride at his son's ruthless rationalism – at how, when a schoolboy, Marcus, tall and lanky with shiny black hair and his deep, assured voice, would declaim over the family lunch-table against the exploitation of popular credulity by the pliant priests who served the military regime. Yet his recollection was rueful, for, on going to university, Marcus had fallen into the grip of the Hand, a decision doubt-less responsible for Nicholas's present captivity.

For Eliza to be reasonable was to live by principles, and by one principle in particular: that to use people was to misuse them, that no-one should be treated as a means to someone else's end or to serve some larger social purpose. Her determination so to live did not derive from reading Kant or any other philosopher but from direct sympathy, observation and experience. Petite and pale like Susanna, she had also inherited all her mother's passionate intensity, which she combined with her brother's bold, indeed reckless, assertiveness and with Nicholas's compulsive urge to envisage how the world could be in the absence of the evils that disfigured it. But unlike her father, she sought to realize that vision immediately, in the here and now, by focusing on and fighting against the most glaring of those evils. She never criticized Marcus's joining the Hand, though she was worried. 'Beware,' she warned him,

'the Hand manipulates.' She also disliked all his Handist talk of 'social forces' and 'structures' and 'mechanisms'. For her, every individual victim of oppression had an immediate claim on her attention and energies; she became a self-generating dynamo for defending the persecuted. She organized the mothers of those who had 'disappeared', arranged escapes for those in danger and cultivated international contacts to publicize individual cases. As the situation in Militaria worsened, Eliza recognized how vulnerable she was and disappeared underground to continue her work.

His domestic world had thus suddenly fallen apart without any proper farewells or settling of accounts. Marcus, now taken in Hand, had disappeared and was in training in one of their camps and Eliza had left in secret with a hastily packed suitcase vowing to continue her work unobserved.

Had he, Nicholas, been reasonable? Neither of his children had really thought so, though Eliza had been the more sympathetic. They both saw him as an escapist, shutting his eyes to the horrors and dangers around him. 'How,' they agreed, 'can you have your ear to the ground with your nose in a book?' Marcus felt genuinely sorry for him, believing his father to be unable or unwilling to grasp either the Hand or its analysis of the situation in Militaria. For Eliza, whose absence Nicholas felt most keenly, he was just an abstracted thinker, conversing with the past rather than acting in the present. Yet his objective was to figure out what was reasonable, something which could not be achieved without consulting others with the same goal. What was it reasonable to hope for? On what principles could a reasonable social order be built? How could trying to answer such questions not be reasonable?

After what must have been several hours, Bullet Head returned, flinging open the door of his cell and waving his pistol at his face.

'On your feet, Professor,' he shouted. 'They want you.'

Pushing him out of the cell into the dimly lit corridor

outside, Bullet Head frogmarched him past a dozen or so cells, all locked, until they reached the open doorway of what looked like a large, square office with bare white walls, in which there was even less light than in the corridor. A single dim bulb hung from the high ceiling. Peering hard, Nicholas could just discern, in the far corners of the room, two figures seated at metal desks, each with a reading lamp turned downwards to illuminate his papers. Otherwise the office seemed empty, like a spartan stage set before the lights go up. Bullet Head departed.

'You can sit down,' said the figure on the left, gesturing to a lone wooden chair in the middle of the room.

His two interrogators seemed strangely contextless and featureless. His poor vision in the low light gave them a cipherlike quality, like two characters in a Beckett play who were there to express the bleak hopelessness of the Human Predicament.

'We are sorry about what happened to your glasses,' said One, on the left, with evident insincerity. 'That was unfortunate. We trust that you have not been unduly inconvenienced.'

Unduly inconvenienced! How was he supposed to respond to this? 'Oh, that's alright – these things do happen'? 'Never mind, I'll manage without them'? The lack of his spectacles seemed to be the only inconvenience it was thought worth mentioning. He said nothing.

'But,' One continued, 'if you cooperate with us, your inconvenience may be short-lived.'

Two, on the right, then leaned forward and addressed him in a tone that seemed to simulate respect.

'Your cooperation, Professor Caritat, would be of inestimable value to your country. Militaria calls on your loyalty and your help in these dark and troubled times.'

He resolved to ask once more the question to which he still sought an answer.

'Why,' he asked Two, 'have you arrested me?'

'Why have we arrested you?' was Two's parrotlike reply. 'We have not arrested you.'

'Why then am I here?' he persisted.

'Professor Caritat,' said Two, impatiently emphasizing the patience he was extending, 'you are a very intelligent man. You are rightly celebrated in Militaria for your intelligence. You have, until now, been paid to think – yet you don't seem to understand the importance of your thoughts.'

'But,' he protested, 'I am a scholar of the Enlightenment.'

'The Enlightenment!' snapped Two. 'There is no light without fire. We are at war, Professor. Our society is being undermined by Optimism. You have been giving aid and comfort to our nation's enemies.'

'I am a scholar,' he repeated, 'a scholar, not (he uttered the word with distaste) an ideologist.'

One reentered the discussion. 'Your scholarship (he mimicked the expression of revulsion) is certainly appreciated by the Visible Hand. Your writings have been found in their training camps. You are included in their reading lists.'

'Unlike you, Professor,' added Two, 'they – and we – take your ideas seriously.'

'What do you want from me?' he asked.

'In the first place,' One promptly replied, 'we know that you have been taking part in meetings at night with Optimistic elements. We want their names. All of them. Second, we want a signed statement from you renouncing Optimism and denouncing all those who continue to entertain it. Third, we want a signed declaration of intent never again to expound Optimistic ideas or cooperate with Optimistic elements.'

'What,' Nicholas asked cautiously, 'if I were to do these things?' It might, he thought, be best to encourage them to believe in his eventual compliance.

'We cannot, of course, offer you any hope,' answered Two.

'But we would be able to replace your spectacles,' said One.

They want me to betray the Enlightenment for a pair of spectacles, he thought to himself. He said nothing, letting some minutes pass. One and Two waited without speaking. One

tapped his pen on the surface of his desk. The lengthening silence began to grow oppressive.

One, obviously frustrated, decided to conclude their discussion for the time being. 'Why don't you give it some thought in your luxurious accommodation?' He pushed a button and Bullet Head instantly reappeared, at the ready to march him back to his cell.

It was now time for further indignities. Bullet Head handed Nicholas a roll of rough, grey toilet paper and pointed to a pail in the corner. He then barked at him to undress and put on prison clothes: an ill-fitting shirt of rough cloth and baggy trousers. (His travelling bag was nowhere to be seen.) A bowl of cold water, a razor, a tiny piece of soap and a grimy towel were provided for his ablutions. Then Bullet Head brought him a meal of appropriate grimness – half-stale bread but no butter, tasteless mashed potatoes, leathery meat, hard cheese and a bottle of water – after which, for the rest of his first day, he was left alone in the small, windowless cell, lit by a single bulb and smelling oppressively of urine, to contemplate his, and Humanity's, future.

He began to lose track of the hours as they passed. With the breaking of his spectacles, his captors had largely removed his control of space. Now, he realized, they were in charge of his faltering perception of time. A grim supper thus came as something of a relief, marking the approaching end of his first day of imprisonment.

After supper, he debated with Immanuel Kant the question, 'What is Enlightenment?'

'Enlightenment,' said Kant, with uncharacteristic directness, 'is thinking for oneself. It is man's emergence from his self-incurred immaturity. The motto of enlightenment is: Have the courage to use your own understanding!'

'That's all very well,' said Nicholas, 'but it's not always so easy . . . '

'Of course it isn't *easy*!' said Kant, rather irritably. 'Laziness and cowardice are the reasons why so many people gladly

remain immature for life. It is so convenient to be immature! If I have a book to provide understanding for me, a spiritual adviser to have a conscience for me, a doctor to judge my diet for me, and so on, I needn't make any efforts at all. I needn't think, so long as I can pay. Others will be only too glad to take the tiresome job over from me.'

'Your ideals are noble,' observed Nicholas, 'but are they within human reach? You offer us a vision of enlightened citizens living in freedom under the rule of law in republics united in a federation committed to perpetual peace. But perhaps Rousseau was right. Perhaps such an ideal is fit only for angels.'

'I know Rousseau says that,' replied Kant, 'but he is too pessimistic. He doesn't see that a well-designed constitution can compensate for human frailties. He thinks that men, with their self-seeking inclinations, would be incapable of adhering to a constitution of so sublime a nature. But, in fact, nature comes to the aid of the universal and rational human will, so admirable in itself but so impotent in practice, and makes use of precisely those self-seeking inclinations in order to do so. All that is needed is for men to create a good organization for the state, a task which is well within their capability, and to arrange it in such a way that their self-seeking energies are opposed to one another, each thereby neutralizing or cancelling out the destructive effects of the rest. The result is the same as if man's selfish tendencies were non-existent, so that man, even if he is not morally good in himself, is nevertheless compelled to be a good citizen. It may sound difficult, but the problem of setting up a state can be solved by a nation of devils, as long as they possess understanding. Even for such devils, justice and peace are inescapable.'

'Even in Militaria?'

'Above all in Militaria. Militaria plays a crucial role in bringing them to fruition. Wars, tense and unremitting military preparations, and the resulting distress which every state must

eventually feel within itself, even in the midst of peace – these are the means by which nature drives nations to make initially imperfect attempts, but finally, after many devastations, upheavals and even complete inner exhaustion of their powers, to take a step which reason would have suggested to them without so many sad experiences – that of abandoning a lawless state of savagery and entering a federation of peoples.'

'But,' Nicholas protested, 'some would say that since attaining such a goal looks so unrealistic, proclaiming it can only be discouraging, that it would be better to set one's sights on feasible objectives – tackling specific injustices, limiting wars, negotiating compromises . . . '

'Justice and peace are uncompromising as well as inescapable,' declared Kant. 'Notice that the Militarian tyrants also claim to act in their name. A conception of the best possible world underlies every attempt – whether genuine or hypocritical – to bring about a better one.'

'Well, perhaps you are right,' conceded Nicholas, and, much encouraged, wrapped in a grey blanket on his hard bunk bed, he fell into a deep, buoyant sleep.

·3·

The Eye Test

Early next morning, Bullet Head delivered Nicholas to One and Two, who were sitting at their desks with their reading lamps on.

'Well?' asked Two expectantly. 'Have you decided to come to Militaria's aid in its time of need?'

He decided to be enigmatic without being discouraging.

'I have,' he said truthfully, 'been debating with myself.' He then fell silent.

'We have also been debating with ourselves,' said One after a few minutes' unproductive silence, 'and we have decided to offer you some encouragement, Professor Caritat. We are going to replace your spectacles.'

'Then,' added Two, 'we are sure you will see things our way.'

'Let us hope so,' he said, without thinking. It was not a very clever reply and he regretted it as Bullet Head dragged him back to his cell, where, he noticed with considerable relief, his pail had been emptied.

It was not long before the morning's encounter bore fruit. After about an hour, his cell door was opened by an officer in smart military uniform, to whom Nicholas took an almost instant dislike. The young man was short and wiry with a

freckled face and glassy eyes and an intrusively familiar gaze. The officer reminded him of something he could not identify but felt sure was not congenial.

'Good morning, my dear Professor Caritat,' said the officer in an unexpectedly familiar voice.

'Good morning,' he replied with some coldness.

'We have heard that you are not in a cooperative frame of mind,' said the officer, slowly and searchingly. Nicholas kept quiet.

'I am sure you have considered the matter with your usual scrupulousness. Come along. Your eyes are to be tested.'

He followed the officer along the corridor in the opposite direction to his previous outings. They entered another office similar to the Interrogation Room but better lit. Seated at a table in the centre of the room was a nervous-looking young man in a white coat with an abundance of ginger hair and a moustache. On the table were several oblong wooden boxes and various optical instruments. Facing Nicholas at the far end of the room was a large white card on which various letters were printed in rows, descending in size from top to bottom.

The officer introduced the optician in the white coat, who looked like a frightened squirrel, ready to shin up one of the pipes on the wall at the slightest interruption. Nicholas nodded in greeting and sat down beside him facing the white card. The officer stood behind them as if chaperoning the test.

'Please tell us what you can see,' said the optician.

He read the top line: 'U . . . R . . . '

The next line was: 'O . . . U . . . R . . . '

'Yes,' said the optician encouragingly.

The next line was smaller but still easy: 'O . . . N . . . L . . . Y . . . '

'Go on,' said the optician eagerly.

The next line down cost some effort, but he managed to read it after some hesitation: 'H . . . O . . . P . . . E . . . '

Odd, he thought, that these letters should make words; they

usually don't. Then it struck him that the whole card, so far, made sense: 'You are our only hope.' The optician was sending him a message.

Below 'HOPE' was a red line below which were three more lines in increasingly smaller print that he could not make out.

'Try the next line,' said the optician, with growing excitement, urging him on.

'I can't see any more,' he said.

The optician placed a pair of heavy spectacle frames on Nicholas's nose and inserted two lenses from one of the boxes. His blurred vision became more blurred and all the letters on the card became indistinct.

'Worse,' he said.

The optician reached for another pair of lenses. These improved matters somewhat but not much. Another pair was inserted and the next line suddenly became legible:

'D . . . E . . . F . . . E . . . N . . . D . . . ' He read it out.

By now the optician was trembling with fear.

'I can't manage the next one.' The letters were dancing about like small black fish in a murky aquarium.

The optician inserted the next pair of lenses. Straining, he slowly read out the next row of letters:

'O . . . P . . . T . . . I . . . C . . . I . . . A . . . N . . . S . . . '

Opticians? he thought. Are they in trouble? How can I defend them? Why don't they defend me?

The optician was clearly upset.

'Move, Professor,' he shouted. 'Move a bit closer!'

Nicholas did as he was told and moved his chair forward. At last the line held steady and he could read it more clearly. It read: 'O . . . P . . . T . . . I . . . M . . . I . . . S . . . M . . . '

Moving further forward, he then read the last line: 'T . . . H . . . E . . . H . . . A . . . N . . . D . . . '

As he read out the last line, the optician rushed forward and flipped the white card over to reveal a chart of jumbled letters that did not make words.

All was now clear. The optician and the young officer were

both obviously working for the guerrillas and at that very moment taking the risk of telling him so.

'These lenses are the best I can do,' said the optician, offering to take the frame with the lenses off his nose, but Nicholas gestured to him that he wished to wear them a little longer. He turned to look at the young officer, whom he could now see clearly for the first time. With a sudden shock of recognition, he realized that he was a former student of his at the University named Justin, a political activist in the days of student militancy and a mentor and friend to Marcus and Eliza. He had been a leading member of the more extreme wing of the guerrilla resistance movement. It was Justin, Nicholas had always suspected, who had persuaded Marcus to join the Hand and to write off – with undisguised contempt – all scholarly pursuits as mere intellectual escapism. Justin offered Marcus and Eliza the image of a philosopher out to change, not just interpret, the world. He taught them to unlearn some of the basic tenets of Nicholas's beliefs: that partisanship should not predetermine analysis, that simple dichotomies should be viewed with caution, that there were different, nonconvergent ways of being reasonable, that the ideas of one's bitterest enemies were worth taking seriously and that spending time interpreting world-transforming ideas was worthwhile. Their encounters had always been frosty. Whenever they had met, Nicholas and Justin had never seen eye to eye.

The young man, Nicholas recalled, had been one of those militants who treat ideas as instruments, and usually as weapons. His only interest in his academic work, it seemed, had been to find material that could be effective in speeches and as slogans. He had once advised Justin to pursue dema-gogy rather than pedagogy, but it now appeared that his former student had chosen a different and unexpected career.

'I never would have thought of you as a budding army officer,' he observed drily.

'Entryism,' explained Justin. 'Join them to beat them.'

A decidedly Optimistic view, Nicholas thought.

'We mustn't waste time,' said Justin in short, rapid whispers. 'We may be disturbed at any moment. We are planning your escape. I will explain the details to you tomorrow when I return with your new spectacles. Meanwhile, behave as before. Now, hand me the frame and lenses.'

Clarity returned to blur, but Nicholas's spirits lifted and he whistled to himself as Justin returned him to his cell. Justin, as he departed, raised his left hand.

·4·

Preparations

*J*ustin arrived early the next morning. He entered the cell, sat down next to Nicholas on the bunk bed and spoke, rapidly in an uncharacteristically low voice.

'You are to be provided with false papers. Your assumed name will be Dr Pangloss. The whole operation is code-named "Helping Hand".'

'Why,' Nicholas asked, 'are you doing this for me? Why is the Hand helping me?'

'Let me be candid with you,' replied Justin. 'We are not helping you. You are to help us. The Hand, Professor Caritat, is not a charity organization. We are sending you to another country. Your mission is to find grounds for Optimism – to find a way of life that will give our people hope. If you should fail to find what we seek in one country, you must then move on to another and then another until your mission is completed. We are relying on you. You are our only hope.'

'But surely,' he protested, 'almost any way of life is preferable to that of Militaria?'

'You say so and so do I,' said Justin, 'but people come to accept the status quo because they have lost faith in the possibility of anything better. They don't believe in what we stand for and we don't know what that is. What alternative

can we offer and why would it be better? For what cause can we fight and demand the necessary sacrifices? We know what we are against, but what are we for?'

This was indeed candid speaking. He began to think better of Justin. Justin seemed to be expressing uncharacteristic uncertainty about what to believe. Perhaps Nicholas had misjudged the Hand. Or had he? Were they looking for arguments that could convince or rhetoric that would persuade? Was this a search for a better world or the most effective illusion of one?

'We want you,' concluded Justin, 'to find us the best possible world.'

'Why,' asked Nicholas, 'have you chosen me?'

Justin's tone hardened. 'Because,' he replied, 'you are responsible for our Optimism, yet you never took your responsibility seriously. You gave us hope, but you never thought it part of your task to see whether that hope was justified. You have always been curious about ideas, excited by them, seduced. When you lectured, you made them come alive for us as well. You taught us that the history of ideas can be a great adventure.'

Strange, thought Nicholas, I never had the impression of teaching Justin anything. How mistaken one can be!

'Now,' Justin continued, 'we are proposing to send you on a great adventure. You used to lecture to us on the thinkers of the Enlightenment and their critics, on their ideas of how society might be, on their imagined worlds. We need to know what it means to live by the former and in the latter. We need you, Professor Caritat, to complete our education. We are relying on you to report to us on how your cherished ideas have turned out in reality. What is left? We need to know what we can hope for.'

'Where are you proposing to send me?' he asked.

'We cannot reveal this to you in advance,' said Justin, 'but you must be ready at any moment to flee.' Justin's tone changed once more as he issued Nicholas his orders. He now sounded commanding, even accusatory. 'We are expecting

you to come out of your academic closet, Professor, to climb off your scholarly fence. I expect to receive regular Progress Reports from you once your travels are under way. You will send them to an address in a friendly country and they will reach me safely. When the time comes for your escape, I shall indicate it to you in the appropriate way (he raised a hand) and you will be taken to the airport. Be vigilant and remain obdurate.'

'Thank you,' Nicholas replied rather automatically.

'Thanks are not in order,' said Justin, preparing to leave.

'May I ask you one last question?' Nicholas asked. 'Can you give me any news of Marcus or Eliza?' Maybe, he thought, Marcus shared Justin's doubts and questionings. He found the thought consoling.

'Marcus,' said Justin, 'is in good hands. He is doing well and he knows of your mission. We will keep him fully informed of your progress and I will personally show him your reports. Eliza is doing good works and is proving helpful to the movement. Whether she likes it or not, she too is in safe hands.'

'Thank you,' said Nicholas once more. Without saying a word, Justin handed him a spectacles case and left.

Nicholas put on his new glasses. Details of his immediate environment that had hitherto eluded him became visible: the unswept floor, dirty sheets, grimy walls, the rusty door with a spyhole from the other side. But he was not disheartened. Lunch seemed less inedible and his new spectacles seemed to have a curiously pinkish tinge.

·5·

Resistance

I n the afternoon, Bullet Head took him once more to the Interrogation Room. The light was brighter and with his new spectacles he could now see One and Two more clearly. Both were in uniform and, he estimated, in their mid fifties, but they displayed very different attitudes towards him. One, who was pale and thin lipped, totally ignored him as he entered. His fixed, concentrated expression conveyed an impression of impersonal, businesslike efficiency, sifting through documents and making notes. Two, by contrast, had an open, expressive face, though the expression was continually changing; his eyes were constantly upon him, observing him closely, and he wore a smile that hovered between encouragement and hostility. One wore dark glasses; Two held his pair in his right hand, waving them at Nicholas, indicating that he should be seated.

'Well now,' Two began encouragingly. 'I see you have your new glasses. So, where have we got to?'

'Let us begin with names,' interposed One briskly, his pen poised.

'I'm very bad at names,' Nicholas said.

Two's smile switched instantly into the hostile mode. He put on his dark glasses.

'Are you prepared to renounce Optimism and denounce all Optimists?' asked One sharply.

'I'm no good at renouncing,' he said, 'or denouncing.'

'Are you willing to swear never again to entertain Optimistic ideas in your mind and Optimistic elements in your home?' One continued relentlessly.

'I don't swear,' he replied, trying to seem cooperative without actually cooperating.

Two continued his hostility. 'You don't seem to realize, Caritat (he had just been deprived, he realized, of his academic post), the nature of the crisis we are in. Optimism is opposed to all that we in Militaria stand for and we shall destroy it root and branch. If you support it – and that includes failing to oppose it – we shall destroy you. This is your moment of decision, Caritat. Are you for us or against us?' Nicholas said nothing.

Two, removing his spectacles once more, switched to encouragement: 'What we offer you is far more substantial than hope. We offer dignity, honour, pride, the satisfaction of serving and saving your country.'

'We can also offer you,' added One, 'a permanent salary at the highest level, a chauffeur-driven limousine at your constant disposal and (he paused for effect) your own television programme.'

'You are a thinker of stature and reputation,' said Two. 'You could be our Cultural Adviser, even perhaps one day our Minister of Culture. You could become the Intellectual Leader of Militaria.'

'You could,' said One, 'replace Dr Orville Globulus.'

Globulus! Nicholas cringed in disgust. Globulus and he had been students together at the University. People always used to say how much they resembled each other in appearance. Yet, except for superficial similarities, they could not have been more unlike. Globulus was an arch-opportunist, superficial to the core, a psychiatrist who pretended to be a 'philosopher', a man who had once flirted with Handism but was now the government's most loyal and – it seemed – trusted

apologist and ideologist. He appeared nightly on television, propounding oily defences of all the current regime wanted defended and fierce condemnations of all it wanted condemned. His psychiatric specialty had been paranoia. His present role, and one in which he excelled, was to propagate it. Enemies ringed and infested Globulus's world.

'The best thing,' concluded Two, 'given your present short-sightedness, would be for us to arrange a meeting between you and Dr Globulus. In the meantime, Caritat, I suggest that you continue to do what you used to be paid to do: Think.'

The bell rang and Nicholas again returned to his cell with an unusually hostile Bullet Head, who brought him a tasteless supper but left the dirty pail to spoil his appetite. That night Nicholas sought to cheer himself up by discussing vanity and its temptations with Dr Johnson and Alexander Pope.

Dr Johnson suggested to him an unfamiliar prospect of the scholarly life, whose comforts and protections he had hitherto taken so much for granted, saying,

> Deign on the passing world to turn thine eyes,
> And pause awhile from letters to be wise;
> There mark what ills the scholar's life assail.
> Toil, envy, want, the patron, and the jail.

Was the recognition that Two had offered worth considering? It certainly wouldn't be recognition of his scholarly merits, as Johnson went on to point out:

> See nations slowly wise, and meanly just,
> To buried merit raise the tardy bust.

But Pope was even more dismissive of the very idea of being tempted by Two's suggestions. 'What's fame?' he asked, 'that fancy'd life in others' breath,

> A thing beyond us ev'n before our death, . . .
> All that we feel of it begins and ends
> In the small circle of our foes or friends.

They were both right. As he dropped off to sleep, he felt fortified for his encounter with Globulus, to which he was not looking forward.

·6·

Confrontations

After breakfast the next morning, there was an un-
expected knock on his cell door.

'Come in!' he said loudly, as though welcoming a
visitor to his office at the University.

The metal door opened slowly and Bullet Head ushered in
a visitor, to whom he showed a hitherto unseen deference,
removing the pail but not, unfortunately, its odour. He closed
the door and departed. The visitor was a clergyman, dressed
in black, priestly garb, with his hat in his hand. He was tall,
young and courteous, and his long, thin, mournful, bearded
face was dominated by the earnest, unblinking blue eyes of a
believer.

'I hope you will permit me to visit you, Professor Caritat,'
said the priest in a low, deep baritone voice. 'I know you are
not a particular friend of religion or religious philosophy, but
I thought that a conversation between us might be of some
use.'

To whom? Nicholas wondered. The priest was right: he was
religiously unmusical. Moreover, with very few exceptions, the
Church had for a long time deployed its forces and teachings
in Militaria in unambiguously ambiguous support of the various
Juntas.

'It is true,' Nicholas observed drily, 'that I prefer clarity to consolation.'

The priest sat down at the end of his bed. 'It is, if I may say so, you, not I, who are blinded by faith,' he said. 'I speak of your faith that the world is hospitable to human purposes. You believe that nature and human institutions are governed by principles that human beings can understand. You believe that human beings, enlightened by that understanding, can progressively predict and control their natural and social environment. And what is your vision of the lives they will lead? They will, you imagine, dispose of their lives as they choose. They will come to regard war as the most dreadful of scourges, the most terrible of crimes. They will no longer be inspired by murderous contempt for persons of another colour or creed. They will live by freely contracted habits that are inspired by nature and acknowledged by reason. They will make laws and devise institutions that identify the interests of each with those of all, rendering the path of virtue no longer arduous. And they will recognize that the natural rights of women are exactly the same as those of men and will no longer tolerate the tyranny of calmly depriving half the human race of its rights to citizenship.

'They will, you suppose, attain what you like to call real equality, where differences in enlightenment or talent can no longer raise a barrier between persons who understand each other's feelings, ideas and language. Some may wish to be taught by others but, to do so, they will have no need to be controlled by them. They may wish to confide the care of government to the more able, but they will not be compelled to yield them absolute power in a spirit of blind confidence.

'Believing all this, it is, I fear, you, Professor, not I, who seek and find consolation. You lament the errors, the crimes, the injustices which still pollute the earth, but you are consoled by your vision of the human race, at last released from the empire of fate and from the enemies of its progress, advancing

with a firm and sure step along the path of truth, virtue and happiness. That is your credo.'

Nicholas was struck by the deftness of this statement of his beliefs. But he was also struck by the extraordinary fact that the priest had summed them up in the very words of Condorcet, written while in hiding from the Terror shortly before his tragic death. Nicholas felt inclined to qualify and develop what had been said, in a number of respects. But, desiring to hear what the priest had come to say, he remained silent.

'Your faith and your hope, Professor Caritat,' said the priest, 'attest to your charity. But I fear they are all misplaced. You have faith in, hope for and charity towards a human nature that does not merit them. For how can you deny that there is no evil of which human beings are not capable, that they are miserable, utterly contemptible creatures for whom no sacrifice, and certainly not a self-sacrifice on your part in the name of your beloved Enlightenment, is worthwhile?'

Nicholas was astonished by these words. This was not the way that priests usually spoke.

'I agree, of course,' he finally replied, 'that we now know that human beings can sink to depths unimaginable to even the most feverish eighteenth-century imagination. But what are we supposed to do in the light of this knowledge? Watch them sink yet further into the filth and slime? Turn our backs and flee to pools of safety? Or should we try to raise them up, individually and collectively, through upbringing, through public instruction, through building institutions, making constitutions . . .'

'The articles of your faith,' continued the priest, 'were written by people lost in illusions. They believed the conditions of human life to be reformable or transformable: their zeal prevented them from seeing that individual human beings are irredeemable and their failings and failures irremediable. The domain of human action is entirely governed by two great principles: Perversity and Futility. The first guarantees

that good intentions pave the road to Hell, that attempts to make this world better are certain only to make it worse. The second ensures that all roads marked "Progress" or "Reform" lead nowhere and run into the sand. Any map that indicates otherwise is not a map of this world.'

'Your certainty is suspect,' Nicholas interposed. 'You presumably base it on the blackest interpretation of the bleakest evidence. And your picture of the future has no indefinite lines. It is fixed, predetermined, unalterable. But how do you know this? Moreover,' Nicholas warmed to the theme, 'you contradict yourself. On the one hand, you say that all human efforts to make the world better demonstrate their extraordinary perverse power to make it worse. On the other, you say that all such efforts are so incredibly feeble that they must end in futility.'

The priest seemed unmoved by this battery of arguments. 'You accuse me of relying on biased evidence, of unjustified certainty, of being illogical. The truth is that you think I exaggerate wildly. But do I exaggerate? What is this "nature" in which your hopes and beliefs are grounded? It is a scene of unending violence, pain and destruction. The whole earth is continually steeped in blood, a vast altar where all that lives must be sacrificed without end. A hidden power is at work that ensures that life on earth proceeds only through violence. From every animal species it selects a certain number charged with devouring the others: insects of prey, reptiles of prey, birds of prey, fish of prey, quadrupeds of prey. And which is the king of all these animals, whose destructive hand spares nothing that lives? Man kills to obtain food and he kills to clothe himself, he kills to adorn himself, he kills to attack and he kills to defend himself, he kills to instruct himself and he kills to amuse himself, he kills to kill. He inhabits a world of perpetual carnage. From the catgut of his violin strings to the clothes on his back to the dinner on his table, it is littered with corpses.

'Nor does he confine his proclivities to the lower orders of creation. These human beings, in whom you invest such hope

and faith and towards whom you extend such charity – with their reason and their moral sense and their natural sympathy and their yearning for justice and their capacity for tears – of what horrors are they not capable towards their fellow human beings? What, my dear Professor of the Enlightenment, do the experiences of this century suggest to you? The experience of being bundled into a cattle truck pressed against the struggling bodies of others, all of you destined for certain incineration. Of trudging in fear along endless dusty roads under the burning sun, carrying tiny children and a few wretched belongings, after your village and your home have been razed to the ground, only to die of starvation or disease. Of lying wounded in a hospital in agonizing pain without medicines or anaesthetics under constant bombardment by people who used to be your neighbours. Of being burnt to death by radiation from a nuclear explosion or asphyxiated by poison gas or penetrated by the fragments of cluster bombs. Of being tied down and raped by a group of laughing soldiers wholly indifferent to your private, incommunicable anguish. Of being confined indefinitely and without hope of rescue in some remote labour camp or psychiatric ward, compared with which (the priest looked around him) this place would seem rather agreeable, because someone has decided you are a rich peasant or a class enemy or belong to the wrong ethnic category or just because you think the wrong thoughts. How many millions of people have been slaughtered in this century for such reasons? How many millions have been sacrificed in the name of ideals that sprang from your very Enlightenment – by zealots and their blind followers who believed that the Universe was so arranged that a future of perfect equality and unity and brotherhood and happiness was at hand, convinced that their enemies were all that stood in its way?'

'I have no idea on what basis the Universe was arranged,' remarked Nicholas. 'Indeed, I have no reason for saying it was arranged at all. Which is one, admittedly negative, reason for thinking it worthwhile to try to make it more liveable in

and life within it more worth living. You, by contrast, seem remarkably confident about such matters.'

'I have no special insight into the purposes of Divine Providence,' continued the priest. 'Nor, of course, do you. What I do know is that we know enough by now to know that the world is not arranged for the benefit of humankind. Perversity and Futility! We may well suppose that all this pain and misery and death is a divine punishment meted out upon the guilty and the guiltless alike, Providence's way of redeeming sinful mankind. There is so much sin in the world, Professor, and it must be expiated by a proportionate amount of suffering. The sins of the fathers will be visited upon the children. A divine fury seizes hold of human beings, making them into innocent murderers, passive instruments of a strong hand, as they plunge into the abyss they have themselves created.'

'You are an extremist!' declared Nicholas. 'Your vision of human history focuses only on the extreme, on the evidence of the worst that human beings can do to one another. I don't, of course, deny or underestimate that evidence. But what about all the rest? Not to speak of the best, what about the good or even the moderately bad?'

'You say that I exaggerate. What, you ask, of the few pools of light amidst all this darkness, those places where some measure of order and peace and prosperity and civilized life exists? I say: look more closely at such places and you will see the surrounding and underlying degradation, destitution and despair, upon which such civilization as exists must depend. And I say that such places are not beacons but decoys, leading foolish people astray by inducing false hopes . . .'

Nicholas interrupted the priest. 'What you are interested in doing,' he said, 'is dazzling people instead of enlightening them, seducing them and imbuing them with prejudices.'

'That,' replied the priest, 'is because the light of your beloved reason is but a pale flickering light that is all too easily extinguished.'

'You have not offered me a single reason,' said Nicholas, 'for accepting your Pessimistic vision.'

The priest laughed. 'So you think I am a Pessimist. Let me tell you,' he leant forward with an intent expression, 'a Pessimist says: "Things could not be worse." An Optimist says: "Oh yes, they could." In this sense, I am a resolute Optimist. And let me tell you something else,' he leant even closer and lowered his voice, 'I have always detested, do now and shall all my life detest military government. Anything perfected in the sphere of the art of war is a misfortune pure and simple. The brazen fools who run this country are certainly not worthy of your esteem or respect, or of mine. They are mere technicians of warfare – and inept ones at that. They have no sense of a divine mission or of any nobler purpose than hanging on to power. But we live in the darkest of dark times. In the face of anarchy and chaos, human beings must huddle together in fear in the comforting shadow of superior force. A degree of ruthlessness, which may not be mild, is often needed to prevent things from being even worse. The torturer and the executioner are our protection against the war of all against all. They are the source of my Optimism, the rock on which it is based. *They* are our only hope, Professor. Certainly, the light of reason offers none.'

The priest rose from the bed. He had finished speaking and seemed to have nothing further to say. Though he had never seen this priest before, Nicholas had recognized his words: he had spoken in the unmistakable words and accents of Joseph de Maistre, bitter and implacable arch-enemy of the Enlightenment and the French Revolution. Nicholas also rose. There was a conversational chasm between them that seemed at that moment unbridgeable. The priest, smiling, appeared to understand this and to draw satisfaction from it.

'It could be that our conversation has been of some use,' he remarked, pressing the bell by the door to summon Bullet Head. Of use to whom, Nicholas wondered once more, as steps approached outside and Bullet Head opened the door to let the priest depart.

For some thirty minutes, Nicholas sat silently, reflecting on the oddness of what the priest had called their 'conversation'. He found the recollection of it disturbing. Each had heard and responded to the other, but had they communicated? Indeed, how could they, if, as the priest maintained, what divided them was a confrontation of faiths where reason was not arbiter but partisan? The morning had not started well.

The door burst open suddenly revealing the ever aggressive Bullet Head.

'Now you're going to see someone who'll put you straight alright,' he rasped, shoving Nicholas out of the cell.

They turned right, in the direction of the Eye Test. At the office door, Bullet Head stopped and tapped respectfully.

'Come in!' boomed a loud, depressingly familiar voice.

Bullet Head roughly pushed him inside and then seemed confused about what to do. He first bowed, then saluted and finally said: 'I have the honour, Your Honour, of bringing the prisoner.'

'Good. Now go,' replied Globulus unappreciatively.

Bullet Head departed, looking rather forlorn.

'Nicholas, what an immense pleasure!' Globulus said, turning towards him. Seated at the table, he was flamboyantly dressed in a dark green velvet suit and bright yellow shirt and sported an oversized red-spotted bow tie. The two of them, Nicholas begrudgingly conceded, were still remarkably similar in their physical appearance. Both were tall, heavily built and slightly stooping, both had abundant black curly hair with greying temples, a high forehead, long straight nose and full, expressive mouth. Globulus's smiling face, however, was suntanned from holidays in expensive resorts and fattened by innumerable meals in the best restaurants while Nicholas's was pale and drawn – the pallor of scholarship. And unlike Nicholas, Globulus sported an elegantly trimmed, greying goatee. Each had grey-blue eyes under black, bushy eyebrows behind gold-rimmed spectacles. Globulus's eyes still conveyed the same look of innocent bewilderment that

there could be anyone who might think ill of him. He had always suspected that Nicholas was one such.

'I always used to enjoy conversations with you,' Globulus began, 'and I have long admired your wonderful writings. Of course, this is not what our friend Habermas would call an ideal speech situation. But we must make the best of it.'

With the priest, Nicholas had felt drawn into contesting an uncompromising view of the world that challenged his own. Now, he reflected, it might be as well to remain silent, to avoid compromising himself.

'Nicholas,' Globulus looked him in the eye and adopted an urgent, confidential tone, 'we are under siege. You mustn't let yourself be fooled by their fine words. They are ruthless, believe me, ruthless.'

'Who are?' he could not stop himself from asking.

'All of them.' And then Globulus proceeded to recite names, name after name of former professors they had known, friends, acquaintances, former students, intellectuals, writers, teachers, many of whom Nicholas knew to be in hiding and others to have disappeared.

'You are just paranoid,' Nicholas remarked coldly.

'The paranoiac,' said Dr Globulus in expert tones, 'is the person who knows what is really going on.'

'It's all nonsense,' he protested, 'utter nonsense!'

'*Is* it?' inquired Globulus. 'Are you sure? Is it less well-founded than those ideas about the Progress of Mankind in which you and your *friends* (he lingered over the word) believe or hope to believe? Where is the evidence to support your "progress"? Do you see any in the history of our country, or the world at large?'

'The idea of progress,' he responded irritably, recalling his conversation with Kant, 'becomes all the more important when the facts tell against it.'

'It's exactly the same with what you call my paranoia. With this difference: that in my case the facts tell in its favour. All the names I cited to you are the names of our enemies, are they not?'

'You have made them your enemies,' he rejoined.

'Come now, my dear Nicholas. I – we – have not *made* them anything. They are free agents and they have taken sides against Militaria.'

He was deriving no pleasure from this conversation, though it was, he had to admit, mildly stimulating. Globulus at least seemed to be trying not merely to frighten or manipulate but to convince him.

'They oppose you,' Nicholas continued, 'because you hound them and persecute them and treat them as the Enemy.'

'But that is what they are,' said Globulus. 'We are defending an ideal against them, the Militarian way of life. You, by contrast, have nothing to defend except a vague and abstract hope that there will be a better future for all. We know there will not. We also know that this whole illusion of Progress is, as our French philosophical friends – Foucault, Lyotard, Baudrillard, Kristeva – say, an exhausted "meta-narrative". The days of meta-narratives, Nicholas, are over. Read Richard Rorty. History has no direction. Everything is contingent and could be otherwise at any time. Unlikely as it might seem to you, I, for example, could be in your position and you in mine. We used to construct fictions, like your Progress tale, as though we could give history a meaning and a direction. But there is no meaning and no direction. Just stories we invent.'

'You are the inventor of stories, stories of imaginary conspiracies plotted by all those you dislike to justify the crimes of the regime you serve.'

'*Justify!*' repeated Globulus. 'Why should my government's actions need to be justified? All that is needed is to persuade. You are evidently not persuaded, and for a very simple reason: your confounded Optimism blinds you to what anyone with good sense can see. As they say, a Pessimist is a well-informed Optimist. Do your Optimistic friends have any clear idea of what the society they seek would be like? Does the Visible Hand have any conception of what the Progress they claim to value would be towards?'

Nicholas was tiring of this exchange, not least because it was clearly doing him no good. Globulus was drawing him out, inducing him to say things that would doubtless incriminate him and would duly appear in One's pile of documents.

'Nicholas,' Globulus's tone changed to that of an old friend offering advice, 'why don't you reconsider your attitude? If you were willing to become my colleague, you would be able to continue with your work in comfortable surroundings and have real influence on the times in which we live.'

Nicholas decided to appear less than totally intransigent.

'What would I have to gain?' he asked contemptuously.

Globulus chose to take his words as a question.

'Freedom,' he answered. 'You would be free not only from prison but to go wherever you liked. You could even (he chuckled) go freely into prison, as I did today. All you would need is this magic little document.' He showed him his pass, in a little plastic folder with a gold embossed crest and a flattering photograph.

'May I see it?' Nicholas asked.

Globulus handed it to him with pride. At that moment, the door burst open to the sound of a tremendous commotion. A fellow-prisoner, massive in size, was yelling and gesticulating in the direction of Dr Globulus. Two officers were restraining him with considerable difficulty. Looking more closely, Nicholas perceived that one of the officers was Justin; the other bore a striking resemblance to the optician.

'You are a malicious, evil, lying bastard!' shouted the prisoner. 'It's all lies you've invented. I never met no foreign agents. I don't even know any foreigners.'

Perhaps because of the presence of Nicholas, perhaps because of their earlier conversation, Dr Globulus tried to remonstrate with the prisoner and calm him down; but as he did so, the prisoner became more and more agitated. While all this was happening, Justin looked at Nicholas and raised a hand.

Quickly Nicholas slipped behind them, as the optician

pointed to a small bathroom adjoining the office. On the toilet seat was a set of clothes with a note pinned to them which read 'QUICK CHANGE'. Like lightning, he discarded his prison clothes and donned a green velvet suit, yellow shirt and red-spotted bow tie, identical to those Globulus was wearing. He also put on a false goatee beard, suitably greyed at the edges. The bathroom had a second door on which was pinned another note 'LEAVE FAST HAND.' He turned left and walked purposefully along the corridor.

He approached a double door guarded by a soldier. He held up Globulus's pass and received a salute and an open door in reply. Acknowledging the soldier's salute with a brief nod, Nicholas strode on up two flights of stairs into the front hallway of the prison. Ahead was the prison entrance, manned by another soldier. As he approached, the prison gates swung open.

Nicholas stepped into the street, where a waiting Ford Falcon car with darkened windows stood, its engine purring.

The driver, in military uniform, raised a hand in greeting. 'This way, Dr Pangloss,' he said, bundling him into the back seat, and off they sped.

·7·

Travelling Light

Next to him on the back seat was another change of clothes and, he noted with relief, his travelling bag. 'Get dressed quickly,' said the driver, 'in case we're stopped.' He did as he was told, putting his Globulus uniform and the false beard in his travelling bag. As Dr Pangloss, he discovered, he was to be altogether more businesslike, in a grey suit, white shirt and pale green tie. In his new jacket pockets he found a passport complete with an excellent photograph of himself, beardless and bespectacled, a quantity of money, a piece of paper with the address to which Progress Reports to Justin were to be sent and an air ticket. He was, it appeared, heading for Calcula, Utilitaria on Utilitarian Airways flight UA 572 leaving in one hour's time.

'What if we're stopped?' he asked the driver, nervously.

'Keep smiling, Doctor,' said the driver, attempting but failing to reassure him.

They came to a security checkpoint.

'Hand me your passport,' said the driver. He flourished it with his own documents at the soldiers. They waved them on.

The driver gave him back his passport and said, with what sounded like sincerity, 'We are counting on you, Doctor, to

find us the best possible world. We have a serious morale problem. You're our only hope.'

'What do I do when I get to Calcula?' Nicholas asked.

'Apply for political asylum,' said the driver.

'What if they reject me?' he persisted.

'Keep smiling,' said the driver, pulling up at the airport car park. 'Now, Doctor, you're on your own. Good luck!'

Nicholas marched briskly into the Departures Hall. There were soldiers everywhere, stalking about, pointing their rifles ahead of them. He made the mistake of looking one of them in the eye. The eye immediately fixed him and followed him about – as did its owner's rifle-barrel. Both followed him to the check-in counter, where there was a queue of three persons.

The eye and the barrel remained glued to Nicholas, making him intensely nervous. The three persons took a painfully long time to be processed, fumbling and fussing about their seats and their luggage. Finally, he presented his ticket and his passport.

'Smoking or nonsmoking, Dr Pangloss?'

'Nonsmoking.'

'Window or aisle?'

'Aisle.'

'Any luggage?'

He pointed to his travelling bag. 'Only this.'

'Here is your boarding card. Board now. Gate A3.'

In near panic, he fled the eye and the barrel to Passport Control. A bored soldier mindlessly took and stamped his passport, and Nicholas rushed to the gate for his flight. Passengers were already boarding. He followed them into a coach and then up steps into the aeroplane. Exhausted, he slumped into his seat. At last, safety belt fastened, Nicholas was free to contemplate his past and his future.

·8·

Entry

*A*s the aeroplane taxied towards takeoff, Nicholas's spirits lifted. Utilitaria was, from all accounts, a land of promise. He was heading for a country dedicated to well-being and exclusively concerned with the future. He knew that Utilitaria's national motto, coined by its revolutionary founder Jeremy Bentham, was 'The Greatest Happiness of the Greatest Number'. If all went well, he might be one of that number.

His spirits received a further boost on noticing that the seat next to his was occupied by a slim young woman in a smart blue suit and black polo-necked sweater, with long shiny brown hair, green eyes, delicate features, a pleasing smile and a laptop computer on her fetching black-stockinged knees. In her early thirties and obviously a professional person, she evidently had some work to do, for immediately after takeoff she briskly let down the table in front of her, opened up her computer and called up a programme involving graphs and tables with figures.

The stewardess offered each of them a drink and a bag of nuts and therewith a conversational opening. There being no room on her table, Nicholas offered her a space on his, observing that the airline was gravely at fault in failing to

·42·

plan for one's need to work, eat and drink all at the same time. Smiling, she thanked him. He introduced himself as Dr Pangloss, teacher and philosopher, visiting Utilitaria for the first time. Her name, she told him, was Stella Yardstick. She was a Utilitarian diplomat who had been working in Militaria. Nicholas asked her what it was she was calculating. Her reply gave him a start.

'Immigration,' she said. 'There are lots of Militarians trying to get into Utilitaria, most of them pretty desperate. Of course, they usually ask for political asylum but that's usually just a pretence and obscures the real issue. What I'm trying to calculate is which types of immigrant, if any, contribute significantly to the welfare of all. It's all rather tricky.'

Nicholas heartily agreed. Yet the bluntness of her answer suggested that trickiness for Stella Yardstick meant the complexity of the calculations involved, not in any conflict of principles.

'Does "the welfare of all" not include the welfare of those desperate Militarians?' he asked.

She gave him a smile that could have been condescending. 'Our computing skills have developed enormously,' she said, 'but the day has not yet arrived when we can take the whole world into our calculations. I'm afraid that until that day comes, we must focus on the consequences of Utilitarian policies for Utilitarians.'

Should he, he wondered, venture to tell her of his own case, so as to discover what to expect on arrival and even perhaps enlist her help? He decided against it. She was not evidently predisposed in favour of political refugees and, besides, he had already introduced himself under a false name. He decided instead to switch the course of their conversation. What, he asked her, had been her impressions of the state of things in Militaria?

'Quite horrifying!' she declared.

Once more he heartily agreed. What, he asked, had especially horrified her?

'The terrible waste of human resources, the disorganization of production, the collapse of the bureaucracy, administrative chaos. The whole place is a managerial disaster! But what else can you expect when the military is in power?'

'I quite agree,' said Nicholas.

'And worst of all,' she went on, 'they've lost the capacity to calculate the extent of the disaster they're creating. Take all those disappearances! No-one knows any more what the population of Militaria really is. Do you know that they haven't had a proper census for *fifteen years?*'

Nicholas had to admit his ignorance.

The stewardess brought them their meal. Stella Yardstick turned off her computer and put it back on her knees. Lunch came on plastic trays with plastic cutlery, packaged in little white squares and rectangles and covered in transparent clingfilm. It was certainly an improvement on the fare served up by Bullet Head – considerably less tasteless, if not quite tasty. The stewardess also offered them each a half bottle of red wine, which they each accepted. The wine, he noted with some relief, came with a glass.

Nicholas asked his travelling companion to tell him about life in Utilitaria, and, as they sipped their wine, she answered his questions with animation, even enthusiasm. She was obviously glad to be going home.

Computers, she told him, were very popular there. Indeed, calculating was the national obsession. All Utilitarians agreed with the principle that what counts is what can be counted. When faced with the question 'What is to be done?' a Utilitarian invariably converted it into the question 'Which option will produce the greatest sum of utility?' Everyone treasured pocket calculators, and Stella had brought several home to give as special gifts. Technocrats, Bureaucrats and Judges – the most powerful and admired people in Utilitaria – were particularly adept at calculating, but they used state-of-the-art computers.

There were, she told him, two political parties: the Act party,

which was in opposition, and the governing Rule party. What divided them was that the Actors were (they claimed) democratic, and encouraged everyone to use pocket calculators on all possible occasions, while the Rulers believed in discouraging ordinary people from using them for all but the most minor decisions. According to the Rulers, people should live by 'rules of thumb' devised and interpreted by the Technocrats, Bureaucrats and Judges, according to their superior calculating methods and skills. Actors tended to call the Rulers 'elitist', Rulers to call Actors 'demagogic'.

'My guess,' said Nicholas, 'would be that you are a Ruler.'

She gave him a smile, revealing two rows of perfectly uniform and perfectly white teeth. He began to find her smile, despite the dimples that surrounded it, less warming than before. Was it, perhaps, also calculated?

'Members of the Diplomatic Service,' she answered, 'are politically neutral.'

They had reached the coffee stage. She had so far painted him a rather untroubled picture of Utilitarian life. Nicholas decided to ask her what were the most pressing problems the country faced.

She heaved a sigh. There was, she explained, a region to the west where trouble had rarely been absent and was now all too present, both there and now elsewhere in Utilitaria. A majority of the region's inhabitants were Utilitarians but a minority supported a movement that was engaged in an implacable struggle for their territory's independence. Utilitarians called the members of the minority 'Bigotarians'. Bigotarians, said Stella, were fixated on the past. They were far more interested in fierce and virulent proclamations and discussions about the meaning of battles four hundred years ago than they were in calculating which of various present options would yield the greatest sum of future utility. They spent most of their time hating, cursing and fighting their Utilitarian oppressors.

Bigotarians, she explained, were also inclined to mount

unsettling campaigns of terror within Utilitaria. Another had just recently begun, with what aims she seemed neither to know nor care. The Utilitarians were, it was clear, wholly indifferent to the concerns of those they called Bigotarians, attributing their violent and barbaric ways to their incomprehensible obsession with the past.

The stewardess arrived to collect their plastic debris. Stella Yardstick smiled at him again, replaced her computer on her table and switched it on. This time her smile was unambiguous: as the computer switched on, the smile switched off.

'Now,' she said, 'I must get on with my work.'

'Of course,' said Nicholas, 'I have so enjoyed our conversation.'

'So have I,' she replied generously.

They had an hour's flying time left. While she compared and evaluated the futures of categories of would-be immigrants to Utilitaria, Nicholas contemplated his own. As she started to tap out theirs, he tried to map out his. He had known a Utilitarian once, an eighteenth-century scholar, an expert on Helvétius, who had attended his conference on Voltaire some years ago. It was, in fact, the conference at which Nicholas's troubles had begun, when the regime had first identified him as a student of dangerous Optimistic ideas. What *was* that Utilitarian scholar's name? He could bring to mind his amiable smile and his clipped and precise way of talking, but his name?

The aircraft began its descent towards Calcula. Stella Yardstick closed her computer and folded up her table. The plane landed smoothly and the passengers arose as in one mass. Nicholas reached for his travelling bag in the overhead compartment and handed his neighbour her coat. He followed her and the other passengers into the airport building. For the first time, he turned his attention to them and noticed a striking fact. They divided into three quite different groups. First, there were brisk, confident and smartly dressed youngish men and women, carrying laptop computers, analogues of Stella

Yardstick. They lined up before a sign on the left that read 'UTILITARIAN CITIZENS'. Second, there were people plainly on holiday: teenagers with backpacks, elderly couples and family groups in carefree mood. They assembled before a sign in the centre that read 'VISITORS – VISA HOLDERS'. The third group, on the right, waited in front of a sign, less informative and altogether less hopeful, that read 'OTHERS'.

His travelling companion made straight for the left-hand queue. As she joined it, she offered him a hand and a smile of farewell.

'I hope you enjoy your visit,' she said, 'and that your stay here will be a happy one.'

'Thank you,' said Nicholas, joining the visitors' queue until she had disappeared through Passport Control. The left-hand queue was soon gone. The central 'visitors' queue was also moving quite quickly. The 'others' was, however, almost stationary. Lamenting his lack of a visitor's visa, Nicholas slunk from the second to the end of the waiting group.

It comprised men and women of different ages, most poorly dressed and several old and infirm. One of the women was pregnant and several were accompanied by small children. The adults clutched their passports nervously. All bore looks of despair made the more intolerable by their surviving hope. Their hope was also evidently his: to be granted political asylum. Their problem – which, he realized, was his as well – was to convince Utilitaria that there was a good reason to admit them. Each had come with an unhappy past, but why should they be granted a happy future? Utilitaria's welfare services were notoriously excellent and costly to the public purse. Each new immigrant represented a certain cost and a disputable benefit. The problem was how to convince Utilitaria that the benefit outweighed the cost.

The queue before him moved forward slowly. One by one, individuals and family groups waited at the glass window before proceeding into an office behind a grey metal door for further interrogation. They spoke in low, urgent, pleading

voices. As he waited his turn, Nicholas reflected that it might be better to abandon his recently assumed identity: the case of the fictive Dr Pangloss was not obviously more convincing than that of the real Nicholas Caritat.

Finally, he stood before the glass and presented his passport.

'Actually,' he said, feeling somewhat foolish, 'my name isn't "Pangloss". It's "Caritat".'

'I see,' said an unsmiling young officer in a peaked cap.

'And I wish to apply for political asylum,' he added in a low, urgent, pleading voice.

'Can you prove you are who you say you are?' asked the official, 'and that you are not who you say you are not?'

Each of these tasks seemed equally and insuperably difficult.

'I can't,' Nicholas mumbled helplessly, 'prove anything.' It felt like a professional defeat.

The unsmiling officer pointed to the grey metal door on which a sign read 'IMMIGRATION CONTROL'. He knocked and entered. It was a small square office with grey metallic walls and a grey metal desk, at which was seated a woman Immigration Officer in a grey uniform. She looked intensely bored. He sat down on the grey metal seat before her.

'Apparently, you are not who you appear to be,' she began, unpromisingly.

He decided to risk his future on the truth, since he doubted his capacity to invent a more convincing fiction. For one thing, he had no clue about what *would* be convincing. So he began his story in detail while the grey-suited officer listened impassively, her eyes closed.

When he had finished, she opened them and started to type onto a keyboard, looking only at the screen in front of her.

'Apparently, you have written books and articles,' she remarked.

'Yes.'

'How much do they weigh?'

Weigh? Did she mean how weighty was his scholarly reputation? He hesitated. Would seeming to be modest worsen his position?

'How many kilos?' she specified.

Better invent, he thought. It might seem a sign of incompetence not to know.

'Thirteen and a half,' he said firmly. She typed this in.

'How many publications?'

He guessed again, 'A hundred and ninety-three.'

'Rate of production?'

'Currently five per month. But I'm working on increasing it.'

'You have produced graduates in your academic field?'

'Yes.'

'How many?'

He guessed wildly. 'Two thousand and three,' he said.

She typed this in and then turned towards him. Her boredom seemed to have diminished.

'Professor Caritat,' she said, 'we may be able to give you the benefit of what is nevertheless a considerable doubt. You are, it would appear, a remarkably productive scholar and teacher. Our aim in Utilitaria, as you may know, is to maximize utility and your contributions could be significant, though we cannot be sure.' Maximize! A bell rang dimly in his head. *Maximize!* That was it. His Utilitarian acquaintance from the past, the expert on Helvétius, was called Maximand, Gregory Maximand.

'Is there perhaps someone,' the Grey Officer was continuing, 'who might know something about you? Someone to whom we might refer in order to estimate your likely productivity here?'

'Gregory Maximand!' Nicholas shouted excitedly, 'he knows me.'

'And who and where is he?' she asked.

He could not remember but made a guess. 'Calcula University. Department of History.'

She typed this in and departed into another office,

presumably to make the fateful telephone call, leaving him in a limbo between helplessness and hope.

After twenty minutes she returned with what seemed like the faintest trace of a smile. 'We had some difficulty in tracing your Professor Maximand,' she said. 'Calcula University has no Department of History. History is a branch of the Department of Futurology. But we managed to locate him. We have decided to issue you with a residence and a work permit for six months. All we need is four photographs and a signature. Please come this way.'

She led him out of the door through which he had entered, handed him some coins and pointed to a large box covered with photographs of apparently happy, smiling faces, alongside which hung a dark green curtain. Feeling happy too, he sat down behind the curtain and smiled at a glass reflection of himself smiling. He pushed a button and, with four flashes, his smile was recorded and became official Utilitarian property. The Officer took possession of it as it emerged from a little grill at the side of the box. They returned to her office and she pinned it to four different documents, two of which she handed him in a plastic folder.

'I am very grateful,' he said, spontaneously.

She looked puzzled. 'You are what?'

'Very grateful.'

'What is that?'

'Grateful,' he explained, 'I mean . . . I feel gratitude.'

'What is *that*?' she asked.

'*Gratitude* (he summoned from memory the definition from Diderot's *Encyclopédie*) is the sentiment for benefits one has received.'

'We don't have that concept in Utilitaria,' she observed. 'We have sentiments only for future benefits.'

Diderot, he recalled, had suggested that gratitude had only appeared in the late sixteenth century and was already growing old in the eighteenth. In Utilitaria, it seemed, it was already dead.

The Immigration Officer rose from her chair. 'Professor Caritat,' she stated briskly, 'Professor Maximand will arrive to pick you up in half an hour.'

She opened the metal door behind her and he followed her through it. They entered a waiting room in which his fellow passengers sat disconsolately, still clutching their passports. The children were crying. At the exit, the Grey Officer turned to leave him.

'You must wait for a Public Announcement,' she said. 'Oh, and you'll need this.' She handed him a pocket calculator.

'Thank you,' said Nicholas. She returned to her office, looking mildly perplexed. He entered the brightly lit Arrivals Hall, full of bustling people and gleaming surfaces, with escalators and well-stocked shops, resounding with a stream of booming, echoing announcements and messages. He sat down on a low seat, his travelling bag beside him, and waited. Eventually, the words he was waiting for boomed and echoed forth.

'Professor Caritat to the Information Desk!'

It seemed like a Public Announcement of welcome – or, at least, admittance.

·9·

Calcula

A midst the crowd at the Information Desk, Nicholas spotted Gregory Maximand. He was in his early sixties but looked much younger. Trim, tanned, fit, smoothly elegant, with wrinkles around the eyes and a friendly, smiling face, he was, exactly as Nicholas remembered him, a decidedly cheering sight. No less cheering was the warm embrace and his flow of solicitous and welcoming words.

'Professor Caritat! It's *so* good to see you after all this time. We all rather lost track of you after the academic boycott of Militaria. You're obviously in trouble, but we'll sort it all out. You'll come and stay with us at home until we find you something. My car's this way. You'll have dinner with us tonight of course. Are you very tired? Would you like to lie down or would you like a drive around Calcula first?'

He gladly agreed to the drive. It would be as well to get his bearings.

The car was silver and purred gently. As they drove from the airport into the city, Nicholas told his story, for the second time that day. Maximand was an eager listener and was especially interested to hear of the mission entrusted him by Justin.

'Nicholas!' he exclaimed, on hearing of it. 'May I call you that?'

'Of course!'

'Your mission, Nicholas,' he said decisively, 'is over.'

'How so?'

'You have reached your destination. I can assure you of that.'

Gregory was plainly a patriot. Could his claim be true? Had Nicholas already reached the best of all possible worlds? Calcula was a busy modern metropolis in which everything seemed well-ordered and under control. Gleaming cars and buses flowed smoothly through long, straight and wide streets. The buildings were tall, elegantly designed, glass-fronted office blocks and shopping malls. The Calculans walking brightly along the broad and tidy pavements appeared uniformly well-dressed, healthy and happy. Looking more closely, he observed that they all seemed to be smiling, not at one another, but to themselves. Looking even more closely he noticed that, as they walked, they would stop every now and then, take small calculators out of their pockets and consult them, as if checking something, then put them back with evident satisfaction. Everywhere he saw efficiency, prosperity, cleanliness and order. No poverty, no litter, no mendicants – or even persons who were aged or infirm or handicapped. He decided to test Gregory's claim a little: were all Utilitarians, he wondered, preserved from misery and misfortune?

'Where,' he asked, 'do the poorer classes live?'

'Ah,' said Gregory. 'There are no poorer classes because there are no classes. Our successes in Utilitaria (he gestured out of the window) are collective, our failures individual. We live in a Meritocracy, where merit consists in contribution to the common good. Of course, some Utilitarians do less well than others. Some individuals are failures, but that is because they contribute less than others to the utility of all. But that is all they have in common. They don't form a class: they're just so many particular individuals who don't succeed as well as others.'

'But,' he asked, 'don't they feel resentment at their inferior position?'

'What is that?' Gregory looked puzzled.

Another word they don't seem to know, he thought. He recalled that Dr Johnson had defined it rather well.

'*Resentment*,' he explained, 'means "a deep sense of injury; anger long continued".'

'We don't have that word,' said Gregory, 'or indeed the strange phenomenon it seems to refer to. Less well-off Utilitarians certainly don't have it. Why should they? By whom have they been injured? At whom should they feel anger? If they contribute less than others, it's either because they are unable to or unwilling to. If they're unable, it's nobody's fault; if they're unwilling, it's their own. We make sure that all can perform to the limits of their abilities, through training and encouragement. And there is a welfare floor nobody capable of contributing to society falls through. In Utilitaria,' he concluded with pride, 'everyone is rewarded according to his or her contribution to the welfare of all.'

'In what sort of conditions,' Nicholas persisted, 'do the less well-off Utilitarians live?'

'I see you have a particular interest in their welfare,' Gregory observed with what seemed to be amusement, 'Very public-spirited! I'll tell you what. I'll show you a less well-off neighbourhood on our way home where (he looked at his watch) we should be heading in any case.'

As they drove out of the city centre, Nicholas reflected on the extraordinary change his circumstances had undergone within the span of a single day. Only a few hours ago he had been sparring with the despicable Globulus in a Militarian prison; now he was speeding along the busy streets of a Utilitarian city, in the company of a guide who had, it seemed, nothing but good news for him.

Suddenly, the car stopped. Up ahead, in front of a line of cars, there was some sort of security checkpoint: a metal barrier manned by two policemen with guns. This was the second road block of the day. He looked at Gregory, who seemed unfazed.

'It's those wretched Bigotarian terrorists!' he explained. 'They've started up another bombing campaign. The police are checking cars for weapons and suspicious persons.'

Suspicious persons! How could he not be such a person, with identity documents in the names of Globulus, Pangloss and Caritat.

'Don't worry,' said Gregory, noticing his anxiety. 'I'll deal with it.'

On reaching the road block, Gregory handed the soldiers his own documents and Nicholas's residence and work permits. 'My colleague here,' he said, rather grandly, 'is a distinguished Professor from abroad, with a very high level of productivity and a very promising future.'

Satisfied, the soldier handed back the documents and waved them through.

They drove on, past a series of about ten high-rise, functional apartment-block buildings, some forty storeys high, set back from the road, and fronted by long, well-kept green lawns.

'Perhaps,' his host suggested, with what sounded like a hint of irony, 'you would like to see how what you would call our poor live. Let's go and have a look.'

Gregory drove into the driveway of the last of the blocks and parked in the large parking space in front of the main entrance.

They entered a spacious entrance hall with a polished black floor and mirrored walls. Passing a bank of elevators, Gregory led Nicholas towards the back entrance. 'Let me show you this,' he said with what sounded like pride.

Nicholas found himself looking upon a large, well-tended and trimmed green lawn that stretched to their right all the way along the length of the ten apartment blocks and was surrounded by more white, gleaming buildings. In front of the building to their left was a children's playground, with swings and a sandpit. Directly to their right, towards the other side, the shimmering streams of a circular fountain on a stone

pedestal rose, turned and fell like an array of liquid plumes into a small artificial lake. The sound of the falling water gave the place a calming, peaceful atmosphere.

'I'm sure you'd like to see how Utilitaria cares for its citizens – even the poorest,' Gregory said, as they walked along the path past the buildings, which were of varying height. They were divided into blocks, each with a separate entrance, with white steps and glass doors on which words in gold letters announced its function.

They passed a nursery, from which Nicholas could hear the shrill sound of young children's voices, and then the elementary school, the primary school and the middle school. Coming to the corner, they started along the path opposite the apartments. The first building, white and gleaming like the others, but somewhat higher, was the senior school. Next was a building announcing itself as 'THE CLINIC'. Here, Gregory explained, all problems that beset the eyes, ears, noses, throats and feet of the residents were attended to by appropriate specialists. The next building offered 'COUNSELLING SER-VICES', provided, Gregory explained, at public expense, for those who needed help with problem solving.

'What kinds of problems?' Nicholas asked.

'Every kind,' replied Gregory. 'There is no problem without a solution. The residents come with their problems and the experts calculate the answers.' Through the windows, Nicholas could see the glow of computer screens.

The next building stood opposite the fountain and the lake. 'This,' said Gregory, 'should impress you. It is an old people's home.'

Nicholas looked up at the glass doors and started as he read the inscription: 'FAREWELL HOUSE'. He was for a moment shocked by the bluntness of the label, but then he realized that the name was distinctively Utilitarian: future-oriented and promising good prospects in the time to come.

Seated at tables around the water's edge were a number of white-haired men and women, some reading, some of the

women knitting, some gazing at the fountain. They sat silently, ignoring the visitors who mounted the steps and went inside. Once in the entrance hall, Gregory knocked on a door on the left. A large, bespectacled woman who looked like a hospital matron answered. Her expression combined an air of authority with what Nicholas would have taken to be a broad smile of welcome if he had not seen it worn by every Utilitarian he had so far encountered. Gregory explained that he wanted his friend to see Utilitarian health care provision at work. She shook Nicholas's hand vigorously.

The room they had entered struck him as a cross between a doctor's waiting room and a nursing home. Some thirty or so old persons, men and women, in varying stages of infirmity were ranged along the dark, olive green, cloth-covered walls, on which there hung vivid pictures in pastel pinks and blues of birds and flowers and furry animals. At the far end were large double swing doors. Written across them in large gold letters was the word 'FAREWELL'. Once more Nicholas was struck by the seeming insensitivity of the message, but he resolved to exercise interpretive charity and try to understand it from the natives' point of view. The room, whose ample windows looked out onto the lake and fountain, was tastefully carpeted and furnished. Some of its occupants were sitting in comfortable chintz armchairs, some were lying propped up in low beds. Some were surrounded by small groups of what were obviously caring relatives and friends. Others sat or lay alone. There was a low buzz of many inwardly focused conversations. Three nurses moved discreetly from one to another of their charges. The whole scene conveyed a sense of soothing restfulness. The matron took evident pride in displaying it to her unexpected guests.

Nicholas looked around him. The aged persons in the room – none of whom he noticed was very ancient – seemed remarkably contented. All were smiling to themselves, no-one was complaining or even frowning. Some were even amusing themselves with pocket calculators.

Against the wall to his right Nicholas noticed an old lady in a blue dressing gown with a white face and large round spectacles, sitting upright in an armchair. Before her sat two young women, evidently her daughters, both trying, with little success, to engage her in a conversation about books they had read, travels they had enjoyed together, mutual friends, but the old lady's attention was flickering and intermittent. Every now and then she uttered a disconnected word or two evoking animated conversations of the past, retreating into peaceful silence. Her eyes fell briefly upon Nicholas. Next to her, another frail woman lay curled on a bed talking softly to herself in obvious physical discomfort, but smiling all the while. Nicholas met her gaze as the nurse drew a screen around her. On a neighbouring bed sat an expansively jolly man in pyjamas who seemed to be entertaining a party of relatives with what sounded like black humour on the topic of his impending demise. A nurse was serving the assembled company cups of tea. Their laughter seemed to convey both enjoyment and embarrassment.

'As you can see,' remarked Gregory, 'the standards of Utilitarian care, even for the least of our number, are of the highest.'

With this remark Gregory thanked the matron for the visit and the two took their leave. Once outside, Gregory indicated with a wave of the arm the rest of the quadrangle's buildings: a banking and shopping area, a cinema, a recreation centre and a very large pleasure arcade.

'I'm afraid this is the best we can do, Nicholas,' Gregory said with a smile of apology, 'in the way of a poor neighbourhood. The people who live here don't see themselves as a *class*, and many of them move out when their productivity improves. They are all likely to have relatives – fathers and mothers, brothers and sisters, uncles, aunts and cousins – who are doing very well. Failure in Utilitaria doesn't come in families.'

From all he could hear and see, it didn't seem to come too painfully to individuals either. Nicholas decided to try a

further testing question or two as they resumed their car journey.

'But,' he asked, 'surely there are still many sources of unhappiness left?'

'We have eliminated all the social sources of personal unhappiness,' asserted Gregory firmly, 'through the public provision of *benefits* for all who need them: maternity care, day nurseries, education at every level, health care, sick pay, unemployment compensation, care for the elderly. Whatever individuals lack, the public provides.'

'But don't individuals then lack a sense of responsibility?' Nicholas could not stop himself from asking.

'That's just another source of unhappiness,' observed Gregory.

'How about the suicide rate?' Nicholas asked.

Gregory seemed to have an answer to every question. 'It is,' he admitted, 'very high. But a high suicide rate, provided the suicides are appropriately distributed, can make a real contribution to the overall sum of happiness. Don't you agree?'

Gregory was very reassuring. He was a friend of whom Nicholas was in need, but was he a friend indeed? He was certainly extremely, even extravagantly, friendly, quite beyond the call of their previous acquaintance. Was this just an impersonal, universal benevolence of which Nicholas was the present, lucky beneficiary? Was he, perhaps, behaving strategically, just to make Nicholas think well of him and of Utilitaria? Or did he really care about Nicholas? Did his friendliness signify friendship? Nicholas hoped for the last, most comforting interpretation of Gregory's solicitude and looked forward with added pleasure to his forthcoming hospitality.

·10·

The Maximands

The Maximands' home was an imposing neoclassical building in a quiet, leafy suburb, set back from a tree-lined avenue. Nicholas was greeted by the other Maximands: Gregory's wife, Charmian, and their teenage son, Graham. The elegant Charmian, whose matchstick-thin body was dressed in the simplest sweater and trousers, smiled charmingly. She was obviously proud of Gregory's having come to Nicholas's aid. 'Gregory,' she explained, 'is terribly good at picking up people in need.'

'Who are very much needed here,' Gregory added. 'Nicholas will soon be on his feet, contributing to our utility, I'm sure of that!'

Graham was smiling to himself somewhat abstractedly and seemed rather eager to dash off.

'He has some calculating to do on his computer,' explained Gregory, 'but will join us later. Let's talk in the library while Charmian gets supper ready.'

Charmian, Gregory told Nicholas with pride, was a wonderful cook. She was also a superlative housewife and mother and was employed as his research assistant, personal, social and political secretary. All her activities seemed geared to support all the various sides of Gregory's obviously successful life.

Nicholas followed him into a large, pleasant room with white walls hung with paintings of flowers and lined from floor to ceiling with books, some new, some old. He recognized, with a faint twinge of sadness, the brown eighteenth-century bindings that were so familiar. He could see entire sets of Voltaire, Rousseau, Bentham and, of course, Helvétius. Nicholas's eyes wandered over the titles and he studied what was evidently the poetry section while Gregory poured them drinks. He pulled out a volume of poetry as Gregory handed him a sherry.

'Fancy some pushpin?' Gregory inquired.

'Pushkin?' he said. 'Well, yes, it's been a good many years since I read Pushkin.'

Gregory looked surprised. 'Well, I do have some Pushkin,' he said, 'but what I actually said was *pushpin*, not Pushkin.'

'Who is Pushpin?' he asked.

'Surely you've heard of pushpin,' said Gregory. 'It's a rather amusing game, of which I'm especially fond, that's always been very popular here in Utilitaria. According to John Stuart Mill, Jeremy Bentham thought that pushpin was as good as poetry, judged as a means of generating utility – and, as you know, Bentham used to say "all poetry is misrepresentation". For some reason Mill seemed to think there was something wrong in these opinions. Personally,' Gregory added, 'I'd say that pushpin is a good deal better than Pushkin.'

Nicholas did not really feel up to defending the merits of Pushkin against a strange game whose rules he did not know. Still less did he feel like playing it there and then, so he decided to stall by suggesting that they looked up 'pushpin' in Dr Johnson's *Dictionary*, banking on Gregory's having a copy. They consulted the brown leather volume. '*Pushpin:*' the entry read, 'A child's play in which pins are pushed alternately' and there followed a quotation from L'Estrange: 'Men, that have wandering thoughts at the voice of wisdom out of the mouth of a philosopher, deserve as well to be whipt, as boys for playing at pushpin, when they should be learning.' The good Doctor, it was clear, thought worse of pushpin, and better of poetry, than did Jeremy Bentham.

Gregory, however, was not to be deterred. Opening a cupboard, he produced a large flat wooden board at each end of which he carefully placed several small silver pins.

'Now,' he explained with growing excitement, 'we have to push these in an endeavour to cross them.'

At that moment Graham burst into the room. 'Oh, I'm so sorry,' he said with evident contempt for what was causing his father intense enjoyment, 'I didn't realize you'd be doing this already.' He turned to Nicholas. 'As you can see,' he remarked, 'the child is father to the man. "To see the son you would admire",' he recited drily, '"Go play at pushpin with his sire."'

Gregory, oblivious to his son's taunts, was absorbed in the pleasures of anticipation, eager to inveigle his guest into the mysteries of this curious pastime. But then, to Nicholas's relief and Gregory's evident disappointment Charmian entered the library to summon them to dinner in the rather sparsely furnished dining room, decorated with abstract, rather geometrical paintings, with a wooden floor and pine furniture. They sat down at a long narrow table as Graham, emerging reluctantly from his calculations, joined them. Gregory presided at one end of the table and Charmian sat at the other. Opposite Nicholas sat Graham and the fifth person at the table: a small old lady dressed in black with neat white hair, eyes like small black pebbles and a particularly enigmatic smile. Gregory introduced her with a cursory wave of the hand as Charmian's mother. Nicholas extended his hand and she shook it with remarkable firmness, smiling vaguely. For the rest of the meal she sat unnoticed and silent, as if enclosed in an invisible capsule.

Nicholas was distinctly hungry. What Charmian served them came as something of a disappointment: a meal whose overriding object was plainly healthiness. They began with an hors d'oeuvre of grated carrots, lettuce and red cabbage. There were also various kinds of bread – high-bran, high-protein, wheatgerm and wholemeal, as Charmian carefully explained to her guest. Nicholas tried several pieces, but they all tasted the

same. The main course consisted of nut steak with spinach. To drink there was a choice of skimmed or semi-skimmed milk.

Both Gregory and Charmian treated Nicholas like a long-lost friend, expressing concern in roughly equal measure about his past troubles, his present comfort and his future prospects. Gregory, it soon emerged, was no mere professor and scholar. He had connections in high places, which he made no effort to conceal, and from which his guest, he promised, would soon benefit. Charmian only added to his growing sense of well-being by assuring him that Gregory always kept his promises. Graham, however, looked on morosely.

'What, if you don't mind my asking,' he asked the young man, 'have you been busy calculating?'

'The likely outcome of tomorrow's vote in Parliament,' answered Graham, 'on the basis of the members' previous voting records. It's difficult, though, because it's such a tricky issue.'

'What is the issue?' he asked.

'Abortion,' said Graham. 'The problem is that, though the Rule and the Act parties' positions are clear, there are enough waverers and mavericks on both sides for the result to be quite uncertain. Moreover, it is a free vote. They don't have to follow their party lines.'

Nicholas tried to guess which party stood for what on the abortion issue but found he could not. 'Tell me,' he asked, 'which party is for the right to choose and which for the right to life?'

All three Maximands looked utterly puzzled. Then a flicker of understanding crossed Gregory's face.

'Nicholas,' he explained to the others, adopting a rather ponderous professorial tone, 'is using an obsolete vocabulary unknown here, but which was, actually, very popular in the seventeenth and eighteenth centuries. John Locke even thought that every man has a right of property "in his own person"! It was in the eighteenth century that the pernicious fashion began of making ringing declarations of the so-called

"rights of man" and the "rights of citizens" and proclaiming that everyone had "natural rights" to this or that. You see,' he continued, turning to Nicholas, 'we don't have the concept of *rights* – and certainly not those supposed "natural" or "human" rights that can't ever be abrogated, against which Bentham railed so fiercely. You remember, Nicholas, Bentham wrote that "there is no right which, when the abolition of it is advantageous to society, should not be abolished". Such alleged "natural and imprescriptable rights of man" Bentham considered "mischievous" and "dangerous nonsense" and the idea that they can't be abrogated for society's advantage was, he declared, "nonsense upon stilts".'

It was odd, Nicholas thought, that Gregory, who was so concerned with the future, should be so fond of quoting from a thinker of the past. He decided to try to frame his question in a non-obsolete vocabulary.

'Which of the parties is in favour of permitting abortion?' he asked.

The Maximands still looked puzzled. This time it was Graham who answered.

'That's not the issue,' he said. 'No-one's against permitting abortion as such. The question is: who is to decide? The Act party says the mother, and perhaps the father. The Rule party says it should be decided – as it is at present – by a set of guidelines interpreted and applied by a committee of experts.'

'Which experts?' he asked.

'Oh, doctors, psychiatrists, demographers, economists – you know, professional futurologists of various kinds,' said Graham, with what sounded like contempt.

'And your view?' Nicholas asked the teenager, who was beginning to remind him of his own children.

'I say, Down with Experts!' Graham replied vehemently. 'The people should have the power to abort themselves. They are the best futurologists. The people make the best decisions.'

'Do they indeed?' interjected Gregory sharply. His sarcastic tone indicated that he was not of his son's mind. 'I would point

out, Graham,' he continued sarcastically, 'that if the system you favour had been in operation fifteen years ago, you would not be here to argue in favour of it.'

'Gregory!' exclaimed Charmian, clearly embarrassed, though Nicholas could not tell whether this was due to her husband's indiscretion or to his use of it to try to squash their son in an argument.

Poor Graham, he thought, unwanted by his parents, the fruit of an administrative decision. His sense of rapport with Gregory and Charmian was beginning to evaporate.

But Graham, unsquashed, responded with spirit, mimicking his father's sarcasm. 'If you let the people decide,' he said, 'they will learn from their mistakes.'

'You can't let ordinary people decide the future of the country,' protested Charmian.

'The future,' retorted Graham firmly, 'is too important to be left to futurologists.'

'Why did you say this is such a tricky political issue?' Nicholas asked.

'Because the issue between the parties is not only who should make the decision about abortion,' Graham explained. 'There's also the problem of how to resolve it. The Act party think it is a fundamental issue and want it to be decided by the people in a referendum, whatever the result. The Rulers, of course, would be happy to win a vote in Parliament, thereby ratifying the status quo. It's all going to be debated tomorrow.'

Charmian served dessert: a selection of hard, green and rather sour apples.

'If you like,' suggested Gregory, 'we could watch television after supper. There are a couple of party political broadcasts in view of tomorrow's debate.' Nicholas gladly agreed.

The apples consumed, they moved to the drawing room, Charmian's mother disappeared upstairs with a vague wave of the hand and the television was turned on. The Act party's programme was rather moving. There were shots of various

weddings. Then you saw newlyweds, all young and attractive, engaged in intense discussions, pocket calculators in hand. Then the scene changed to hospital beds, with young mothers proudly fondling babies with promising futures. Then you saw other young women, apparently childless, cheerfully explaining their decision to forego the pleasures just witnessed when they realized what the consequences would be. 'But,' said an interviewer sternly, 'why didn't you practise birth control?' At this point there was stirring music with a voice-over saying, 'Never too late to calculate', and the programme came to an end. Graham cheered and left the room.

The Rule party's broadcast was much more sober and informative. There were shots of young couples, in various degrees of perplexity and helplessness being visited by marriage guidance counsellors, doctors, psychologists, and so on. Then there were interviews with various knowledgeable people, mostly in white coats, sitting beside computers, explaining the complexity of the decision whether or not to have a baby, with lots of facts and figures and diagrams superimposed on the screen to show how difficult it was to arrive at a clear decision in any given case. Then there were further shots of the experts sitting around tables, interviewing the perplexed young couples. Finally, a young woman asked the experts: 'But how on earth can I decide?' and a voice concluded the programme saying: 'You can't. They can.'

Gregory and Charmian were clearly delighted with the second programme. 'Very professional,' said Gregory. 'Just the job. Some questions are technical ones and technical questions are for experts to decide. To pretend otherwise is just sheer sentimentality. Perhaps (he turned to Nicholas) you'd like to come with me to the debate tomorrow? It'll give you a sense of what politics is like here. And I can introduce you to people in the government.'

Nicholas agreed and retired to bed, where he began to reflect upon his impressions so far of Utilitaria. He decided to begin his first Progress Report for Justin, to announce his

safe arrival. But, faced with a blank sheet of paper and with his pen poised, he puzzled over what style and tone to adopt. His relationship to Justin was not, after all, simple and straightforward: it was that of teacher to ex-student, but also that of ex-victim to saviour and of spy to spymaster, albeit a spy seeking, rather than defending, a cause. But what was he seeking? He decided to start with this question.

He wrote:

<div align="right">

c/o The Maximands,
Calcula,
Utilitaria

</div>

Dear Justin,

Perhaps I should begin by saying how I interpret the rather ill-defined mission on which you have chosen to send me. I shall try to think of it in two ways. First, from my own point of view – I can't, after all, start from anywhere else. Which place would I settle for and settle in, given the choice? In fact, for me this is not just an academic question (which is what people tend to call a question of no real significance or practical import). I have to live somewhere from now on, and I don't mean to denigrate your movement by observing that my chances of returning to Militaria in the near future do not look especially rosy. So I am, first of all, looking for a new home, a place where I might persuade Marcus and Eliza to join me. Second, I shall try to think of it from *anyone's* point of view. Where would I advise someone not yet born to be born, if I knew nothing of his or her talents and capacities, wealth, gender, race, religion, social position and life prospects? Where would it be best to take the fateful, irreversible risk of birth? Where would such a potential person have the best chance of a decent life? I hope you will agree that this is a reasonable interpretation of your rather imprecise instructions.

As you can see, I have arrived safely in Utilitaria, though not without considerable difficulties. Fortunately, I have been taken in by an old acquaintance, Gregory Maximand, who, it turns out, is well connected to the local Powers That Be. He is very informative about the Utilitarian system and I've

already learnt a lot from him and his son and from a rather remarkable young woman I sat next to on the aeroplane.

It's too early, of course, to give you my impressions of life here, but I am struck by how well-organized and efficient everything appears to be and how those I have met so far seem to take this for granted. There seems to be an extraordinarily well-developed welfare system of health care and education and a particular concern for the well-being of the elderly.

One strange thing I have noticed: the Utilitarian language seems oddly deficient and certain words and concepts are simply unknown here. The limits of their language seem to be the limits of their world. I must investigate this further.

And there is another matter which puzzles me: the Utilitarians I have so far come across all seem to be *smiling*, but the meaning of their smiles is not altogether clear. Is it *happiness*?

But what, after all, is happiness? Is it a sort of inner glow, an individual state of mind, a 'quiet state' as Diderot thought, 'sprinkled here and there with a few pleasures which brighten up its depths'? Or is it an aspect of interaction with others? Was Pope right in thinking it 'must be *social*, since all particular happiness depends on the general'? And is it something to be consumed or does it require effort and activity? Was D'Holbach right to say that 'happiness, to be appreciated, cannot be unbroken; work is necessary to mankind to place some distance between its pleasures'? Is it just the satisfaction of whatever desires people happen to have, including those harmful to themselves and others? Or does happiness consist in the satisfaction of the desires people should have, or would have if they were well-informed or sensible? Or is it something negative – the avoidance of misery, pain and suffering? Could that be why Tolstoy said that all happy families resemble one another, while every unhappy family is unhappy after its own fashion?

And are happiness and these concrete forms of unhappiness really to be measured in degrees on the same scale, the former as positive, the latter as negative? In fact, how *do* Utilitarians measure whatever it is they are maximizing? What *are* they maximizing? I must try to find out.

That is all for the time being. The prospects here look decidedly promising. Please send all my love to Marcus and Eliza.

Yours truly,
Pangloss

Lying in bed, Nicholas continued to worry over the last question in his letter to Justin. What was the object of Stella Yardstick's calculations and of all those Calculans calculating in the streets? What, he asked Alexander Pope, *is* happiness? 'Oh Happiness!' replied Pope, 'our being's end and aim!

> Good, pleasure, ease, content! whate'er thy name:
> That something still which prompts the eternal sigh,
> For which we bear to live, or dare to die,
> Which still so near us, yet beyond us lies,
> O'erlook'd, seen double by the fool and wise.

'But what is it?' Nicholas persisted.
'Some,' said Pope, 'place the bliss in action, some in ease,

> Those call it pleasure, and contentment these;
> Some, sunk to beasts, find pleasure end in pain;
> Some, swell'd to gods, confess even virtue vain;
> Or, indolent, to each extreme they fall,
> To trust in everything, or doubt of all.
> Who thus define it, say they more or less
> Than this, that happiness is happiness?

'Thanks very much!' said Nicholas. 'That's a lot of help.'
His thoughts turned to the Maximands. Were they a happy family? Take Charmian. Her life appeared to be entirely devoted to Gregory's comforts and professional career. Was it a happy life? Were its satisfactions really satisfying? Did Utilitarians ask themselves such questions? As a matter of fact, he had not seen a single sign of endearment pass between Gregory and Charmian, both seemed to entertain an active dislike of Graham (which was fully reciprocated) and all three had totally ignored Charmian's mother. Yet the family members

appeared thoroughly satisfied, even self-satisfied. Their self-satisfaction, he concluded, came from their evident conviction that their personal lives demonstrably contributed to some overall impersonal good. All three clearly held two firm beliefs: that their activities (in Charmian's case, her contribution to Gregory's) and the political parties they supported made a significant addition to the general sum of well-being, and that one could prove by calculation that this was so. Yet surely their goals were admirable and admirably public-spirited? And if calculation, using the most up-to-date methods, could bring them nearer to realization, then the Utilitarians' obsession with calculations could only be beneficial in its consequences. Of course, the important question remained: who was best placed to make them?

Without resolving the matter, Nicholas fell asleep. All in all, it had been a busy day.

·11·

The Great Debate

As they drove towards the Parliament next morning, Gregory raised with Nicholas the issue of his future in Utilitaria.

'We will, of course, appoint you as a Visiting Professor in the University in the Department of Futurology,' he announced, 'You can lecture on the future of the Idea of Progress. But I have a further suggestion.'

'What's that?'

'I'm Chief Cultural Adviser to the Government,' Gregory said, 'and actually (he leant towards him confidentially) I'm really rather close to the Prime Minister. I've proposed to her that you be given your own television programme which would explore all the virtues of life here in Utilitaria from an outsider's perspective. You can tell about your mission and explain why it has come to an end.'

Why, he wondered, do people keep wanting me to present television programmes?

When they reached the city centre, the traffic slowed and eventually the cars in front of them came to a complete stop. In the near distance he could see what looked like a crowd approaching. As it came nearer, he could see it was a demonstration. A procession slowly marched past them along

the wide street, shepherded by policemen. The marchers were waving banners and carrying placards aloft.

'That,' said Gregory derisively; 'is the Opposition. It's the best the Actors can do. When they haven't got any arguments, they demonstrate.'

The marchers wore anoraks, donkey jackets and polo-necked sweaters. Many were teenagers and students, but there were older people as well, grizzled and determined. Most were waving pocket calculators high in the air. The leaders were chanting slogans through loud hailers: 'BE ACTORS, NOT REACTORS' and 'UP WITH CALCULATORS, DOWN WITH COMPUTERS.'

'Demagogues and Luddites!' Gregory snorted.

Nicholas read some of the slogans on the banners and placards as they passed by: 'OUR RULERS ARE OUT TO FOOL US' and 'DON'T TRUST OUR FUTURES TO THEIR COMPUTERS'.

'Just calculate,' said Gregory, 'what the consequences would be if that lot were in power!'

At that moment, Graham passed them, one in an advancing line of teenagers holding a long red banner which read: 'WE MUST BE THE ABORTERS OF OUR SONS AND DAUGHTERS'.

Gregory snorted even louder.

The Parliament Building was large and imposing, a modern, functional building ten storeys high, with innumerable glass doors, stone floors and echoing halls and corridors, full of people rushing about clutching papers and briefcases. As they entered the main hallway, the soldiers on guard saluted Gregory. 'I'm a Member of the Upper House,' he explained, as they walked towards the Visitors' Gallery. 'This debate is in the Lower House. They're more rumbustious than we are. But the issue will then have to come to us in any case. The Act party keeps trying to push this one through. Think they know what "the People" want. Actors don't, of course, and they won't get anywhere with it. The people want the most efficient way of producing the most utility, but they don't know what it is.'

Nicholas and Gregory entered the Gallery and looked down on a semicircular Chamber. From where they sat, they could see the two parties, seated to the left and the right of the President's chair. The difference between the two groups was immediately apparent. Those on the right were sparse in number, evidently relaxed and terribly bored. Some were asleep with legs propped up on the seats in front of them, some were chatting to each other informally and some were idly reading news- papers. The left-hand side, by contrast, was a hive of activity. The deputies here looked angry and agitated. Some were taking notes, or whispering urgently to one another. All seemed attentive to the speech that was being declaimed by one of their number: an aggressive, rather grim-looking man of about sixty with a shock of white hair and a deep, booming voice.

'That,' said Gregory, 'is Ned Erskin – the Actors' most powerful demagogue. He's their blunt man, prepared to say the things that others wouldn't dare. He's also sharp. He's also a perfect idiot.'

' . . . and,' Ned Erskin was saying, 'we can't trust them an inch. Not a bloody inch. They're not interested in the Happiness of the Greatest Number. All they're interested in are the Pleasures of Number One. Look at their so-called expense accounts, and their business lunches and their free trips abroad. They hide behind their computer screens and tell us that they know what we don't. Well, I'll tell you this: all they see on their screens are reflections of themselves. They don't know anything about ordinary people. Where I come from we call them *toffs* (several members behind him cheered) – but (he paused for effect) that's not all we call them.'

Erskin turned to address the members of his own party. 'And it's not only the party opposite I'm talking about. We've got some stool pigeons on our own side. People who think they've got a special insight into what the people want. Snobs who think they know better than we do what we want. "The people want more opera and poetry!" they say. Well, I've got news for them. What the people want is football and pushpin.'

'Erskin,' explained Gregory, 'is the spokesman for the populist faction of the Act party. He calls the others "elitists". They hate him for it.'

'What the toffs and the snobs had better do,' Erskin continued, 'is read their John Stuart Mill.' Nicholas sat stunned. 'He once said an intelligent thing. He said that what's desirable is what's desired . . . '

'You don't make a logical blunder any less of a blunder by pointing out that John Stuart Mill committed it,' observed Gregory tartly.

' . . . he said: if the majority desire something, then they must have it . . . '

'A further blunder,' commented Gregory. 'Mill feared the uneducated masses and rightly thought the educated know better.'

' . . . and so we say: let the people who desire to abort get on with it. That's how to make the people happier.' And he sat down, to raucous cheering from a minority of his own party and a group of supporters in the Visitors' Gallery.

The next speaker was also from the Act party. He was dressed in a crumpled, ill-fitting suit, with flowing white hair and horn-rimmed glasses. He spoke in long, flowing cadences, pausing only in the middle of sentences, thereby discouraging interruptions.

'My esteemed and honourable colleague,' he began, 'has an enviable familiarity with the writings of that great Utilitarian John Stuart Mill. I don't admire Mill any less than he does. But he really ought to have given us more of the fruits of his considerable scholarship. He should perhaps have reminded us that Mill made a famous distinction between higher and lower pleasures. And that he said that a Socrates dissatisfied is better (and he turned to look hard and fixedly at Erskin) than a pig satisfied.'

'That,' Gregory explained to Nicholas, 'is Eustace Legge. Another demagogue, but an intellectual. You couldn't accuse Erskin of that!'

'And if we take a Millian and Socratic view,' continued Legge, 'we can only conclude that the people must inform themselves. How? By making their own decisions. People can only discover what they want by confronting alternatives. No-one can do it on their behalf, even with the aid of high-powered computers. Those who have already faced choices between different kinds of pleasures are in a superior position to those who have not. That is why (he turned again to Erskin) we pay heed to those who are better placed to appreciate the value of opera and poetry. But it is also why (he turned in peroration to the President of the Chamber) we should reject the crass and egregious effrontery of unelected experts, the arbitrary arbitration of our destinies, the featureless futurologists, the commensurators of the incommensurable, the numberless number-crunchers, the countless counters of the uncountable, the innumerable enumerators of the unnumerable, the presumptuous, pretentious, portentous, preposterous impostors in white coats who have usurped our wills and would do our choosing for us.'

With this he finished, and the majority of his party rose to their feet, cheering wildly. Eustace Legge sat down.

Now it was time for the Rulers to speak, and interest in the debate visibly revived on the right-hand side. Empty seats filled up, newspapers were folded away and chattering ceased, as a wiry man with silvery grey hair, elegantly dressed in waistcoat and bow tie, addressed his fellow deputies in a languid, rather supercilious drawl.

'That,' explained Gregory, 'is Milton Candew. Leader of the so-called "minimalist" faction in our party. They believe in the quick, simple fix: achieve maximum happiness by removing frustration, eliminating all desires that can't be satisfied. Candew's got this mad idea that by introducing this new drug "Frustricide" into the water supply you can create instant mass happiness. Harebrained. It's all he can talk about, and yet it has a kind of mad logic.'

' . . . and if our purpose is to eliminate pain and suffering,'

drawled Candew, 'what better way could there be? Frustricide can be produced extremely cheaply. It can be introduced into the water supply without any difficulty. In short, it is virtually costless. It is also odourless, colourless and tasteless, as well as harmless and painless . . . '

'Now they're trying to poison our bloody water!' shouted Erskin.

Candew continued unruffled: 'A baseless accusation, typical of the members of the Opposition party, and in particular of that member. After the administration of Frustricide, no-one will be unhappier. Indeed, no-one will be unhappy. I cannot think of any argument a Utilitarian can advance against this policy!'

'Life would become extremely boring!' declaimed Eustace Legge.

'Boring!' Candew repeated, with mock surprise, 'Is misery interesting? Is suffering exciting? Is frustration diverting? If you remove all the symptoms of unhappiness, what have you left? Happiness. Why do any more? We have a wonderful solution to our nation's problem on our hands. That's why we say: *We must decide for Frustricide!*' Candew sat down to a thin ripple of applause from the thin ranks of his supporters.

Now there arose from among the Rulers a speaker who was clearly of sterner and solider stuff. She wore a steel blue suit, her peach-dyed hair was in perfect trim, her gait assured, her poise immaculate. The Chamber became silent in anticipation.

'That,' whispered Gregory, 'is Hilda Juggernaut, the Prime Minister.'

'It might be as well,' she began icily, 'to return to the question before us: Who will decide who is to abort? The Act party proposes that no-one should. Leave it, they say, to what they like to call "the People". What a monstrous doctrine! How can you leave a matter of such public moment to the blind play of arbitrary, private whims?'

Her tone changed, becoming softer, huskier, more urgent: 'Our great object is to produce more and more utility. We must not be deflected from that noble task by subversive ideas,

such as the idea the Opposition seems to favour that you must respect the whims of actually existing persons. *Why* should you? What is there to respect? Nothing. Because (she paused dramatically) there is no such thing as *persons*. We must get rid of obsolete ideas like "personal identity", "personal dignity" and "personal integrity". People are just the producers and consumers of utility.'

Her tone now became steely: 'Our task is to produce people who are more efficient at producing and consuming utility. The issue before us is just one aspect of that larger programme. We must control population growth so as to optimize it relative to available resources. We must also breed more efficiently. We must develop and perfect our reproductive as well as our productive technologies. We must not only produce utility but also Utilitarians capable of producing more and more utility and capable of consuming it efficiently. The point is not to make people happier. The point is to make happier people.'

A great roar of applause greeted this remark. Her speech rolled on relentlessly. 'The question of abortion is only one of very many questions to which our larger vision provides answers. Committees of experts are to decide who is to be born. From whom are the sperm and the eggs to come? Who shall give birth? There is of course no necessity that these should be the same persons. And who is to mother and father them? Utility may well dictate that this be done by yet other persons. These questions concern the beginnings of life, but we must also consider its termination. Just as experts are in the best position to determine who is to be born and how and by whom they are to be brought up, so too are they best able to calculate when useful lives have reached the limits of their usefulness.

'Which leads me to a very important new policy initiative. We have decided to reconstitute the administration of our Welfare State by dividing its functions between two new Super Ministries. From now on, all that concerns the positive functions of nurturing and fostering the efficient production

of ever greater utility will be dealt with by the new Ministry of Welfare. And all that concerns the negative, but no less important, task of removing from the scene those no longer able to contribute to that production with adequate efficiency will be under the aegis of the new Ministry of Farewell.'

Nicholas heard these words with a sudden shock, recalling the peaceful scene in the House of Farewell. So it was a waiting room after all. He could not stop himself wondering how it was done. Did the nurses do it in public view, with syringes perhaps, wheeling out their charges through the doors marked 'FAREWELL'? Or did they wheel them out alive and do them in on the other side?

'What the party of the Rulers believes in,' the Prime Minister continued (she seemed to have reached her peroration), 'is a *real* Welfare State – one which will be safe with us. A State in which those best able to calculate what will bring about the best consequences for the general welfare are left alone to do so. A State in which in every sphere of life *experts* make the significant choices. A State in which we trust medical personnel to decide whom to treat and for how long, social security personnel to target those who genuinely require support, teachers and education officers to allocate our children to the appropriate schools and colleges, weighing the alternatives and selecting the most efficient. A State in which we trust bodies of qualified experts to determine who will be born, how they will be educated, who will receive medical treatment and whose lives will have to be brought to a conclusion.'

The Prime Minister, having reached her conclusion, sat down, to an explosion of clapping, stamping and cheering on the Rule party side. The Actors sat still, looking grim. None looked grimmer than Ned Erskin.

It was time for the vote, the motion being 'that this House favours granting mothers, in consultation with fathers, the power to decide to terminate pregnancies'. The deputies all pressed buttons attached to their seats and the result came up

on a large screen behind the President's chair: against 403, in favour 106. Graham had obviously been over-hopeful about the waverers and mavericks. The Rulers were firmly in the saddle. Gregory looked pleased. 'Come and meet the PM,' he said.

They descended the marble stairs and walked down several long corridors, past bustling people carrying papers and briefcases. They passed through a red curtain and reached a door marked 'PRIME MINISTER'. Gregory knocked and entered. The room was painted in pastel pink and softly furnished in deep red velvet. 'Hello, Hilda,' he said jovially. 'Marvellous speech, absolutely marvellous! You pulverized them! I've brought Professor Caritat to meet you.'

She rose from her desk, piled high with official papers, her hand outstretched, 'Professor Caritat,' she said, softly and huskily, 'we're so glad to meet you, and so glad that you have come to Utilitaria. Gregory has told us all about your mission to find the best possible world.'

'A mission,' intervened Gregory, 'that is now at an end.'

'Untrue!' she retorted with some force. 'Gregory, I regret to say, is much given to exaggeration. Of *course*, this is not the best possible world. But (her tone changed to the hard, metallic register) it will be when our policies come to fruition.'

She returned to husky softness: 'Gregory tells me you are one of us. I'm so glad.'

He felt an impulse to demur but, not wanting to seem impolite, resisted it.

'We're *very* much looking forward,' she continued, 'to your first television programme.' The impulse recurred and once more he suppressed it.

The conversation (in which he had not actually spoken) was now evidently at an end, for she was shaking his hand in farewell. It appears, Nicholas thought, that conversations in Utilitaria come to an abrupt end when no longer useful. He wondered what effect that would have on debate and discussion.

'Please don't hesitate,' the Prime Minister was saying, 'to be in touch if there is *anything* we can do. If you ever need any help, you can count on us!'

Better not indicate gratitude, he thought, recalling his encounter with the Immigration Officer. 'Goodbye,' he said, 'I look forward to our next meeting.'

'So do I,' she said, with a smile he found oddly unreassuring.

'An extraordinary woman!' remarked Gregory, as they walked down the corridor towards the exit. For once, he decided, Gregory was not exaggerating.

The rest of the day was spent in establishing the framework of his future in Utilitaria. Gregory took him for lunch at the University Faculty Club, after which he was given an office, assigned a secretary and provided with computer, telephone and fax machine.

'Your first lecture,' Gregory informed him, 'will be the day after tomorrow at nine a.m. You can explain the origins of the Idea of Progress in the Enlightenment. Why don't we advertise it under the title "Breaking Free from the Past"?'

Gregory then took him to what was to be his new home, on the ninth floor of a block of University apartments. It was spare and rectangular, with parquet floors and walls in white and bright orange: functional, geometrical and sparsely furnished with tubular metallic Scandinavian-style furniture that was also white, orange, functional and geometrical. He winced, remembering his book-lined inner sanctum in Militaria.

He had dinner that evening *chez* Maximands. Graham was absent – called away, Gregory suggested with a sneer, for some higher political purpose. Once again Gregory presided, sitting opposite Charmian. Once again Nicholas found himself sitting opposite Charmian's silent mother. On his left there was another dinner guest: an expansive, ebullient, well-groomed, well-dressed woman in her late fifties, with a loud, ringing voice and a great deal to tell the assembled company. She was Priscilla Yardstick, Minister of Health in the current government and, Gregory proudly announced, a very good

friend. The menu was different but no less healthy and his hosts as attentive to him, and as little to each other, and to Charmian's mother, as ever.

Nicholas mentioned that he had met a young woman diplomat on the aeroplane called Stella Yardstick. 'My daughter!' explained Priscilla proudly. 'Splendid girl. She's been doing excellent work on immigration. We often joke about it: she focuses on the flow and I on the stock. Of course you can't in the end distinguish the two, can you Professor? (She turned to Nicholas but did not wait for his answer.) After all, this abortion business is a flow question: who is to be born and who isn't. And that, you could say, is also a matter of stockbreeding. And weeding out the old and infirm – that's also a matter of maintaining the quality of the stock. That's what my job essentially amounts to. Maintaining the quality of the stock. Maximizing its productivity – its capacity to produce goods and services that generate utility – and maintaining its capacity to enjoy those goods and services and to obtain satisfaction! It's all a question of maximizing efficiency.'

'And how do you go about doing that?' Nicholas asked.

'Well,' answered Priscilla, obviously delighted at being asked to expand upon a favourite theme, 'it's all a matter of *weighing* alternatives. For instance, our medical administrators have to decide how to allocate resources and when and how to treat patients.'

'How do they do that?' asked Nicholas.

'They weigh the alternatives!' exclaimed Priscilla. 'They *calculate*. Measurement and publicity, that's our motto! What is a human life worth? Every six months the Statistical Office publishes an updated valuation and that figure is used as a basis for assessment. We make adjustments, positive and negative, for various factors. We examine specific capacities for productivity and consider capacities for efficient consumption. Generally, it takes less to make the old happy, once ambition has been fulfilled, or died.'

'I see,' Nicholas said, though he was not altogether sure that he did. Then he noticed that Charmian's mother's stony eyes were fixed intently upon the Minister. For the first time, the old lady spoke. Her voice was surprisingly firm and clear, given her advanced age: she must have been over eighty.

'You are absolutely right,' she said with obvious conviction. 'The policy of your government is wonderful. I think so – and so did Charmian's dear father, didn't he, dear?'

Charmian nodded enthusiastically.

'Such a happy man he was, always laughing and joking. He was a civil engineer for the whole of his life. He built our roads. Then, at the age of sixty, they said he needed a hip replacement. He was in terrible pain, but he never let it show, in case anyone should think his capacity for being happy had been impaired. And so they operated and he got his hip replaced, because they said he was contributing so much to transport and was so happy and uncomplaining. A few years later, he had a stone in his gall bladder. Terribly painful, but he bore up and never let on how much he was suffering – though I knew. Once again they operated because he was still designing roads and smiling all the time. But then, when he reached seventy, he had a cataract in his eye which prevented him working. He'd reached retirement age but had carried on working by contract. The surgery wasn't justified, they argued, after weighing the cost against the benefits to others and to himself. He never complained about the decision. He thought they were absolutely right and so did I. And when he went completely blind, he said that he'd made his contribution and didn't want to be a burden on society. He was glad when they took one of his kidneys for transplant to give to some young productive worker. When he had his stroke and was denied a hospital bed, he and I both agreed that it was time for him to go. After all, there wasn't much utility in his staying around, was there? Charmian and Gregory were of the same opinion.'

Nicholas was struck by the sincerity of the old lady's

speech. She was obviously a true believer in Utilitaria's health policy and a firm supporter of the Minister. Or was she? Priscilla Yardstick certainly assumed so and was looking delighted at these words of support. But one thing puzzled Nicholas.

'About the kidney transplant. You said they took one of his kidneys. But surely he had to give them permission?'

Priscilla intervened. 'Well, not since our recent law,' she explained. 'The transfer of body parts is now included in the tax system, and, where needed, such contributions have to be paid, just like income tax and sales tax. But unlike those taxes, you can know exactly what you have contributed to.'

'I see,' said Nicholas. The whole health system sounded remarkably efficient and, to judge by the old lady's story, supported by patients. And it had, he reflected, further advantages. For instance, it obviously gave everyone an incentive to avoid expensive illnesses, to devote themselves to productive activities and to be, or at least *seem* to be, happy and contented, so as not to appear inefficient.

Nicholas asked the Minister a further question. 'One other thing I don't quite see: how do you organize the transfer of body parts?'

'Ah!' replied Priscilla, 'like clockwork! The system works especially well from the point of view of the unproductive handicapped.'

'Why are they particular beneficiaries?' asked Nicholas.

'They're not *beneficiaries*,' Priscilla corrected him. 'They're *benefactors*. It's their distinctive way of contributing to the general welfare. They can't produce goods or services, but they can provide organs that will enable others to do so. It gives them a purpose in life, and that's especially valuable as we've largely phased out medical care for that particular category.'

'You mean,' said Nicholas, 'that the handicapped who can't work don't receive medical care?'

'Well, of course, it's a question of degree,' explained Priscilla, 'like everything else. It's all a matter of how many

points your handicap scores. So, for instance, if you're lame in one leg you score three, if you're blind you score six, if you can't use a pair of scissors you score eleven and if you're totally paralysed you're awarded fifteen. The higher your score the less your entitlement to medical resources. As you can see, the whole system is very finely tuned.'

There were those in the Rule party, Priscilla went on to relate, who favoured the active elimination of the unproductive handicapped and the incurably ill, but, for the time being, the experts were of the opinion that it was most advantageous to retain these categories as sources of supply of body parts and as resources for medical experimentation.

The rest of the dinner conversation was taken up with Priscilla recounting political gossip about various members of the government, all known to Gregory, of which Nicholas could make little sense. At the end of the meal, she rose to depart in abrupt Utilitarian style, explaining that she had to attend to her papers. Shaking Nicholas's hand, she wished him good health. Thanking her for her informative conversation, he resolved to keep his health robust, his work productive and his happiness apparent.

After Priscilla's departure, over coffee, Gregory made another suggestion to Nicholas: 'Why don't you come with me to the Court of Appeal tomorrow? There's a major case being decided. You've had a glimpse of Utilitarian politics at work. Now perhaps you should take a look at Utilitarian justice?'

This, Nicholas agreed, sounded like an excellent idea.

Back in his stark Utilitarian flat, he reflected on that evening's dinner-table discussion. Charmian's mother intrigued him. One thing puzzled him: how had the old lady managed to escape the government's farewell services? Why was she still at the Maximands rather than at Farewell House? Perhaps she was herself still performing some valuable welfare service: as health adviser on the family's meals perhaps? And how was it that she did not seem to feel any resentment at the manner of her husband's death?

But then, he remembered, Utilitarians didn't understand resentment – or gratitude, concepts that only made sense by looking backwards across a person's life. Why didn't they? Perhaps it was because they didn't believe in *persons*. In the debate the Prime Minister had said 'there's no such thing as persons'. What did she mean? Of course *people* existed, but perhaps she meant that no deep importance is to be attributed to an individual's life seen as a whole, stretching from birth to death. There was, he recalled, a philosopher called Parfit who suggested that such a life is simply a series of experiences and deeds: that there's no further fact in addition to these, no separate entity called a 'person' which owns those experiences and performs those deeds. Perhaps for Utilitarians all that matters are experiences, some more happy, some less so, connected only by memories. Just as the composition of the body continuously changes in the course of a lifetime, cells replacing other cells, so one could see a 'person' as no more than a flux of successive and more or less interconnected experiences. In which case, there would be no special reason to attach importance to the fact that earlier and later experiences occur within the same lifetime. So someone contemplating death shouldn't say, 'I shall be dead', but rather 'There will be no future experiences that will be related, in certain ways, to these present experiences.' Perhaps, Nicholas surmised, all that matters to a Utilitarian is maximizing the number of happy experiences, not whose experiences they are. So perhaps ending a particular life would have a lesser significance for Utilitarians than for non-Utilitarians. It would be much less important than diminishing or not increasing the number of happy experiences. The unity of a so-called person's life would simply be a series of interconnected experiences – and the earlier ones could be very distant from the later ones. But, he wondered, what implications would such a viewpoint have for guilt and innocence, for punishment and responsibility? Why should someone feel guilt now for a barely remembered deed

committed earlier in his lifetime? And would it matter so much *whom* one punished for a crime, provided that the punishment had the desired deterrent effects? But it was too late at night to work all that out and in any case he was very tired.

·12·

Justice

At 8.45 next morning, there was a knock at his front door. He opened it to a young man in a peaked cap, who identified himself as a University driver sent at the request of Professor Maximand.

Sitting in his new office, Nicholas reflected upon the theme of the next day's inaugural lecture, which had been announced as 'Breaking Free from the Past', and wrote some lecture notes and a rough outline. He would chart the ways in which the past reasserts its hold on those who most fervently seek to escape it. His message would be that a preoccupation with the future can be self-defeating, that seeking after novelty is not always the best way of achieving it and that the study of the past can itself be a source of innovation. He would illustrate this last thought by reference to a range of Enlightenment thinkers, among them Voltaire, Hume and Rousseau. He gave the lecture notes to his newly appointed secretary to be typed up for the following morning.

At eleven Gregory arrived and they set off for Court.

'The case,' said Gregory, 'concerns five Bigotarians who planted a bomb in a café in Reckonham fifteen years ago. Killed twenty-one people and wounded many more. Caught virtually red-handed while playing cards on a train on their

way home from their crime. They confessed, of course. Sentenced to life. It's an open-and-shut case.'

'On what grounds are they appealing?' Nicholas asked.

'No real grounds,' answered Gregory. 'Of course, they claim they've been framed and that the police forced them to confess and fabricated evidence against them. A whole campaign has been mounted on their behalf. Won't cut any ice though.'

As they approached the Court, he could see that there was another street demonstration. Unlike the previous day's, it was separated into two distinct factions, one on each side of the street. On one side was a group of rather solid, respectable looking, middle-aged persons holding a banner which read: 'THE RECKONHAM FIVE SPELL THE WRECK OF US ALL'. On the other, the demonstrators were younger, shabbier and scruffier. Among them he saw Graham, standing with the same group of teenagers as yesterday, holding up another red banner which read: 'THE RECKONHAM RECKONING IS BECKONING'.

'Does Graham ever go to school?' Nicholas asked.

'It has been known,' Gregory replied. 'But,' he added drily, 'one has to be indulgent. He has a great future in advertising.'

They parked the car and approached the Court Building, an imposing nineteenth-century neo-Gothic structure. At the summit of its façade was a statue of Utilitarian Justice: a female figure holding a pair of scales in one hand. She was, however, without blindfold and sword. Instead, she held a telescope to her eye, peering, Nicholas surmised, into the calculable future.

They passed through the security check into a long, dimly lit and echoing entrance hall, with a mosaic marble floor, on either side of which were white busts of various eminent Utilitarians – Beccaria, Helvétius and Bentham – and mounted a spiral stone staircase to a door marked 'COURT NUMBER FOUR'. The Courtroom was large, gloomy, echoing, oak-pannelled with a very high ceiling. It had high mullioned windows through which a greyish light filtered. The wooden

benches of the Public Gallery were packed with people listening attentively. In front of them was the Judges' bench, illuminated by three green-capped lanterns, behind which there sat three elderly gentlemen. To the left of them, behind a metal grill, sat three men and two women, their eyes cast down and their faces ageing, wasted and expressionless, flanked by two guards. Below them was a large table, at which sat the Court Clerk, scribbling and shuffling papers. The Judges, the Clerk and the Lawyers facing them, with their backs to the public, were all begowned and bewigged.

'The Judge in the middle,' whispered Gregory, 'is Judge Tantamount, the Lord Chief Justice. On the left is Judge Barker and on the right Judge Growler.'

As Nicholas and Gregory sat down, the Defence Counsel, a forceful woman with long eyelashes and manicured finger nails, had just begun her summing up and was waving her spectacles in the air theatrically.

'You have heard evidence from a variety of scientific experts that the tests for gelignite, on the basis of which the Appellants were convicted, are entirely unreliable – as unreliable as the evidence of the forensic scientist on which the Prosecution case has relied. You have heard from independent experts that the traces found on their hands could equally well have resulted from the playing cards that they were holding when arrested on the Reckonham–Fishport Express – or indeed from chemicals supplied from unknown sources to assist the police in their enquiries.

'You have heard evidence from a number of prison officers that the Appellants were badly beaten up and that their black eyes and broken ribs and cuts and bruises were not, as was officially claimed at the time, the results of a curious proclivity they all five of them shared for throwing themselves down staircases.

'You have heard and seen compelling evidence that the written records of interviews with the Appellants were falsified by the police investigators after the event. We have

conclusively proved that, not content with extracting confessions from my clients by bullying and intimidation, the policemen in charge of this case have doctored their own evidence by rewriting the relevant pages of their notebooks.

'You have heard evidence from a variety of friends and neighbours of the Appellants that they were openly begging and borrowing money to pay for the train journey on which they were subsequently arrested. That would seem an odd activity for conspiratorial bombers working for a terrorist organization to engage in.

'It is obvious the police investigating this case decided from the start to pin the crime on these easily available suspects. They did not look elsewhere, even though known Bigotarian leaders were known to be in the area. Five birds in their hands were worth any number in the bush, especially if they could be made to sing. The investigators' powerful imaginations led them to look for homeward-bound, card-playing Bigotarians on trains. Their considerable powers of persuasion enabled them to convince five innocent people (she waved her spectacles at the grill) to confess to a crime they never committed – confessions which my clients all repudiated at the first possible opportunity. There are no grounds for believing that they committed this horrible crime. It has certainly not been shown beyond reasonable doubt that they did. What possible reason, then, can there be for continuing to keep them in custody?'

She sat down as decisively as she had spoken, to a rustle of excitement among the public and a muffled cheer from the back of the Court. She seemed well satisfied with her performance.

Gregory leant over and whispered to Nicholas. 'That's Clarissa Preen, the Bigotarians' Friend. The press has dubbed her "Queen Preen". As you can see, she has several admirers, but the greatest is herself. Now we're going to hear some serious argument. That's Augustus Rapier.'

The Counsel for the Prosecution rose to speak. Tall and

perfectly erect, his robes draped elegantly around him, his tone was aloofly supercilious.

'My Lords, my Learned Friend has asked an excellent question – which I shall endeavour to answer. The Appellants' case, which she has so very *ably* presented to us, amounts to this: that on the say-so of various assorted so-called scientists, of a few doubtless disaffected prison officers and of a bunch of friends and neighbours, who are associates of and plainly sympathetic to the Appellants, we are asked to call into question the results of an elaborate and painstaking police inquiry and the outcome of a solemnly conducted trial by Judge and Jury.

'My Learned Friend asks us to accept that there is a reasonable doubt that the Appellants caused the Cat and Cucumber Café to explode. What, my Lords, *is* a reasonable doubt? *When* is it reasonable to doubt? *Whom* is it reasonable to doubt? Is it reasonable to doubt the very words of these self-confessed criminals, just because they changed their minds, or because a few unreliable prison officers tell tall tales? Is it reasonable to put one's faith in the arbitrary judgements of a few maverick scientists and so-called handwriting experts? Is it reasonable to place any trust in Bigotarian supporters rallying around their friends? And does anyone doubt for a second that these five Appellants are supporters of the so-called Bigotarian cause? Isn't that enough to render them more than suspect?

'My Lords, I must ask: is it reasonable to suppose that these are *not* the perpetrators of this horrible crime, when, fifteen years after the event, there is virtually no chance of discovering alternative candidates to prosecute? Is it reasonable to abandon a plausible hypothesis in the absence of any plausible counterhypothesis? I observe that the Appellants' case contains no hint of a suggestion as to who might have committed this crime, if they are in fact innocent.

'In view of these powerful considerations, my Lords, I submit that the convictions and sentences must stand and that these five dangerous terrorists, whose purpose was, and doubtless

remains, to disturb our peace and diminish our happiness, must remain in custody for the rest of their days.'

He sat down heavily. Many of the people around him seemed restive and angry but the prisoners behind the grill showed no trace of a reaction.

Judge Tantamount rose and declared: 'We will retire' and, as the three Lord Justices departed, the public and the Lawyers rose and bowed. A buzz of excitement pervaded the Public Gallery. Journalists were comparing notes, Lawyers were conferring, conspirators were conspiring. Gregory seemed well satisfied.

'Fine speech that!' he said. He clearly meant the Prosecution Counsel's. 'He'll be a Judge before long. Very judicially minded.'

'But,' Nicholas remonstrated mildly, 'he didn't contest the *evidence* adduced by the other side.'

'Of course not!' said Gregory. 'He discredited it.'

After a short interval, the Judges returned, and the Court rose, bowed and sank back in tense expectancy as Judge Tantamount began to speak:

'On August the third, fifteen years ago at 18.05, a bomb exploded in the Cat and Cucumber Café in Reckonham, claiming twenty-one lives and twenty-seven injured persons and causing considerable damage to property. Some one and a half hours later, the police discovered five persons on the 19.35 Reckonham–Fishport Express, playing cards, and arrested them as prime suspects. Tests subsequently showed them to have handled gelignite, and they freely confessed, while awaiting trial, to the crime of planting the aforesaid bomb. In the subsequent trial, they were duly convicted and sentenced to life imprisonment, of which they have so far served fifteen years.

'We have heard an admirable, an elegant and eloquent speech from their Counsel. She has endeavoured to persuade us that there exists a reasonable doubt as to her clients' participation in this dastardly, inhuman and senseless crime, by trying to impugn the police evidence and by suggesting

that the Appellants' confessions were extracted by force. These are, of course, exactly the arguments to which those accused of crimes typically resort. When considering them, we must indeed ask, as the Learned Prosecution Counsel has so wisely done, *what* and *whom* is it reasonable to doubt? On the answers to these questions much depends.

'It cannot be too often stressed in this Court that the underlying maxim of Utilitarian justice is *Utilitas populi suprema lex est.* That maxim applies not least to the questions before us. It is only reasonable to doubt when the people's utility requires such doubt and it is unreasonable to do so when it does not. Will overall utility be enhanced by doubting the veracity and probity of our police and the sagacity of our Judges and Juries? Whose interests are served by the instilling of such doubts?' He looked hard at the grill.

'The Law is a vast machine for producing future goods out of past ills. The Criminal Law, in particular, responds to past injustices, crimes and misdemeanours by applying a vast system of finely graded sanctions in order to maximize, through deterrence, future good behaviour. If this machine is to function well, three conditions are necessary. First, crimes must be punished. Second, the punishment must fit the crime. Third, there must be a general belief that criminals are punished. This last belief must, at all costs, not be undermined. That is especially the case in our present situation, faced as we are by a campaign of terror directed against our Utilitarian way of life by those who are implacably opposed to it. Potential terrorists and criminals must be held in check by the fear of the consequences of their actions. That fear would not be enhanced by the doubts we have been invited to entertain today. Some have been known to say that Justice should be blind. That is false. Justice must be *deaf* – deaf to the doubts that would undermine its very existence. That is why I say that the longer this hearing has gone on, the more convinced this Court has become that the verdict of the original Jury was correct.'

At this point Judge Tantamount took his pocket calculator out of his waistcoat pocket. 'This Court,' he continued, 'has devoted much time and expense to this case. We have heard seventeen witnesses for the Appellants who, along with their counsel's lengthy speeches, have taken up one hundred and seven hours of Court time. At the rate I calculate per minute to run this court, that works out at a very large sum indeed. In the ordinary way, this Court would require the Appellants to bear the entire burden of these costs. In this particular case, however, we are prepared to assume them, in the interests of the wider justice we are dispensing. What cannot be contemplated is that our society should pay the costs of uncertainty and loss of confidence in the forces of law and order, were the perpetrators of evil crimes such as these not to be brought to book.

'As always, in our system of Utilitarian justice, we must look at the consequences of what we decide. One may well ask whether this case should ever have been allowed to come to Appeal. If these five persons fail in their Appeal, it will mean that much time and money have been expended by many people for no good purpose. If the five persons were to win, it would mean that the police were guilty of perjury, that they were guilty of violence and threats, that the confessions were involuntary and were improperly admitted in evidence and that the convictions were erroneous. This is such an appalling vista that every sensible person in the land would agree that it cannot be right that their Appeal should win.

'This case shows what a civilized country Utilitaria is. Here are five persons who have been proved guilty of the most wicked murder of twenty-one innocent people. They have no money. Yet the State has lavished large sums on their Defence. They were convicted of murder and sentenced to imprisonment for life. In their evidence they were guilty of gross perjury. Yet the State continued to lavish large sums on them in actions against the police. It is high time it stopped.

It is simply an attempt to set aside the convictions on a side wind. It is a scandal that should not be allowed to continue. The Appeal is dismissed.'

'I concur,' growled Lord Justice Barker.

'I concur,' barked Lord Justice Growler.

Consternation broke out in the Public Gallery. 'So much for Utilitarian justice!' yelled a young man to their left. 'Courage! We'll fight for you!' shouted others. 'Silence in Court!' ordered the Clerk.

The five were swiftly escorted out of their places into the nether regions below and behind. At the same moment, the three Judges rose and also departed, as some of the public stood up and bowed once more. As protesting voices continued to protest, the Clerk of the Court ordered 'Clear the Court!' and a crowd of agitated people pushed through the doorway. Nicholas and Gregory walked back to the entrance of the building.

'I think you should meet Lord Chief Justice Tantamount,' said Gregory. 'I know him rather well. Close friend, actually. I'm sure he'd like to meet you.' He picked up a telephone, made a call and, within minutes, a uniformed woman usher arrived. She led them along a corridor, lined with Judges past and present: busts of Judges, hanging portraits of Judges and even mannequins of Judges in glass cases wearing caps and fur-lined gowns of various shapes and colours. They ascended another spiral stone staircase and came to a locked door. She opened it and led them along another corridor through imposing oaken doors, until they reached yet another door marked 'THE LORD CHIEF JUSTICE'. She knocked and they were admitted into Judge Tantamount's study.

His room was impressive. It was lined to the ceiling with law books and had the same grey light filtering through high mullioned windows. Judge Tantamount rose from his desk and greeted them with an expansive smile. Gregory introduced Nicholas and explained once again about his mission and its happy completion.

'Delighted to meet you, Professor Caritat,' said the Judge. 'Would you care for a glass of claret, gentlemen?'

Gregory nodded enthusiastic assent, Judge Tantamount pressed an imperious bell and a male servant duly appeared with a full decanter and three glasses on a silver tray. Gregory and Nicholas reclined in deep leather armchairs sipping their wine, and the Judge sat before them behind his desk.

'I should be most interested to know,' he asked Nicholas, 'how you thought Utilitarian Justice acquitted herself today.'

Nicholas chose his words carefully: 'I'm not sure, but, so far as I could observe, she didn't seem to weigh the Appellants' case in her scales.'

Judge Tantamount looked slightly surprised. 'She weighed,' he replied, 'the risks of their case being accepted as true.'

'But,' replied Nicholas, 'isn't there a risk that their case might be true?'

'Professor Caritat,' answered the Judge, 'our whole system of justice can only work if everyone believes it is working well. Potential wrongdoers must be convinced that the wrongs they would do will not pay, and everyone else must be convinced that they are so convinced. In that way we minimize law-breaking and maximize both our security and our sense of security. Take the case you have witnessed today. The original verdict against the Appellants sustained everyone's belief in the functioning of the system. The one conviction, you might say, preserved the other. Overturn the first and you undermine the second.'

'Are you saying,' asked Nicholas, 'that, if innocent, these five people are to be *sacrificed* for the public good?'

'Your language is very colourful, Professor,' said the Judge. 'Speaking for myself, I don't use words like *sacrifice*. As a matter of fact, it is a concept barely understood in Utilitaria. It is a religious metaphor, inherited from the past, hardly appropriate to our circumstances. I much prefer an economic or commercial metaphor. Let us say that what we faced today was a *trade-off*.'

Nicholas persisted, for the question continued to trouble him.

'But suppose,' he asked the Judge, 'that a journalist sees a man on the roof of a prison claiming he is innocent. Should he investigate the claim or walk away?'

'Oh, walk away!' said Judge Tantamount. 'Ignore him. I have a lot of letters from people in prison who say they've been wrongly convicted. I'm afraid I put them into the wastepaper basket.'

Their meeting was, it seemed, drawing to its abrupt Utilitarian close, for the Judge had risen from his chair, his hand extended towards Nicholas.

'I'm extremely pleased to have met you, Professor, and I have taken careful note of your penetrating questions. I hope your stay here will be happy and profitable for all of us. Don't hesitate to be in touch if there is any way we can be of help. We will if we can – you can count on that. Goodbye, Gregory.'

They left and were ushered down the stairs and past the statues of the Judges. 'An outstanding Judge!' remarked Gregory. 'Utterly reliable. Man of principle. Bit old-fashioned, though.'

'How do you mean?' asked Nicholas.

'Still believes in the jury system. Thinks it preserves the appearance of justice, maintains people's faith that the verdicts are well-founded. But, I ask you, consider the case we've just witnessed. The Bigotarians and their supporters would have had much less ground for hope if the whole thing had been dealt with summarily by a magistrate. They might never have appealed! Think what a lot of time, trouble and money could have been saved! In fact,' he added, 'if they'd been executed there and then, we wouldn't have heard any more about the case. We're going to have lunch today with the Chief Prosecutor. She's spearheading a campaign to abolish juries and make our whole Utilitarian system more efficient. Close friend of mine, actually.' Nicholas was beginning to

wonder whether there was any important Utilitarian who was not a close friend of Gregory's.

The Chief Prosecutor, Felicity Hawk, made a strong impression on Nicholas as they lunched in a smart, discreetly lit restaurant surrounded by important-looking people speaking in low voices. She was thin and intense and wore an elegant dark grey trouser suit and short-cropped hair. Fiery, fierce and forthright, with a no-nonsense manner of speaking, Felicity was plainly a true believer, a Utilitarian evangelist. Gregory at least had a scholarly interest in those parts of the past that prefigured a Utilitarian future. Felicity, by contrast, appeared to regard the entire past as an encumbrance upon the efficient management of the justice system.

'Medieval junk!' she remarked as she picked at her cottage cheese and celery salad. 'Sentimental mumbo-jumbo! I ask you,' she asked Nicholas, 'what reasonable person would think of leaving the most important decision in the legal process to twelve ignorant amateurs?'

Nicholas started to say something about the right to be tried by one's peers but she did not seem to want to pursue the idea.

'It's farcical,' she continued, 'unprofessional, inefficient and a total waste of public funds.'

'It's also politically motivated,' said Gregory. 'The Act party's in favour of juries, and we all know why. It's their usual demagoguery – flattering people into thinking that everyone can be an expert. But don't worry,' he added, in an attempt to reassure Nicholas, 'the jury system's doomed in Utilitaria.'

Nicholas was not seeking reassurance but saw little point in arguing the issue. His lunch companions were so sure of the self-evidence of their view that they simply assumed that Nicholas must agree with them and did not try to persuade him. Their obvious interest in securing convictions did not, it appeared, extend to him.

He spent the rest of the day in his office, preparing his

inaugural lecture. When he returned late to his apartment, he found a note on his front door which read: 'You will be collected at 8.15.'

In bed, he debated with Constantin-François Volney about the relations between past, present and future. Volney was less confident than his friend and fellow-campaigner against slavery, Condorcet, about the prospects for human progress, but he looked forward, like Condorcet, to a time when 'the whole species will become one great society, one individual family governed by the same spirit, by common laws, and enjoying all the felicity of which human nature is capable.' But looking backwards, he contemplated ruins:

> To the tumultuous throng which crowded under these porticos, the solitude of death has succeeded. The silence of the tomb is substituted for the hum of public places. The opulence of a commercial city is changed into hideous poverty. The palaces of kings are become the receptacle of deer, and unclean reptiles inhabit the sanctuary of the Gods. . . . What glory is here eclipsed, and how many labours are annihilated! . . . Thus perish the works of men, and thus do empires and nations vanish away!

'Who can assure me,' he demanded mournfully of Nicholas, 'that their present defoliation will not one day be the lot of our own country?'

'No-one,' replied Nicholas. 'We just have to find a way of not finding the past too discouraging or the future too encouraging.' And, maintaining that the past is a house in which to live and make improvements, rather than a set of ruins on which to build anew, he fell fast asleep.

·13·

The Collection

At 8.15 the next morning there was a knock at the front door. He opened it to reveal another young man in a peaked cap who, as on the previous day, announced himself to be a University driver sent at Professor Maximand's request. Nicholas followed the driver along the corridor. This time they did not use the lift but walked down the stairs instead and out through the back entrance of the building to a waiting car. The driver opened the back door. Nicholas sank into his seat, and the car sped off.

After several minutes, he noticed that they were taking a different and wholly unfamiliar route to the University. It slowly dawned on him that they were actually driving away from, rather than towards, the city centre. Leaning forward to speak to the driver, Nicholas noticed a metal and glass grill that separated them. He began to sweat, thought of opening a window, and then realized that there were neither window nor door handles on the insides of the back doors.

The car was speeding along a deserted street past low, drab houses. Suddenly, it swept into the driveway of one of them and came to a sudden halt in a dark garage. Immediately, the garage door rolled shut with a sharp, metallic sound. He could hear both back doors of the car being opened. Two

·100·

people got in, one on either side of him, and he again felt himself being handcuffed and blindfolded. He heard the garage door rolling open once more and the car backed out and resumed its journey. No-one spoke.

The notice on his door had read 'You will be collected at 8.15.' I have, he thought, indeed been collected – harvested, garnered, plucked – but by whom and why? He decided to ask his taciturn fellow travellers.

'Why do I have to be treated like this?' he asked.

'You'll learn soon enough,' was their morose reply.

Silence resumed. The journey continued for some twenty minutes or so. Once again, the car swung into a driveway and came to an abrupt halt.

The back door was opened and he was ejected through it by his companions, one pushing, the other pulling. They frog-marched him into a building, down a stone staircase, into a room onto a bed, and then departed, locking the door behind them. Alone, Nicholas felt distinctly disconsolate.

Some minutes passed. He could hear the muffled clamour of several voices. There seemed to be an argument going on somewhere in the building.

Finally, there were more heavy footsteps and someone unlocked and entered his room. Freed of handcuffs and blindfold, he saw that his liberator was a tall, thin young man with straggly black hair, a sallow face, jutting chin and a stubbly beard, but whose most distinctive feature was his right eye – unblinking, with a glint of flint and the faintest hint of a squint. Its intense gaze was fixed on him as though through the viewfinder of a firearm.

'The title of your lecture was announced,' said the Eye, 'as "Breaking Free from the Past". We don't like the idea of that. We don't like the idea of your encouraging such Utilitarian illusions. Where else is there to live but in the past? Our goal is to break free from the future – the future that the Utilitarians are trying to impose on us. Bigotaria (he concluded with a fierce emphasis) can only be built on Utilitarian ruins.'

'Of what possible use could I be to you in pursuit of that goal?' asked Nicholas.

'You are of great value to them and therefore of even greater value to us,' said the Eye.

'What makes you think so?' he asked.

'We saw Professor Maximand boasting about it on television. He said that you had concluded that Utilitaria is the best possible world and would be telling us so every week on television. So far as we are concerned, you are a dangerous Utilitarian ideologist.'

Wrong on three counts, he thought to himself, but better not to dispute the point. It might be to his advantage to be considered valuable to the enemy.

'But how are you proposing to make use of me?' he asked.

'First,' said the Eye, 'your being captured is a powerful symbolic statement of our presence and our vigilance and our indomitable will to resist. Second, we need cash. We are going to ransom you. It'll be interesting (he eyed him coldly) to see how much they think you are worth.'

Nicholas began to sweat again.

'What,' he asked, 'if they don't pay up?'

'In that case, said the Eye, picking up his keys, 'you'll very quickly be breaking free from the present.'

He opened the door and departed, locking it from the other side.

·14·

Mediation

*T*he Eye's departure left him free to survey his new surroundings. The decor was certainly an improvement over chez Bullet Head. He was in a room in a house, not a cell in a prison – a dingy and rather damp room with a wardrobe and sink, and a framed picture of a bird in a cage on the wall. A small window gave out on to a grey stone wall six inches away. If Nicholas looked through the window and craned his neck, he could just see a small patch of blue sky. However, in a cell you at least knew where you stood: a prisoner in an institution run by professional incarcerators and interrogators, however arbitrary and ruthless. Now he was a hostage, an altogether less predictable condition, at the mercy of passionate fighters for a cause he could barely comprehend.

He spent the rest of the day preoccupied by such musings. Rough, unshaven young men brought him cold, unappetizing meals and a change of clothing for the night and supervised him silently along the corridor outside his room to the establishment's rudimentary toilet facilities. Here, as in the Militarian prison, he began to lose his sense of time.

It was, in short, a miserable day.

Day Two

The next morning he was awoken by the Eye, who was in a state of high excitement. 'Look at this, Professor!' he said, thrusting a tabloid newspaper at him. 'You've hit the headlines!'

On the front page in bold print he read: 'TERRORISTS CAGE SAGE'. Below the headline was a large, blown-up photograph of his smile at the airport and the following story:

> Early yesterday morning Bigotarian terrorists made a daring strike. From his Calcula apartment they kidnapped Professor Nicholas Caritat, newly arrived political refugee from Militaria and famous thinker and writer.
>
> 'He was about to give his first lecture to our students,' said Professor Gregory Maximand, Cultural Adviser to the Government. 'He is a man of vision and wisdom who has recognized our system to be the best possible. His kidnappers are clearly afraid of his message.'
>
> The Prime Minister has expressed the Government's concern that such an act should befall such an 'honoured guest' and has promised that 'all that is possible will be done'.
>
> A security alert has been declared in the University area. Calcula's Police Chief has ordered an intensive police operation across the city and has declared that 'no stone will be left unturned until the terrorists are brought to book and Professor Caritat has been freed'. A telephoned message to the Police confirmed that Bigotarians are holding the Professor and that further messages can be expected.

'What messages will you send?' asked Nicholas.

'We are fighters, not writers,' answered the Eye, handing him paper and pen. 'You are a famous writer. The newspaper says so. You'll write the messages. We'll deliver them. I suggest you write to your friend Professor Maximand right now.'

'What am I to say to him?' Nicholas asked nervously.

'Tell him that we mean business, Professor. Tell him that if your Utilitarian friends don't comply with our demands, which we've sent them but they haven't responded to, then it'll be the

worse for *you*. And you might as well know that *if* (the Eye moved closer to its target) they take too long about it, we'll have to knock you about a bit, and send them photographs to encourage them. I'll be back in ten minutes.' With this he departed, locking the door behind him.

Nicholas realized that he was sweating again. He began to write:

Dear Gregory,

I must apologize for failing to attend my lecture yesterday. I hope the students were not too disappointed. My captors here say they 'mean business'. I think this phrase is to be understood in both of its possible senses. First, they are serious about the ransom demand they have sent and will presumably release me if the money is paid. Second, they have threatened me with violence if it is not paid soon, and they seem quite prepared to do me in.

I'm awfully sorry to have put you and others in such a ticklish situation. I would not presume to offer advice about what should be done. This would in any case scarcely be objective. All I can do is rely on our recently cemented friendship and hope for the best.

With all good wishes to Charmian and Graham,
Nicholas

He had barely finished writing when the Eye returned, read through his text and commented: 'Good work, Professor. Ten out of ten. They'll get your letter very soon. I just hope, for your sake, that they get your message.' With which menacing thought, he left Nicholas in confinement for the rest of the day, disturbed only by the delivery of meals and the supervision of natural functions by the Eye's two surly, silent companions.

Day Three

The Eye arrived with the morning's newspaper. His face conveyed an expression of triumph. Nicholas read the headline:

'CARITAT'S BARGAIN PLEA SPURNED'. Again his airport smile was reproduced, as was the text of his letter to Gregory. The story was brief and to the point, and it was not encouraging:

> The kidnapped Militarian Professor Nicholas Caritat has sent a letter (see BOX) making plain the Bigotarian terrorists' terms for his release. He is believed to be incarcerated somewhere in the Capital. Several clues to his whereabouts are currently being followed up.
>
> The Ministry of the Interior has issued the following statement: 'There is simply no question of bargaining with terrorists. This has always been and always will remain the Government's unshakable position.'
>
> Eustace Legge, for the opposition Act party, declared his party's 'total and unqualified support for the Government's stand'. 'To negotiate with terrorists,' he declared, 'is an act we cannot contemplate.'
>
> Professor Gregory Maximand, Cultural Adviser to the Government and friend and colleague of the kidnapped Professor, said, 'We must not allow our personal feelings to interfere with the impersonal calculations to which we are committed, above all in extreme circumstances such as the present.'

'Marvellous!' said the Eye. 'It's all going splendidly!'
'How so?' asked Nicholas in disbelief.
'That's what they say when they're about to negotiate.'
I hope you are right, he thought.

Day Four

Next morning, the newspaper carried a much shorter item. There was, it seemed, little to report other than that the Prime Minister had restated the government's line with her characteristic force:

> We simply cannot do deals with those who are out to destroy our very way of life. They have made us an offer we cannot but refuse.

'Wonderful!' said the Eye. 'You'll be a free man within days.'

Nicholas continued to hang on to hope but felt uneasy. For one thing, he was troubled by Gregory's words. Had it really been necessary to put things quite so explicitly? For another, he was not wholly confident about his captors' powers of prediction. They seemed altogether more at home in the past than in the future.

Day Five

The fifth day brought no new news. It did, however, bring a change in his social life which had up to now been largely confined to short conversations with the Eye and silent encounters with the Eye's accomplices. Now the latter began to talk. One brought him lunch and lingered at the doorway to tell him about a thousand years of Bigotarian history. This appeared to consist entirely of battles, alien invasions and heroic resistance. When his companion brought supper, he continued with the same theme but from a more specialized perspective, focusing almost entirely on the battles of four hundred years ago, which he recounted in vivid detail – weather, scenery, commanders, soldiers, even the various stages of the fighting – as though they had just taken place. Nicholas was a captive audience, yet although military history had never been even a minor interest of his, he found himself intrigued by the ways in which the past was present for his captors. And it was, at the very least, more pleasant than contemplating the uncertainties of his own future.

Day Six

There was little in the newspaper about his case, only a report of continuing police and army searches and raids on houses

in suburban areas. Meanwhile, the daily discussions about historic battles, agonized defeats and glorious victories intensified. Lunch dragged on for two hours and supper extended into the late evening, as all three captors crowded into his room. Bottles of beer were shared among the four of them. He found their storytelling enjoyable, except when he thought of the story they would one day tell of their current battle, in which he was the ammunition.

Day Seven

Again, nothing new about his case. Indeed, it no longer figured on the front page. The Eye looked displeased. 'By now we should have had some movement,' he said. 'This is not good. Time for another letter.' He handed Nicholas pen and paper. 'I'll be back in ten minutes.'

He wrote the following:

Dear Gregory,

Do forgive my writing to you once again. I can imagine what an awkward situation I have placed you in, caught between the calls of private friendship and public duty. I know, of course, how much importance Utilitarians attach to calculating consequences and I realize that you must deal with my case in that spirit. All I ask is that all relevant factors are taken into account, since my life may depend on it. My captors are ruthless and will, I believe, stop at nothing. They are, I am convinced, sincerely committed to their cause. As for myself, I continue to hope for the best.

<div align="center">

Best wishes to Charmian and Graham,
Nicholas

</div>

The Eye returned with his two companions. He picked up the letter and read it through. 'Eight out of ten,' he said. 'You need to add a phrase after "sincerely committed to their cause".'

'What phrase?' Nicholas asked.

'" . . . and their cause is just",' said the Eye.

'But,' Nicholas remonstrated, 'wouldn't it be against your interests for me to do that? It would make me appear as a sympathizer of yours and thus less valuable to them.'

The Eye was unimpressed.

'Add it!' he snapped.

'I'm afraid I can't,' said Nicholas politely.

The Eye advanced towards him, ripped his glasses off and struck him in the eye with his fist. This event was so sudden and unexpected that Nicholas fell over onto the floor in a heap. Eyeing the Eye with circumspection, he scrambled to his feet.

'That,' said the Eye, with satisfaction, his anger suddenly gone, 'will make an excellent black eye. *Now* are you going to add the phrase?'

'Leave it Chief,' said one of the others. 'He may be right.'

'O.K., but photograph him when the eye turns black!' All three then departed.

A few hours later after he was photographed, his letter was collected and Nicholas was left alone for the rest of the day to nurse his bruised face.

Day Eight

The eighth day was spent in tense suspense. Nothing about him in the newspaper, no talk of battles, no beer and no more black eyes. All four of them awaited the next development.

Day Nine

The next morning's newspaper gave him a shock. It also seemed to have surprised the Eye who looked decidedly out of sorts. The headline read 'DOUBTS EMERGE ABOUT CAGED

SAGE', and below it was a photograph of Nicholas with a huge black eye looking exceedingly miserable. Alongside it were photographs of the Prime Minister, Judge Tantamount and Gregory. His letter was also reproduced. The story read as follows:

Nicholas Caritat, the kidnapped Militarian refugee, has sent another letter from his Calcula hiding place, urging his 'friend', Professor Gregory Maximand, Cultural Adviser to the Government, to obtain his release by bargaining with his Bigotarian captors (see BOX).

The Government's uncompromising stand against such negotiations has been once more reiterated by the Prime Minister, who added, 'It is, in any case, not obvious that this individual is altogether committed to our way of life or that his potential contribution to overall utility is as great as was originally hoped.'

The Lord Chief Justice, Judge Tantamount, confirmed that Caritat had voiced suspect reservations about the principles and the practice of Utilitarian justice. These doubts were confirmed by the Chief Prosecutor Felicity Hawk. And Professor Maximand confirmed rumours circulating in the University that the notes for the lecture Caritat intended to give on the day of his kidnapping contained 'reflections about the past and the future that give cause for concern'.

There followed a short report, datelined the previous evening, from 'Our Special Correspondent in Militaria', headlined: 'PSYCHIATRIST CLAIMS LINK BETWEEN CARITAT AND "CAPTORS"':

Dr Orville Globulus, the famous psychiatrist, has offered his interpretation of Caritat's second letter from captivity, claiming that his is a case of the 'Stockholm Syndrome' in which hostages come to identify with their captors.

'I am,' the doctor said on television here this evening, 'an expert on both the syndrome and the man, I know him well. The letter speaks of the Bigotarians being "sincerely committed to their cause". What clearer evidence does one need?'

'In fact,' he added, 'I would go further. I wouldn't be at all surprised to learn that Caritat had engineered his own kidnapping, just as, I believe, he planned his escape from prison here. He is a master of deception and trickery. Even as a student, one could detect in him signs of incipient fanaticism.'

He handed the newspaper back to the Eye.

The Eye was in a very ill humour. 'You've let us down badly, Professor, very badly. You're certainly doing us no good.' Cursing vehemently, he left him alone.

Nicholas felt abandoned, a stateless person positively unwanted by three nations. His kidnappers left him alone, save for meals and the supervision of visits to the toilet, and they resumed their previous surly silence. Nothing happened for the rest of that day.

Day Ten and Day Eleven

Or indeed the next day or the next. The Eye did not even bother to bring him the morning newspaper. He was no longer deserving of even that much attention.

Day Twelve

As day twelve dawned, Nicholas decided that the time had come to write his second letter to Justin to sum up the impact of his Utilitarian experience so far, to report on his miserable situation and dismal prospects, and to inquire whether these might not be improved by outside intervention. Might he get out with a little help from the Hand? He would have to think of how to despatch the letter later. There was paper left from his earlier, abortive letters to Gregory, so he sat down to write:

Dear Justin,

I am writing to you from a prison cell. You doubtless have learnt of my kidnapping and detention for blackmailing purposes by the Bigotarians. I can only assume that you are rather familiar with their means, if unsympathetic with their ends. But are you familiar with any Bigotarians? Are there connections in the secret underworld of resistance movements that could be exploited to secure my release? I have the strong impression that my captors would like to get rid of me. The problem, as I see it, is to help them to do so in a manner consistent with my survival.

It is odd, isn't it, that in Militaria I was imprisoned by the authorities and freed by the resistance, whereas in Utilitaria I have been imprisoned by the resistance, while the authorities are showing little interest in my freedom. But, come to think of it, I am not sure that Utilitarians have much interest in anyone's freedom.

They do, however, have an unrelenting, all-absorbing interest in something else – in whatever it is that is the source of all their smiling and the object of all their calculations. They debate over who is to decide how to maximize it, they punish those whom they see as diminishing it, they defend themselves against those whom they see as threatening it. But what is it? I have to confess that I have yet to find out. And none of its various names – 'utility', 'happiness', 'well-being', 'want-satisfaction' – help. It's as though their whole way of life is founded on an arcane mystery, a sacred essence, an unfathomable secret, a value unrelated to any other. It seems to be quite unconnected with any particular social relationship or community, such as friendship or the family, and, as I have said, caring for it does not appear to imply a desire for freedom. Yet they believe in it totally and act as though they can calculate its extent with precision and by their actions bring about the maximum amount of it possible. It is the strangest religion I have ever come across.

All things considered, I don't think that I could settle in Utilitaria, even if I were to become *persona grata* here once more, which is, in any case, rather unlikely. Nor would I advise my children to emigrate here. It would not suit either of them in the slightest. Marcus would undoubtedly be put off by the mysticism of its religion and I'm sure he would be as mystified as I am about what the problem is to which all that calculating is meant to provide solutions. As for Eliza, she would be concerned at the human rights situation here – or rather, at the lack of a human rights situation since the Utilitarians find the very concept of human rights quite unintelligible.

What would I say to you if you were an inquiring embryo in search of a society to be born in? I would say: forget Utilitaria. You might be alright to begin with, provided you didn't turn out to be handicapped, or unproductive, or inefficient at converting resources into pleasure, or cursed with an incorrigible interest in the past. Of course, once born, Utilitarians would do all they could to inculcate in you a Utilitarian mentality. Worst of all, they might succeed and you would end up happy.

So much for Utilitaria. Love to Marcus and Eliza. In the hope of better times ahead.

Yours truly,
Pangloss

Nicholas folded the letter carefully, placed it in an envelope, addressed the latter and put it in his trousers pocket. The rest of the day passed uneventfully.

Day Thirteen

At last there was a new development. The Eye appeared with the day's newspaper. This, for once, ran what seemed like an encouraging headline: 'PRELATE COMES TO CARITAT'S RESCUE'. Below was a picture of a smiling clergyman, with a dog collar, a shaggy beard and kindly eyes. He read on:

The stalemate over the captured Caritat may soon be broken by the intervention of Goddington Thwaite, the Communitarian

clergyman with a taste for troubleshooting. Thwaite, notorious hostage-helper, has offered his services to resolve the deadlock that has arisen over the Utilitarian Government's resolute refusal to bargain for Caritat's release.

The Prime Minister has expressed in Parliament her Government's willingness to cooperate in this mediation attempt to allow Caritat safe passage out of the country for Communitaria. Eustace Legge has indicated the opposition Act party's enthusiastic support. The only criticism voiced in Parliament came from Ned Erskin. 'They're only cooperating to prevent the Bigotarians from murdering Caritat, because they're worried that might stem the flow of productive Militarian refugees to Utilitaria,' he said.

The terrorists are also believed to be ready to cooperate. They are thought to be eager to wash their hands of Caritat, who has turned out to be a major liability to them. Indeed, informed observers have even suggested that, were they to kill him, they might be thought to be doing Utilitaria a favour.

'Are you cooperating?' Nicholas asked the Eye.

'You bet we are!' said the Eye. 'Why should we kill you to do them a favour? Be ready to leave at any moment.'

The Eye departed. He did not, in fact, have anything to get ready except for his false passport in the name of Dr Pangloss, Dr Globulus's pass, permits in his own name to work and reside in Utilitaria and his letter to Justin. He waited and hoped for the rest of the day, but nothing happened. Eventually, he fell into a deep sleep. A couple of hours later he was suddenly awakened by the noisy entry into his small room of all three of his captors. Once again, they blindfolded and handcuffed him, before marching him out into the cold night air. He found himself being stuffed into the back seat of a familiar car, a companion on each side. The car sped off.

After half an hour's high-speed driving they came to a halt, and he was pushed and pulled out of the car. They seemed to be in open country. He could feel a gentle breeze wafting across his face and he could hear the sound of trees rustling

in the wind. His captors marched him to a low wooden seat and ordered him to sit down.

'Well, Professor,' said the voice of the Eye, 'it seems that thirteen is your lucky number. It is a real pleasure to say goodbye to you.' Footsteps retreated, doors slammed and the car sped away.

He sat there, eyes covered and hands tied, for an hour or so, listening to the dawn chorus of birds in the nearby trees and savouring the early morning fresh air and the prospect of impending freedom. Finally, he heard the noise of an advancing car. Footsteps approached. There was the sound of someone clearing his throat.

'May I remove your encumbrances, Professor Caritat?' said a voice.

'Please do,' Nicholas answered with relief as his blindfold was gently removed. In front of him was the familiar face of Goddington Thwaite, who stood before him in the early dawn at the edge of a wood, unlocking his handcuffs. He was very tall, bearded and burly and clerically attired in black with a dog collar. His shaggy beard was a bird's nest of grey and black and his eyes were wide open and sincere. His friendly, reassuring face radiated goodwill and encouragement.

'I am *very*, *very* grateful,' Nicholas exclaimed with real feeling. It was such a relief to have this remark not meet with puzzlement.

'Charity,' replied the Reverend Thwaite, 'I've always said, begins abroad. But I'm taking you to a place where you will feel welcome. Believe me, Communitaria is where one can feel truly at home.'

They got into the car and drove off. On the back seat Nicholas found his travelling bag.

'I brought your things from the apartment. Thought you might need them, though let's hope your travelling days are over. You've had a lot of bad luck, Caritat,' said Thwaite, 'and you deserve a break. We've heard all about your mission to find the best possible world. Soon we'll take a plane directly

there. You will be welcomed and valued. In Communitaria, people are valued for what they are.'

What am I? Nicholas wondered, but he put the question aside for the time being. Truth to tell, he was feeling rather exhausted.

Before long, they arrived at the airport, where they were met by an official who led them directly to the VIP lounge. While they waited, Nicholas noticed a mailbox in the corner. He took from his pocket the envelope containing his letter to Justin and scrawled on the back of the envelope: 'Free at last. Next stop Communitaria.'

'Do you, by chance, have a postage stamp?' he asked his travelling companion. Goddington obliged and Nicholas posted the letter. At Passport Control, Nicholas handed over his Pangloss passport.

'Thank you, Professor Pangloss,' said the official, handing it back, duly stamped.

Next to the Passport Control office stood the grey-suited Immigration Officer who had interviewed him on his arrival.

'Leaving us so soon, Professor Caritat?' she said. 'I do hope you'll be coming back to visit us before long.'

As he boarded the bus for the aeroplane he reflected that that was one hope he did not share.

·15·

Arrival

*H*igh in the sky, strapped to their seats and sipping martinis, Nicholas and Goddington finally had a chance to talk. Nicholas's saviour exuded an earnest and heartfelt religiosity that verged on the exuberant. A minister of the Communican Church, Goddington clearly believed in good works. He regaled Nicholas with tales of his rescue missions. On occasion he had been imprisoned and even tortured but he had always bobbed up victorious in the end. Goddington managed to avoid sounding self-congratulatory only because he attributed all his successes (there were, it seemed, no failures) to the Higher Force whose mere instrument he did not doubt himself to be. Nicholas wondered why the Higher Force should be congratulated, since It could presumably have avoided putting him to such trouble in the first place, but he thought it better not to voice such an impious thought.

Communicanism, Goddington told Nicholas, had historically been the dominant religion of Communitaria. In those times, the country was far more homogeneous – ethnically, culturally, religiously, and in every other way. Old Communitaria was a cohesive and settled nation bound together by many ties, among which the Communican religion was preeminent. The

national poets and philosophers of the past were much given to using agricultural metaphors. From their writings, Goddington explained, one could see how Communitarians were attached to the *soil*, cultivated their *roots* and felt in truly *organic* connection with one another. They despised the Utilitarians' calculating way of life and chose instead to rely on unspoken understandings, unexamined traditions and slowly evolving customs.

Since then there had been great changes in Communitaria. Waves of immigration and modern communications had unsettled the old ways and created a more heterogeneous society. New Communitaria was a patchwork quilt of communities, each claiming recognition for the peculiar value of its own specific way of life. New Communitarians, Goddington told Nicholas, believed in 'multiculturalism' and practised what they called the 'politics of difference', recognizing different identities with scrupulous fairness in the country's institutions. Positive discrimination was used to encourage those communities that had been disadvantaged or were in danger of extinction; employment quotas ensured that all were fairly represented in the professions and the public services. Each minority had its allotted share of the public monies. The schools were segregated but they taught curricula that gave equal value to all of the various cultures, and no way of life – and certainly not the Old Communitarian way of life – was ever given preference. In short, each Communitarian citizen managed both to attach supreme value to his or her way of life and to recognize its equality with all the others.

As for the Communican religion, Goddington explained, it too was heterogeneous and pluralistic. There were High Communicans and Low Communicans. The former believed in the importance of priests, authority and formal rituals; the latter did not. Then there were Broad Communicans and Narrow Communicans. The Broads favoured maximum flexibility in interpreting the doctrines of their Church; the Narrows were keen on strict orthodoxy. And then there were the Ecumenical

Communicans (the 'Ecus'), who thought of themselves as occupants of a huge mansion with room for all the creeds of Communitaria, or, better still, as a flower among the many that bloomed so luxuriantly in Communitaria's fertile but well-cultivated garden. They contrasted with the Anti-Ecumenical Communicans (the 'Anti-Ecus'), who focused on their own affairs, while tolerating the rich diversity around them.

'Speaking for myself,' said Goddington, 'I'm very Low, Broad and Ecu.'

'I see,' said Nicholas.

'My family will prove it to you,' said Goddington proudly. 'You'll meet them this evening. You'll stay with us as our guest.'

'I'm most grateful,' said Nicholas.

'Charity can also be found at home,' Goddington conceded.

The stewardess brought them their lunches, on plastic trays, packaged in little white plastic squares and rectangles and transparent clingfilm.

'I see we are flying on Utilitarian Airways,' said Goddington. 'Believe me, if we had been on a Communitarian Airways flight, we'd have had a good, solid, tasty ethnic meal, instead of this rubbish!' Nicholas looked forward with relish to the evening meal in the Thwaite household.

Over their plastic lunch, Goddington told Nicholas that he should be prepared for questions on arrival about his identity.

'Everyone will want to know,' he said, 'what you are.'

Nicholas began to see his problem. He explained to Goddington that he was confused about how to answer. To begin with, he was in possession of four identity documents, all bearing his likeness under three different names. Moreover, quite apart from this doubtless surmountable material problem, he felt unsure about how to identify himself to inquiring Communitarians.

'Well,' said Goddington, 'there are many possibilities – thirty-four ethnic communities and seventeen religions, actually. You'll be given the official list at the airport.'

The aeroplane was beginning its descent towards the capital city of Polygopolis, Communitaria's capital. Nicholas continued to worry about what he might be.

Once landed, Goddington took him briskly to Passport Control. A pleasant-faced Officer in a grey beret looked him up and down, as Goddington explained the complications of his mutually inconsistent and severally inaccurate documents. The Officer made a telephone call and eventually accepted the explanation. He then turned to Nicholas and asked the tough question: 'Immigrant or visitor?'

'Immigrant' was altogether too determinate a term to fit his condition. Perhaps 'migrant' would be better. He was *en route*: a voyager, a wanderer, a missionary in search of a message, an innocent abroad. 'Immigrant' implied a firm statement of intention: after all, Nicholas had yet to be convinced. On the other hand, 'visitor' seemed too weak and too superficial: he had come to discover, not just pass through, the best possible world.

The Passport Officer could see that Nicholas was troubled by the choice and was indulgent. 'I'll mark you down as "Pending" and you have sixty days to decide. If you decide to apply for Immigration Status, you have to fill in this form and specify which religious and ethnic communities you identify with, pull off the backing paper, stick it on to your identity document and present it to the Immigration Office. Here is the Official List of Communitaria's communities.'

'Thank you,' said Nicholas. 'But may I ask, once I have identified my communities, is it then possible to change my mind?'

The Passport Officer looked at him even more indulgently. 'It's a question that may bother you now,' he said, 'but I'm sure it will never arise.'

They walked through to the Baggage Claim to pick up his travelling bag. The green form he had been given was short and to the point. It simply required the Applicant to identify his or herself with an official ethnic and religious community.

In the top right-hand corner of the form were the words 'SELF-ADHESIVE'.

'But,' thought Nicholas, as they walked towards the Arrivals Hall to get a taxi, 'that's the problem. *Is* my self adhesive?'

·16·

Neighbourhoods

Nicholas continued to ponder over the problem as they drove towards the capital city. How was his self to be described? He reflected upon the recent, sudden and total transformation of his life. He was no longer a professor and scholar, a respected professional and parent. He was now a lone undercover agent travelling across the world for the resistance with false papers and an assumed name. As he contrasted his present with his past identity, he felt a sharp pang of loss.

Could he now acquire a new *persona* by identifying his self with a new culture and way of life? But if he did that, it would be his present self that would be doing the identifying. Could he actually become a different person with a new, communal identity? Did he (his present self, that is) want to? *Why* should he (or it) want to? Goddington sensed his unease and sought to reassure him.

'Communitaria is a very caring society,' he said. 'You'll feel secure and at peace with yourself, once you've found your niche, your resting place, your cultural home (Goddington, he noticed, had a curious habit of speaking in threes). You will be secure in your identity, your personality, your selfhood, like all other Communitarians.'

All of them? Did the Communitarian way of life really suit all of its citizens equally? Were they all recognized in the way they wanted to be? Did they all want to be recognized in the way they were? He asked Goddington these questions. Goddington replied:

"'To thine own self be true" is a principle all Communitarians believe in. But to *what* is one to be true? What is the self? It isn't some ghostly essence, atom, monad. We know that the self, the person, the individual is socially constructed. How is the "I" to recognize the "me"? Only through the eyes of others. How can one recognize oneself unless through being recognized by others? How can one have an identity without being identified? I am what my community makes of me. To be true to one's self is to be true to one's community, and vice versa. As it says in our Holy Book, "Love thy Neighbourhood as thy Self".'

His sermon-cum-lecture over, Goddington began to explain to Nicholas how Communitarian society was organized. The officially registered communities were of two kinds: ethnic and religious. Membership in the former was decided mainly by facts about your historic and geographic past. Where were you born? Where were your parents, or your grandparents, or your ancestors born? Were you a participant in a particular way of life and the bearer of a certain shared collective memory, invoking common heroes and common enemies? Different ethnic communities were more or less strict in their criteria for adhesion. Some required genealogical tables or authenticated birth certificates; others were more relaxed, admitting anyone prepared to acquire the appropriate memories, heroes and enemies. As for membership in the religious communities, this simply depended on your faith. Every Communitarian had to be a member of one ethnic and one religious community, though there were several 'fused' ethnico-religious communities. Generally, each religion tended to be associated with one or more ethnic communities, so that neighbourhoods tended to be ethnically and religiously homogeneous, though

religion was sometimes a source of division within a single ethnic community that would be split along religious lines.

As Goddington expounded, Nicholas glanced down the list of communities he had been handed at the airport. They were almost all unfamiliar to him, referring to peoples, cultures, beliefs and practices of which he knew nothing. He found 'Atheists' under *A*, but he could not find 'Agnostics'. Out of curiosity, he looked under *I* but did not find 'Independents'. Nor did he find 'Cosmopolitans' under *C* or 'Humanists' under *H* or 'Misfits' under *M* or 'Nonconformists' under *N*.

Each community, according to Goddington, had its own way of selecting its leaders who sat in the two Houses of Parliament: the House of Ethnicity and the House of Religions. Appropriately enough, the latter was known as the Upper House and was supposed to deal with 'spiritual' matters and to look after the 'spiritual health' of Communitaria as a whole, while the Lower House dealt with the issues of everyday life. The problem was that different communities had different views about where to draw the line between the spiritual and the mundane, and some (including both the Atheists and some of the mystical religions) denied that it should be drawn at all. As a result, the two sides had come to a working arrangement by which contentious issues were decided by both Houses meeting in joint session. Otherwise, the Lower House mainly initiated and amended laws of central concern to the ethnic communities, while the Upper House did the same for the religious communities.

Communitaria was a Republic with a largely symbolic President, Goddington told Nicholas proudly. Old Communitaria had been a Monarchy, but the rise of ethnic and religious pluralism had forced the ruling family into retirement. It had been too identified with the dominant community in Old Communitaria, the Bees (which meant the 'Better Established Elements'). As indigenous and immigrant communities entered the mainstream of Communitarian life, the old Bee ethos and way of life became just one among many. The Royal

Family lost prestige. After several scandals involving widely publicized and much discussed illicit liaisons, the Old Queen Bee had abdicated, tearfully but gracefully accepting the inevitable. The Prince was deemed uncrownable because of his past behaviour and the monarchy abolished.

The dominant religion in Old Communitaria, the Communican Established Church, had suffered the same fate. It too had become simply one among many denominations in an increasingly heterogeneous country. Nevertheless, Goddington insisted, the Church continued to have a special place in Communitarian life: as he saw it, Communicanism was the religious expression of the very ideal of Communitarian life.

The taxi was approaching a built-up area.

'This,' said Goddington, 'is where the Emmets live and work, but especially work.'

First, they saw rows of large dilapidated houses on either side of the main road, many-storeyed and roomy, each seemingly occupied by several families, with children on the pavements and mothers calling out of windows. Off the main road were many narrow side streets lined with similar but more modest houses. Then they came to what looked like a business and shopping area. Goddington asked the driver to slow down, as Nicholas observed the scene. There were groceries, butchers, bakers, clothiers, hardware stores – but also many single-storey buildings in which innumerable people were frenetically working. Through half-open doors, Nicholas could see rows of men and women bent over long wooden tables under neon strip lights: stitching, sewing, weaving, cutting, hammering, scraping, sawing, welding, making clothes, jewellery, leather goods, furniture and all kinds of handicrafts. The intense busyness around them was relentless. No-one even looked up or paused from their buying, selling and making.

'The Emmets,' said Goddington, 'are incredibly hard workers and much respected for it. Thoroughly imbued with the work ethic of their Parsimonian religion. But they weren't

always respected. In the days of strife before the Constitutional Settlement, they were envied and despised. Then they were called "Pismires".'

The taxi drove on through the business area and came to another residential area, where the houses were now more packed together and poorer and shabbier and even more crowded with families. Everything here seemed less ordered and organized and the pace of life seemed to have slackened.

'Now we've come,' Goddington explained, 'to the Mellifluan quarter. As you'll soon see, the Mellifluans are very different from the Emmets. Today, by the way, it's the Fifth of June, a National Holiday which commemorates the Constitutional Settlement. The Mellifluans will be celebrating in style.'

'Don't the Emmets take a holiday?' asked Nicholas.

'No,' said Goddington. 'They celebrate the Fifth of June by working harder.'

The residential streets now gave way to a shopping area. A carnival was in full swing. But the first thing that struck Nicholas was the *smell* through the open car window – the pleasant, rich, sharply sweet aroma that made you realize you were in a particular place. He now realized that Utilitaria had been odourless.

Most of the shops were closed, except for food and drink shops, but the bars, cafés and restaurants were all full. Stalls lined the pavements selling food and trinkets of all kinds. Small bands of musicians played infectiously rhythmic music at street corners to which all were swaying sympathetically. On several side streets, the pavements were occupied by long tables covered with white tablecloths and abundantly laden with food and wine, at which there sat families shouting and laughing and around which waiters rushed with steaming dishes. Couples danced to the music in the streets. Young children sported brightly coloured carnival costumes.

'The Mellifluans,' Goddington told Nicholas, 'as you see, know how to enjoy themselves. In Old Communitaria, there was real antagonism between them and the Bees, who they

claimed exploited them by extracting most of what they produced without adequate recompense. But things have been different since the Settlement. You can see how enthusiastically they're celebrating it – though come to think of it, the Mellifluans will celebrate anything enthusiastically.'

The taxi speeded up through another residential area, still, it appeared, inhabited by Mellifluans. But then, the character of the houses and streets became more ordered and tidy and altogether more suburban. Rows of houses became separate detached dwellings with front gardens, and well-groomed trees lined the placid streets. The parked cars were larger and more expensive and even the road signs looked freshly painted. Eventually, the road started to slope upwards.

'We've reached the outskirts of Mandeville, otherwise known as the Hill of the Bees,' said Goddington. 'This is the most fashionable Bee neighbourhood. The higher up the hill you live, the more fashionable you are. The Old Queen's Palace is at the top opposite the Parliament. We live about a third of the way up.'

'Aren't the Bees celebrating the Fifth of June?' Nicholas asked.

'Oh, yes,' said Goddington, 'but we do it as a family occasion at home, over dinner. The family is an institution that is important to all our communities, but especially the Bees.'

As they drove up the hill, the houses grew in size and elegance. Set back from the winding, ascending road, they bespoke a settled and prosperous elite that valued order, privacy and domesticity. The taxi stopped outside a large, rambling house, with gables and a bright green door. Goddington led Nicholas up the driveway, opened it and invited him into his home.

·17·

Celebration

O n entering the hallway, he could hear a cacophony of many children's voices. Down the stairs came a plump, rosy-cheeked woman who looked harassed but cheerful. 'I'm Thelma Thwaite. I'm so glad that Goddington rescued you,' she said warmly, extending her hand. 'You were certainly a difficult case.'

Goddington flushed with pride. 'You'll be meeting another one shortly,' he said. 'But first Thelma will show you to your room. You must be very tired. You should have a good sleep. We'll wake you up for dinner.'

Thelma Thwaite was a social worker who had worked with many of the country's communities. Nicholas found her agreeably down-to-earth. Like her husband she led a life devoted to Good Works but, unlike him, she went about her business privately with little public fanfare. Her speciality was repairing family breakdowns. The problems were, of course, she explained, very different in the different communities. Among the Emmets, for instance, the chief cause of breakdown was workaholism; among the Mellifluans, fecklessness.

'What about the Bees?' Nicholas asked.

Among the Bees, she answered, there was no single factor. She felt the Bees had a special obligation, as the former ruling

class, to try to foster social integration throughout Communitaria. Plainly, she accepted this responsibility herself, for she had moved from the service sector to the productive, creating with Goddington what she hoped would be a model multicultural family drawn from several different communities.

'You'll meet them at supper,' she said. 'For now, sleep well.' He did.

Three hours later and much refreshed, he joined the company seated around the Thwaites' huge round dining table in their large, spacious kitchen. The company consisted largely of playful, chattering children – five boys and five girls, ranging in age, he guessed, from eight to sixteen. His attention was caught by one of the girls, aged about twelve, with lively, beautiful, green darting eyes, long black hair and mobile dimples. She was playing a hand game with two of her neighbours, urging them on to increasing heights of hilarity, watching her parents out of the corner of her eye for the moment when they would order her to calm down, which duly came. She reminded him irresistibly of Eliza at the same age.

Apart from Goddington and Thelma, there was one other adult, a young man in a black leather jacket who sat silently and somehow withdrawn from the jolly scene around him. Slight in build and deadly pale in complexion, he wore a distinctly sombre expression and dark glasses. Goddington introduced him as a house guest and friend of the family called William.

As Nicholas took his place at the table, Goddington rose to say grace and the children's boisterous antics quietened down. 'Dear children, family and friends,' he said, intoning his words as though preaching, 'we are gathered together here today to honour our country's Glorious Settlement, to welcome our guests (he nodded to Nicholas and William) and to commune with one another. For what we are about to receive may our various Gods make us truly grateful. Let us pray.'

At these last words, a surge of movement occurred around the table. The two youngest children, both boys, rose from

their seats: one stood upright, while the other stood on his head, using the table's edge for balance. The next youngest pair, a boy and a girl, crouched on the floor : the boy with his left ear to the ground, the girl with her right. Next were two somewhat older girls, who remained seated but gazed upwards at the ceiling with dreamy expressions, one chanting softly, the other silent. Then two slightly older boys stood up and swayed rhythmically, in opposite directions. The last children to express themselves were the oldest: a boy and girl who clasped their hands on their heads in prayer, the boy kneeling, the girl sitting. Goddington and Thelma also sat with their hands on their heads. William remained seated with a long face.

After a few minutes there was a relaxation of tension, everyone resumed their original positions and Goddington turned to Nicholas to interpret what had just occurred.

'As you can see,' he said, 'we are a truly Ecu family. We embrace not only different religions but different branches of the same religion.' Goddington explained that the two oldest, his natural children, were Communicans, one High and one Low. The rest were adopted. (Goddington spoke in threes, but it seemed he adopted children in twos.) The rhythmic swayers, he explained, were Mellifluans and practised Akimboism, a syncretic mixture of folk religions. One was a rather devout Acute Akimboist, the other what was called a Loose Akimboist. The ceiling gazers belonged to different sects of an otherworldly mystical religion known as Nimbism. The crouchers with their ears to the ground were Netherenes. Their creed was the opposite of otherworldly; their God was internal to the Earth itself. And the youngest two were followers of the deity Stala. One belonged to the Stalagmites who believed that life on earth was an upward progress towards spiritual perfection. The other belonged to the Stalactites who saw it as a process of descending decline from a state of initial spiritual perfection.

Thelma departed from the table to bring the food and

returned with a trolley laden with dishes already prepared. Nicholas marvelled at what she proceeded to provide. To each pair of children she served a different meal: a meat stew, a fish dish, a piquant rice dish, a vegetarian meal, a concoction of shellfish. The other adults were served the meat stew which, she explained, was typical Bee fare, but she offered Nicholas the choice of any of the other dishes. He settled for the stew.

'Man,' said Goddington, 'is what he eats. In eating their different meals and saying their different prayers, our children are becoming what they respectively are and they are doing so respectfully. Our whole way of life can be summed up in the phrase *Respectiveness plus Respectfulness*. Before the Settlement we only had the first. People fled here from their various ethnic and religious wars, but they brought their conflicts, their strife, their antagonisms with them. What we celebrate today is the great invention of our Way of Life which has put all our various ways of life on an equal footing. Every way of life has its own value and none is less or greater than any other; and every religion is true in its own way. The great principle by which we live is the Principle of No Offence. It is the very foundation of our law. What we value is Diversity, Plurality, Heterogeneity. What we respect is Difference, the Other, the Alternative.'

Nicholas had the strong impression that the sombreness of William's mood was deepening considerably during this speech. Indeed, the young man looked positively miserable.

Goddington continued to speak, addressing the children. 'I'm sure you all want to know who our friend Nicholas is and why he's here. Well, he's a very famous Professor who has come from abroad where he's been in some very nasty places and been through some very exciting adventures. He's come here because he is seeking the Best Possible World. Let us all be thankful that he has found it. So I propose a toast: to Communitaria – the Best Possible World – and the flourishing of Nicholas Caritat therein.'

Goddington and Thelma raised their glasses. William raised his too, but, it seemed to Nicholas, without enthusiasm.

The rest of the meal was rather jolly. The children asked Nicholas about his adventures. They were excited and much amused as he told them about Bullet Head, One and Two, about Justin and Dr Globulus, about the Maximands and about his kidnapping by the Eye and his friends. Even William seemed to take an interest in Nicholas's stories and to look a shade less depressed.

When dinner was over, the children went off to bed, but not before making Nicholas promise to tell more stories on another day. As Thelma looked after the children, Goddington invited Nicholas to join William and himself in the drawing room.

'I want,' he said to Nicholas, 'to introduce William to you properly. I think you may find him very interesting to talk to. You may even be able to help him.'

·18·

The Rock Star's Tale

They entered the drawing room and Goddington closed the door carefully, as if to ensure the confidentiality of their conversation. They settled into deep leather armchairs around a coffee table. Goddington lit a pipe and began to speak softly.

'First,' he said, 'I must explain that this (he gestured to William) is not William. We call him that in front of the children. His real name is Jonathan Cypselus, as in Jonny Cypselus, the rock star. Most of the children know who he really is but we keep up the pretence for safety's sake. He is living with us under an assumed name because he is in hiding. Indeed, his life is in serious danger.'

Nicholas had heard of Jonny Cypselus. Marcus, he recalled, used to find his music inspiring. They were about the same age. Jonny-cum-William removed his dark glasses. He must have been in his mid twenties but had a gaunt, sallow, troubled face that was lined beyond its years and sunken, sad eyes. He leant forward and started to speak, in a low monotone, gesturing expressively with his hands.

He began, appropriately enough, by identifying himself in Communitarian terms. 'I'm a Malvolian and a Stalactite,' he said, 'or at least I was. But both the Malvolian and the

Stalactite communities have declared war on me. Now I am their Enemy Number One. And all because of a rock opera.'

'What is it about?' asked Nicholas.

'It's called "Yellow Stockings and Red Pyjamas". It is about the world in which I grew up, about *my* people and *my* religion. The guys in my group are all Malvolians and Stalactites and the opera was a tribute to our communities. I wrote it during our last international tour and we performed it in several of the world's capitals. It was a total, roaring success. We filled stadiums. Then some dumb critic wrote an article about the opera, praising it to the skies, but describing it as a brilliant work of *satire*, depicting, and I quote, "the insularity of ethnicity and the fanaticism of faith". We had no idea what "satire" meant – or "insularity" or "fanaticism". These concepts don't exist in Communitaria. I now know that satire is a form of *humour*, but that concept doesn't exist here either. Apparently, to call something a satire is to imply that its subject matter is held up to ridicule, but in our case that's just not true.

'You know how it is with the critics, though. Soon everyone abroad started describing the opera as satirical. They called it "a satirical masterpiece" and "the world's first satirical rock opera". This happened just as the opera was about to open here in Polygopolis. The leaders of the Malvolian and the Stalactite communities got to hear of all this hype and demanded that the opera be banned.'

'And was it?' Nicholas asked.

'Yes,' said Jonny, 'but that wasn't all. We were denounced as traitors and heretics. They were beside themselves with anger and rage, and wanted us to renounce the opera and publicly apologize for what we had done.'

'And did you?' Nicholas asked.

'Well, our lead guitarist couldn't handle the pressure and did himself in. Suicide. The other members of the group not only renounced the opera, they denounced me for having lured them into it.'

'And you?' asked Nicholas.

'I resisted,' said Jonny defiantly. 'I thought I had nothing to be ashamed of. For me the opera was a way of honouring my communities and I was prepared to defend it as such. Why should I renounce it just because some critic found it funny? If he laughs why am *I* to blame?'

'So what happened?' Nicholas asked.

'The two communities met, first separately and then together to decide what to do about me.'

'The Malvolians,' Goddington explained, 'are the most hypersensitive of our communities in Communitaria. They are so prickly that they employ special vigilantes to ferret out any criticism of the Malvolian way of life. For them, Jonny's opera was a true betrayal. As for the Stalactites, they are always militant against what they see as blasphemy.'

'So I was accused,' Jonny continued, 'of treachery and blasphemy and charged with sacrilege.'

'That,' said Goddington, 'is the most serious crime in Communitaria – worse than insult, ridicule and mockery. It alone carries the death penalty.'

'When my case came to court,' Jonny went on, 'it got enormous publicity, partly because I was so famous but mainly because I had once been the Malvolian and Stalactite poster boy. The public turned against me. I was accused on television and in the papers of attacking the very foundations of Communitarianism. No-one dared take my side.

'I tried to defend myself through my lawyer by insisting on what I had meant the opera to be – a sympathetic portrayal of my communities' ways of life. But the judge ruled against me, arguing that authorial intention is irrelevant to the interpretation of the meaning of a work. Meaning, he insisted, is socially constructed: everyone in Communitaria knows that. But that's what saved me. My lawyer argued that I couldn't be held to be responsible for what everyone agreed was a "satire". So I was freed on a technicality. But you could hardly call my condition one of freedom. The Malvolians and the

Stalactites were furious. Their leaders met for a whole day and decided to *excommunicate* me – a kind of social death here in Communitaria. Frankly, I'm not sure that that is to be the only kind of death to which I shall be subjected. To whom could I turn but Goddington?'

'I offered Jonny refuge and sympathy,' said Goddington, 'but I cannot, I hasten to say, sympathize with what he did. One must be endlessly vigilant in the defence of freedom: the freedom of others from insult. Our whole society depends on our not criticizing one another's ways of life, or indeed our own, and it is undeniable that Jonny's opera gave deep offence to two of our communities. Perhaps it could be argued that satire constitutes some other authentic way of life, and therefore we must make a space for it in our many-roomed mansion. If that is the case, though, we must try to enable satire to exist without causing offence.

'That, Nicholas,' the minister continued, 'is where you may be able to help. We must try to be practical and find a way out of this sorry mess that Jonny has got himself into. It seems to me that there might be an outside chance that, as a distinguished visitor from abroad, a refugee from persecution whose case has reached our newspapers, you might be able to act as a kind of peacemaker and try and persuade the Malvolians and the Stalactites to be less . . . ' Goddington searched for a word.

'Intolerant?' suggested Nicholas.

'Perhaps,' said Goddington, doubtfully. 'I've come across this concept of "tolerance" while abroad. We don't have the concept here in Communitaria. As far as I understand it, it seems to imply that one should put up with being offended. But why should one? Why should one have to be offended in the first place? But our immediate problem is to find a way of persuading the leaders of Jonny's former communities to view his offence less drastically. Perhaps we can persuade them to be less offended. We can only hope they have the acumen to see things more ecumenically.'

'Well, I'll do my best,' said Nicholas helpfully.

Goddington shook him warmly by the hand. Jonny looked doubtful.

'Tomorrow I'll take you to them. It won't be easy but it's certainly worth a try. But in the meantime, perhaps you'd like to see the source of all this trouble?'

He switched on a video machine and inserted a tape. The three of them sat back to watch. Nicholas did not much like the music which was, for the most part, loud, metallic and tuneless. But the acting was engaging and enjoyable, the whole thing was very colourful and there was a great deal of dancing. There were two main groups of protagonists. The first wore cross-gartered yellow stockings, the second red robes over red pyjamas. Every now and then, at moments of high tension, the latter removed their robes and stood on their heads. Various other characters in outlandish costumes kept appearing from time to time. He found the story line rather difficult to follow. It seemed to have something to do with the main protagonists' repeated but seemingly unsuccessful attempts to be recognized by the others as supremely virtuous and praiseworthy. None of the characters was especially sympathetic but nor were they obviously figures of fun.

When the video was over, he bade Goddington and Jonny goodnight, thanking them for the entertainment. It was, unfortunately, the wrong response.

Jonny looked forlorn. Goddington said: 'Make no mistake: this is dangerous material. You must never reveal that you have seen it here.'

Lying in bed, Nicholas discussed tolerance with Voltaire, who rather grandly asserted that 'Human law must in every case be based on natural law.'

'I would have thought,' countered Nicholas, 'that the historical evidence suggests that human beings find intolerance rather natural.'

Voltaire was unimpressed. 'How could it be natural,' he asked, 'for one person to say to another "Believe what I believe

and what you can't believe, or perish!'"? If that were the basis of human law, then the Japanese should detest the Chinese who should execrate the Siamese; the Siamese, in turn, should pursue the Tibetans, who should fall upon the inhabitants of the Indus. A Mogul should tear out the heart of the first Malabarian he finds; the Malabarian should slaughter the Persian who should massacre the Turk; and all of them should fling themselves upon the Christians, who have for so long been devouring one another. A right to intolerance is thus absurd and barbaric. It is the right of tigers – only much more horrible, since tigers only tear each other apart to eat, whereas we exterminate one another for paragraphs.'

'What, then, do you propose?' asked Nicholas.

'I propose,' replied Voltaire, 'that each citizen be allowed to believe his own reason, and think whatever that enlightened or deluded reason will dictate, provided he doesn't disturb public order.'

'The Communitarians seem to have found another solution,' observed Nicholas. 'They don't seem to have much confidence in the individual citizen or much faith in the dictates of reason. Their idea seems to be that all their communities should respect other ways of life and all the paragraphs be declared equally valid.'

Voltaire looked sceptical and more than slightly puzzled. 'How,' he asked, 'can one *respect* prejudices and delusions? And how can mutually contradictory assertions be equally valid?'

Nicholas in turn felt puzzled and, dropping off to sleep, decided to postpone his answer.

·19·

Malvolians and Stalactites

Next morning, Nicholas awoke to the sound of children getting ready to be taken off to their various schools. After they had gone, he went downstairs and found Jonny slumped over a cup of black coffee.

'I greatly enjoyed your opera,' he said.

'Thank you,' Jonny muttered.

'What I cannot judge,' he went on, 'is how much of it is fantasy.'

'That,' said Jonny, 'you will be better able to judge by the end of today.'

Goddington returned from delivering the children to school and joined them for coffee.

'We will visit the Malvolians first,' he said. 'A meeting has been fixed for eleven this morning. Of course they don't know that you're going to make an appeal on behalf of Jonny. They simply take it for granted that a famous visitor would visit them first; otherwise they would take offence. And they know about your mission.'

'And will probably tell you that their way of life is what is best about this best possible world,' remarked Jonny, wrily.

The minister shot him a disapproving glance. 'In the afternoon,' he added, 'we'll visit the Stalactites. But remember,

you must be extremely discreet and on no account reveal that you have met Jonny.'

Goddington and Nicholas set off for the House of Ethnicity to meet the Malvolians. The two Parliament Buildings stood, side by side opposite the former Royal Palace, on a grand public square at the very top of the Hill of Bees. They had been rebuilt after the Settlement, and were characterless, rectangular structures (presumably to avoid offence). Outside each House stood a Guard of Honour of soldiers dressed in a wide variety of colourful costumes. Inside, the House of Ethnicity was decorated with the flags, crests and portraits of all the official ethnic communities. Each community was given an equal section of the imposing entrance hall for display.

They walked along a corridor with doors on each side bearing the names of the different ethnic groups in alphabetical order. Passing 'BEES' and 'EMMETS' and many others, they came, eventually, to *M* and stopped outside the door marked 'MALVOLIANS'. Goddington knocked.

A nervous page in an ill-fitting uniform opened the door to a committee room. Seated at a long table were five men of varying ages, all wearing cross-gartered yellow stockings and grey tunics. The eldest sat at the centre facing the door. He had a white pointed beard, a shiny bald head and a fierce, intense expression that did not soften on the arrival of the visitors. The others wore the same disinterested glare. Neither friendly nor unfriendly, their hostile facial expressions were directed at the outside world in general, of which Nicholas and Goddington were simply two representatives.

The old man with the beard introduced himself as the Chairman of the Malvolian Parliamentary group. The others were his colleagues. Everyone shook hands. Goddington and Nicholas sat facing them.

The Chairman spoke slowly and deliberately. Nicholas noticed that he tended to use the first-person plural indiscriminately. Sometimes by 'we' and 'our' he seemed to mean

himself and his colleagues, sometimes the Malvolian community, sometimes the Malvolians and the Stalactites, sometimes the citizens of Communitaria as a whole.

'We are honoured,' he said to Goddington, 'that you have shown us the courtesy of bringing the Professor to visit us first, before all other communities in our country. We value such respect highly. From which community do you come, Professor?' he asked Nicholas.

'Professor Caritat comes to Communitaria from Militaria via Utilitaria,' explained Goddington hastily. 'He is extremely interested in how you live.'

'Ah, yes,' said the Chairman, 'We've heard about your mission. We are proud of our way of life, although naturally we respect those of our fellow citizens. Unfortunately, such respect is not always mutual. That is a fact of which we are continuously aware.'

'Is it a big problem for you?' asked Nicholas ingenuously.

'It is perhaps our biggest problem. We cannot tolerate disrespect towards what we hold to be sacred: it is like the spillage of our very lifeblood.'

'But,' Nicholas ventured, is there not something to be said for tolerance?'

'The problem,' said the Chairman, 'lies in the giving of offence. What you call tolerance, so far as we understand it, is to be subjected to an offence without objecting; respect is refraining from causing it. Our whole society is committed to the second, not the first.'

The atmosphere in the room grew noticeably chillier, the expressions around the table more hostile. A bony, bespectacled colleague of the Chairman intervened.

'Why are you interested in such problems?' he asked sharply.

'I am a philosopher,' Nicholas replied. It was an answer that did not go down well.

'Have you seen a so-called opera by the so-called J. Cypselus?' asked an elderly man to the left of the Chairman.

'I think I've heard of it,' said Nicholas, carefully.

'It is a sacrilegious work that renders us contemptible in the eyes of others,' said the Chairman. 'It denigrates and diminishes us; it is a piece of despicable filth and foulness. Unfortunately, the judge misunderstood the law, and we have had to act ourselves against this criminal and may well act against him further.'

'How?' asked Nicholas.

'By depriving him of his social identity,' said the Chairman, coldly. 'If he does not recant soon, he'll lose his physical identity as well.'

'But I suppose someone might argue,' Nicholas ventured, 'that such drastic punishments fail to respect his rights . . .'

'Rights!' snapped the Chairman, banging his fist thunderously on the table. 'Rights! The language of our enemies! Let us talk about wrongs! Individuals don't have rights. If we are to talk of rights, we should say that in wronging us Cypselus has violated our absolute right to respect.'

The coldness in the room turned icy. A Malvolian with a moustache leant forward menacingly.

'You don't seem to show us much respect, Professor,' he said.

'We respect people for what they are. We also condemn them, if need be, to death for what they are,' said the Chairman. 'Cypselus is a traitor whose sole aim is to destroy us and all we live for. We wonder, Professor, what you are. In showing sympathy for him, you fail to show us respect.'

'Please don't take offence at my questions,' protested Nicholas. 'I only wish to understand.'

The temperature did not rise even one degree. Ten fiery eyes were fixed on Nicholas in disbelief. A silent minute passed.

'I think that it may be time for us to be going,' said Goddington gently. 'I would ask you gentlemen to be charitable in your view of our conversation today. My friend Caritat is new to our ways and is, I assure you, genuinely seeking to under-

stand and not to judge. Where he comes from, one does this by asking questions that can sometimes be taken amiss. Please forgive him for any offence he may inadvertently have caused.'

Ten eyes remained focused on what seemed to be an object of increasing hate. The Chairman rose.

'I too think it is time for you to leave,' he said. 'We must come to our own conclusions about the meaning of this encounter.'

The nervous page opened the door. Nicholas and Goddington hastily left the room.

'That was not a great success,' Nicholas remarked, as they walked towards the entrance.

'That,' said his guide, 'was a total disaster.'

Over lunch in Goddington's favourite Mellifluan restaurant they discussed how best to deal with the Stalactites that afternoon.

'They'll be fully informed about this morning's fiasco,' said Goddington, 'so we'll be starting off at a disadvantage. They'll be suspicious from the start. It's hopeless to try to convince them that there is a case for what you call tolerance. The idea just doesn't exist here. On that point at least the Malvolians were right: in Communitaria the virtue most prized is *respect* and that means not giving offence.'

'But they *have* taken offence at Jonny's opera,' said Nicholas.

'Yes, but were they right to do so?' Goddington asked. 'Perhaps you could try to persuade them that they may have *misunderstood* the opera? It is difficult, since you can't admit to having seen it: to admit that would immediately brand you as their enemy. We have to accept that it is satire since everyone, including the judge, says it is. But perhaps you could talk to them about satire and its purposes – try to convince them that satire could have a constructive, even a religious meaning. If that fails, I suppose our only hope is to appeal to their compassion.'

Lunch over, they drove directly to the Stalactite Temple at the other end of town. It was a beautiful, reddish pink,

circular building set in a park full of trees and flowers. The main portal was open. A pale, reverential young man dressed in a red robe greeted them and led them inside to a large, semicircular chamber into which light poured from the high windows all around. The high ceiling was golden and from it there hung many statues of robed figures, their expressions grave and pious, their heads and their outstretched arms pointing resolutely downwards towards the stone floor in a kind of supplication. On a small dais facing them were placed a throne and a low table on which there lay a large book. Next to the book was a glass case containing a small brown tubular object on a purple cushion. As Goddington later explained to Nicholas, the book contained the sacred words of Stala told to his followers in an underground cave and the glass case his toe bone. Behind the throne was a door, through which the young man led them into what was evidently the priests' area. They entered through a large golden door into a long room lit at the far end once again from a window that gave out onto the park. There were more statues suspended from the high golden ceiling. Against the wall ten priests dressed in red pyjamas stood on their heads, while a young Stalactite acolyte moved back and forth sprinkling a sweet-smelling powder on their upturned feet. At the centre on a high-backed golden chair sat the High Priest in a deep crimson robe. As Goddington and Nicholas entered, the priests came off their heads, donned red robes and assumed sitting positions on ten gold chairs lining the far wall. As they did so, the High Priest rose. There were two chairs in the centre of the semicircle of priests facing them. The High Priest motioned for the visitors to sit there before them. Nicholas and Goddington obeyed. The High Priest returned to his throne and began to speak, addressing his words to Goddington.

'You have requested a meeting with us. This we have been willing to grant. But we wish to know of your purpose in seeking this meeting.'

'The first purpose,' said Goddington, 'was that Professor

Caritat here should meet you. As you may know, he is in search of the best possible world.'

'The best possible world lies beyond this one,' observed the High Priest, 'and belief in its possibility is granted only to those who have faith in its reality.'

'Quite so,' said Goddington.

'And the second purpose?' The question came from a youngish, bearded priest whom Nicholas and Goddington both recognized. He was the fifth member of the morning's group of Malvolians, the only one who had not spoken. The question was asked with obvious hostility. There seemed no point in beating about the bush.

'Professor Caritat,' said Goddington, 'is a distinguished scholar from abroad who can perhaps view our concerns calmly and dispassionately. He has heard about the Cypselus Affair and he is naturally concerned.'

'About what is he concerned?' asked the bearded priest.

'Not least about the rule of law,' said Goddington. 'The judge decided . . . '

The priest interrupted sharply: 'The judge misinterpreted the spirit of the law.'

'There is a difference between divine and human law,' added the High Priest. 'This is a case of sacrilege and in such a case the former prevails.'

'But,' said Nicholas, entering the conversation at last, 'can you be sure that this was a case of sacrilege?'

'We can be sure. We are sure. What do you think it was a case of?'

'Could you not see it as a case of satire?'

'What, according to you,' the High Priest asked Nicholas, 'is satire?'

'Satire,' replied Nicholas, quoting Dr Johnson's *Dictionary*, is "a poem in which wickedness or folly is censured". But it could, of course, also be a rock opera. To engage in satire is to censure human wickedness and folly by making those vices appear ridiculous.'

'To what end?'

'"The true end of satire",' answered Nicholas, quoting Dryden, '"is the amendment of vices." And thus to indicate the path of virtue and wisdom. Perhaps,' he ventured, 'to remind human beings of what the divine law enjoins.'

'That,' snapped the High Priest fiercely, 'is the role of the priesthood. Are satirists to replace priests?'

'They could assist them,' Nicholas suggested. 'They have the same ends. They just use a different technique.'

'The technique of ridicule,' commented the bearded priest. 'Satire employs ridicule to profane what is sacred. It undermines reverence and awe for the words of Stala as revealed in our Holy Book and vouchsafed to our Divines. It destroys respect for the authority or our Teachers. How could the Divine Law be taught through ridicule? The very idea is ridiculous. You are speaking absurdities.'

Nicholas felt the ground slipping from beneath his feet. He decided to make one last reckless try: 'But surely such respect should not be blind? Perhaps through satire we can gain some understanding of human weaknesses, including our own, and thus learn humility?'

'What you call human weaknesses can only be counteracted through the strength of faith. You have succeeded, Professor, in convincing us that your so-called satire is the enemy of faith. Have you anything else you wish to tell us?'

Nicholas looked helplessly at Goddington, who also looked helpless, and said: 'Of course, gentlemen, I am unfamiliar with the tenets of your faith. From what little I know, I hold you and your religion in the highest esteem, and I earnestly wish to learn more. One thing I want to know now is whether there is not within it a place for compassion.'

'Compassion is at the very heart of our faith,' said the High Priest, 'You have guessed right. Compassion, together with its inevitable accompaniment: implacable hatred of all that threatens to undermine the basis for that compassion.'

At that moment the ten other priests jumped onto their

heads and twenty angry inverted eyes glared at Nicholas and Goddington from the floor. Meanwhile, the High Priest rose from his chair and pointed his forefinger directly at Nicholas. His voice became louder and shriller: 'Implacable hatred,' he shouted, 'for satire, satirists and their accomplices!'

Goddington grabbed hold of Nicholas's sleeve. 'Quick,' he whispered. 'It's time to go and fast.' They rose and bowed.

'Let them go,' the High Priest ordered the red-robed priest who had delivered them. 'But be warned,' he added as they turned to leave, 'beware and take heed.'

Nicholas opened his mouth, intending to apologize.

'We wish to hear no more,' said the High Priest. 'We have heard far more than enough.'

The visitors departed through the golden door into the praying area and through the portal into the street. They returned home, disconsolate and depressed, and broke the news of their double failure to Jonny, who took it sadly but without surprise.

'I fear,' Goddington said to Jonny, 'that you will have to renounce your opera and make a public apology. I see no other way.'

'Never!' said Jonny, his voice quivering with barely controlled anger, 'I will not submit!' With these words, he left the room, slamming the door behind him.

Goddington looked uneasy.

'No good will come of this,' he sighed, shaking his head. 'But you must not judge our society harshly because of this one little difficulty. Tomorrow we are to see what can be done about finding you a job.'

'At the University?' asked Nicholas.

'We call it the Unidiversity,' said Goddington. 'The Rector of Polygopolis Unidiversity has invited you for a meeting tomorrow morning and I shall be glad to take you there. I'm sure they will be honoured to have you join the Faculty.'

Nicholas retired to bed that night with a growing sense of disquiet. He had, he felt, not only let Jonny down but also some larger cause.

Why, he asked Pope, were Communitarians so hypersensitive? In reply Pope told him how effective ridicule could be:

> Yes, I am proud; I must be proud to see
> Men not afraid of God, afraid of me:
> Safe from the Bar, the Pulpit and the Throne,
> Yet touch'd and sham'd by *Ridicule* alone.

But Jonathan Swift, who had joined their conversation, observed that, in fact, most people enjoyed satire because they *didn't* feel touched and shamed. 'Satire,' he remarked, 'is a sort of glass, wherein beholders do generally discover everybody's face but their own, which is the chief reason for that kind of reception it meets in the world, and that so very few are offended with it.' Moreover, Swift added, satire was pretty helpless against the wicked, its point being 'to preserve well-inclin'd men in the course of virtue but seldom or never reclaiming the vicious.'

In Swift's view, the readers of satire could avoid or shuffle off or live with shame and insult. Yet here in Communitaria everyone seemed ready to take offence and went to extraordinary lengths to avoid it. Condorcet, Nicholas recalled, had once said of satire that it was a weapon to be used only against those who by virtue of their rank or their power were sheltered from every other chastisement. In Communitaria, it seemed, they were sheltered from satire too.

·20·

The Unidiversity

As they drove to the Unidiversity on the next morning, Goddington offered Nicholas some advice.

'Now you must be careful in what you say to the various people you meet,' he said. 'Please don't engage in any of this so-called humour of yours; it can so easily be misunderstood. Of course, you must be especially careful if you talk to any Malvolians or Stalactites. Remember not to call the Emmets Pismires. And another very sensitive minority are the Indigens. They're a rather large group who lived here before the Bees colonized the country, and they have a long history of being exploited and discriminated against. You must be especially careful with them. I'll take you first to the Rector who I know will offer you a post. But then I'll have to leave you.'

The Unidiversity was a sprawling complex built in the same unspecific, inoffensive style as the Parliament – large white buildings that could not be identified with any particular culture or period. Nicholas followed Goddington into the most imposing building, up a stone staircase and down a spacious hallway. Goddington knocked on the brass knocker of a majestic door. A secretary opened it and showed them into a luxurious inner office where the Rector, a silver-haired

gentleman of great elegance and poise greeted them with a winning smile.

'Allow me to present Professor Caritat,' said Goddington, 'philosopher, historian and seeker of the best possible world.'

'I have indeed heard of your mission, Professor Caritat,' said the Rector. 'As a fellow philosopher, I can only encourage you in your quest. As a Communitarian, I can only applaud your good sense in pursuing it here. The answer to your question "Where is the best possible world?" lies, I am certain, before your very eyes. Yet, as Rector of this Unidiversity, I must tell you that we regard your question with disfavour, for it implies that worlds can be compared and judged superior or inferior to one another. That violates the multicultural relativism to which we, as a community of communities, are committed. On the other hand, I have to admit that I cannot resist taking pleasure in the agreeably paradoxical thought that one cannot improve upon a world in which your question is no longer thought fit to be asked.'

To this bewildering flow of words Nicholas could not think of a suitable answer. It was probably best to avoid discussing the question. He did not, after all, wish to cause offence.

The Rector continued unabated: 'I am delighted, moreover, to inform you that you have been nominated to an Honorary Visiting Chair at our Unidiversity – the honour is of course entirely ours. If you accept, you will occupy the post of Professor jointly in our Departments of Ethnic Studies and Religious Studies.'

Nicholas was moved to intervene. 'But', he protested, trying not to sound ungracious, 'I am an expert in neither field. My field is the Enlightenment and, as Goddington has said, I am a philosopher and a historian.'

'No matter,' said the Rector. 'Philosophy and history are taught here only as subfields in the Department of Ethnic Studies and the Department of Religious Studies. You'll have plenty of scope.'

'But what are you expecting me to teach?' asked Nicholas.

'As you are a scholar of the Enlightenment,' replied the Rector, 'we propose that you should teach a course entitled "Why the Enlightenment Project Had to Fail".'

Once more Nicholas was moved to protest. 'But,' he said weakly, 'I'm not altogether sure that it *did* have to fail.'

'Ah, quite so,' said the Rector. 'We mustn't jump to conclusions. We must keep an open mind. How about "Did the Enlightenment Project Have to Fail?"'

'I suppose that would be alright,' Nicholas conceded doubtfully.

'So you accept!' said the Rector. 'Excellent news. We'll discuss all the practical details later. But I've taken the liberty of arranging meetings with your future colleagues and students in the expectation that you would agree. They are waiting for us in another part of the building. Would you care to join us, Reverend Thwaite?'

Goddington made his apologies, explaining that he had some urgent matter to attend to, and departed. Nicholas wondered whom he was off to rescue.

He followed the Rector from his office to a door marked 'MEETING ROOM'. Inside some twenty or so persons were seated around a long polished table. At one end were four seats, the middle two empty. The occupants of the other two rose in greeting as Nicholas and the Rector walked towards them.

'Allow me to introduce Professor Grenzen, Head of the Ethnic Studies Department,' said the Rector. Nicholas shook the hand of a tall, dignified, pleasant-looking man in his mid sixties. 'And this is Professor Glaube, Head of our Religious Studies Department.' Nicholas shook the hand of Professor Glaube, a man of a similar age but greater solidity and a severer aspect. All four sat down at the head of the table.

The Rector made a surprisingly short, rather formal speech: 'We are honoured and delighted that Professor Caritat here has agreed to join our Faculty. I need hardly remind you that he is a most distinguished scholar of the Enlightenment

from Militaria who will teach – and no doubt direct research – for the two Departments represented here. Allow me to call on Professor Grenzen to say a few words on behalf of the Department of Ethnic Studies.'

Professor Grenzen rose to speak, clearing his throat. 'For me,' he said, 'for us, it is, as the Rector has said, an honour that you should be joining us. You are a scholar of the Enlightenment, and we have, I must emphasize, the greatest respect for your scholarly concerns . . . '

'And I for yours,' interposed Nicholas.

' . . . but I should perhaps explain to you that our Communitarian way of life, and thus our educational philosophy, has a rather special attitude towards the Enlightenment. It is not that we are, in any simple sense, against it. But we do think that it requires to be – how shall we say? – superseded, or – better perhaps? – put in its place.

'Perhaps I can best explain what I mean by citing Voltaire. As I'm sure you know better than I, he writes in his *Treatise on Metaphysics* that he proposes to study man exactly as one might study the movements of the planets, as though from a standpoint beyond the earthly globe. Only from such a standpoint, he says, can one compare the apparent movements that one sees from the earth with the real movements that one would see if one were, as it were, in the sun. Similarly, he writes, "I am going to try, in studying man, first to put myself outside his sphere and outside interest, and to get rid of all the prejudices of education, of country and, above all, of philosophy."

'It is this ambition – to seek a view of our world from nowhere within it, to escape from the world-view of one's community – so typical of Enlightenment thinkers that we think is so dangerous. It is dangerous, Professor Caritat, because it is *ethnocentric*: the supposed "view from nowhere" always turns out to be a view from somewhere which its proponents claim is universal and objective and then seek to impose on others – as our Bees used to do both here at home

and in far-flung colonies across the world. In Communitaria we take it for granted that every view is a view from somewhere, and that none is superior to any other.

'This principle is the foundation of our teaching here at the Unidiversity. Our curriculum reflects the presence of multiple cultures in every specific body of knowledge. We have what we call a "basic canon" of works which all students must read. It consists in selections from all the various traditions represented in Communitaria. No tradition must be left out and none must predominate. Some of our traditions, it is true, such as those of the Indigens and the Mellifluans, are for the most part oral, not literary, and in those cases we study their folk tales, folk songs and folk dances.

'Then, when our students specialize, they always do so with the utmost sensitivity to the sensitivities of those they study. Indeed, we regard it as a failure of scholarship if a piece of research should give offence to its object, just as we regard it as a failure of our teaching if our students should give offence in this way.

'We think it will be an excellent thing for you to teach our students about the Enlightenment at the beginning of their course, so that they can see what dangers may lie in their paths – above all, the danger of ethnocentrism. I'm sure your lecture course will be a marvellous and enlightening introduction for them.'

Professor Crenzen finished speaking, to the evident satisfaction of the Rector, who then turned to Professor Glaube. 'I now call on Professor Glaube to say a few words of welcome on behalf of the Religious Studies Department.'

'I wish to endorse,' said the unsmiling Professor Glaube, 'all that my colleague has just said. We are honoured that you should be joining us and, after considering the matter very carefully, it seems a good idea that you should introduce our students to the ideas of the Enlightenment. I agree with what my colleague has said about the latter but would wish to add a few further remarks about how my Department views your

field of study – for which, of course, we have the greatest respect.' Nicholas nodded obligingly.

'We all know, of course, that the Enlightenment was not especially friendly to religion. It was sceptical of miracles. It was critical of Revelation. It regarded the existence of evil as a challenge to the credibility of religious faith. It cast doubt on the authority of divinely inspired Holy Books. It was even inclined to *satirize* the faithful and their priests. (As he said this, his eyes met Nicholas's and a certain *frisson* went around the room. Was Professor Glaube, he wondered, a Stalactite? Was he about to stand on his head?) But none of that is for us the cardinal point. For us what is important is that the Enlightenment made a promise which it could not keep: to find a basis in Reason for justifying morality.

'We know that there is no such basis. There is certainly no basis in Reason, with a capital R, that can demonstrate one morality to be superior to all others. Different moralities encourage different virtues, inculcate different duties, embody different notions of what is valuable in this life on earth. How could Reason arbitrate between them? What, I ask you, is Reason? There is no such thing as Reason – only different ways of reasoning, each of them internal to a tradition and a way of life. And how could there be any basis for morality other than a religious basis? Even so-called secular societies must draw on the legacy of the religions they claim to reject. And there is no single religious basis that all can be brought to accept as such. The Gods are irreducibly and eternally diverse. There was a time of terrible religious conflicts, before our Glorious Settlement, when they were at war. But then we negotiated a peace treaty, establishing the principle of *Respectiveness plus Respectfulness*, which forms the basis of our life together here in Communitaria.

'So I fully agree with Professor Grenzen. Let our students learn about the Enlightenment and its illusions. Let them see to what disasters these illusions have led – to the dominance of one culture and body of knowledge over all others, exporting

and imposing particular ways of life and denigrating others, disrupting and destroying traditional cultures in the name of Universal Reason and Truth. I am sure that your introductory course on the Enlightenment, Professor Caritat, will only serve to strengthen our students' faith in their respective religions and their respectfulness towards the religions of their fellows.'

As Professor Glaube sat down, murmurs of approval sounded around the table.

'Amen to that!' said an enthusiastic, bespectacled woman with her hair in a bun. 'Speaking as a Communican Bee and Professor of the History of Exploitation, I must confess that there is much in our history of which we should be ashamed. We have been relentless and ruthless in our pursuit of hegemony over other ways of living and thinking. We were once much influenced by your so-called Enlightenment, Professor Caritat. We exercised our hegemony in the name of the so-called "Progress of Civilization" in which the Enlightenment believed and which it sought to promote. But we no longer speak of the "Progress of Civilization". There is no such thing as "civilization", only different cultures. And there is no such thing as "progress", only different ways in which different cultures develop that can only be judged by their own standards. Your "progress" is just a code word for one culture's dominance over others. It will be an excellent thing for our students to learn that from your course!'

An eager young man in an open shirt on the other side of the table leant forward. 'Absolutely!' he said. 'As a Mellifluan, I must agree. My subject is literature, a field in which the hegemony of which my colleague has spoken was especially operative. Its presence manifested itself, if I may put it so, in its systematic construction of absences. The absent texts and their invisible authors were the well-kept secret of our traditional curriculum. Indeed they imperceptibly shaped its manifest content: Bee culture and Bee values dominated our hearts and minds only because all other cultural possibilities were systematically suppressed. We could only hear the

buzzing of Bees because all other voices were silenced. And what happened when people tried to raise them? They got *stung*!' An approving murmur sounded round the table.

'But, happily, all that has changed. We have drawn the Bees' sting, and our voices are now heard. We don't sing the same tunes, and the buzzing of the Bees is just one theme in the overall polyphony. We have been empowered. Our respective writers and philosophers and poets and folk tales are respected as they deserve. We practise *criticism*, by invoking our own standards, but we only criticize ourselves. No community criticizes any other community's cultural achievements. Your course, Professor Caritat, will help us greatly. Our students will learn from you where the real roots of their past oppression lay: in the illusions of the Enlightenment, in the dogma that there are standards which apply across cultures and in the nightmare vision of a cosmopolitan culture that would embrace the whole world.'

Nicholas was beginning to feel uncomfortable. A pall of cloying unity on the topic of diversity seemed to be congealing around him. The next speaker brought him considerable relief, in several ways. She was a young, strikingly attractive woman with delicate features and a porcelainlike complexion, deep, dark eyes and long jet-black hair, whose soft and gentle voice belied the vehemence of her words.

'I am an Indigen,' she began, adding rather redundantly, 'and a woman. I teach Gender Studies. I am concerned that we may be giving Professor Caritat a thoroughly misleading picture of what multiculturalism means. In the history of our movement (he was not sure whom she meant by "our"), we have had to struggle for it to be understood in a transformative not just reformist sense. For us multiculturalism involves the effective dismantling of Beecentric hegemony and the construction of an entirely new curriculum. It is a goal that is always before us and that we can never wholly achieve. All too often (she turned to her bespectacled female colleague) "multiculturalism" is just a fashionable buzz word that merely

serves as a cloak for complacency. My Mellifluan colleague (she addressed the young man in the open shirt) says we have been empowered, but can we be sure that our minds have been decolonized? Have we really freed ourselves from the Beecentric world-view and from class privilege, racism and (she paused for effect) sexism?' There was an uncomfortable shuffling around the table.

'Which brings me,' she continued, 'to the vexed issue of sex and gender. Some people still pretend not to know what the difference is between them. I'll tell you what it is. Sex is the difference between my bodily functions and those of Professors Grenzen and Glaube. (The shuffling increased. Nicholas found himself visualizing the difference indicated). Gender is what explains why I am not going to be appointed Head of the Ethnic or Religious Studies Departments. Unfortunately, gender is still a source of oppression in Communitaria. We still think that only women have a gender and that everyone else is a human being. Our great 'Glorious Settlement' never solved that problem. Gender was on the agenda then. The women's movement then was strong and fought for the recognition of female identity. But, unfortunately, women are neither a community nor a minority, so we got left out of the settlement. All we are left with is tokenism.'

'Come now, Professor Bodkin,' interposed the Rector. 'We hardly regard you in that light.'

'I don't wish to be patronized,' said Professor Bodkin, her voice for the first time registering anger. 'I am merely referring to our lamentable failure to respect women as women. Only ethnicity and religion are deemed worthy of respect, so we allow fifty-one communities to treat their women as they please – which is, for the most part, badly. (Wearily knowing looks were exchanged across the table.)

'We do have the Body of Gender,' protested the Rector.

'Exactly!' said Professor Bodkin. 'A useless, lifeless, virtually toothless institution, the point of which nobody understands or remembers. We are, I fear, not yet living in the Best

Possible World, Professor Caritat, at least as far as women are concerned. I only wish that, by following your course, we might learn how to make it so. But your Enlightenment was not very enlightened on the subject, was it?' She cast Nicholas an unmistakably combative glance.

Nicholas felt agreeably provoked. What she said was not false, yet the point was arguable. What, in particular, about Condorcet? In 1789 he had come out in favour of admitting women to citizenship, denouncing the behaviour of even the most enlightened men of the time. 'Have they not all violated the principle of equal rights,' he wrote, 'by coolly depriving half the human race of the right to take part in the formation of the laws?' And he had demanded to be shown 'a natural difference between men and women that could justify such an exclusion from rights'. Nicholas imagined that he would greatly enjoy discussing the Enlightenment and feminism at some later date with Professor Bodkin – and preferably in private. Not, however, there and then. The feeling around the table was plainly becoming restive and the Rector diplomatically closed the proceedings.

'I think your future colleagues have given you some idea of what to expect here,' he said. 'I suggest that you might care to go with them to the cafeteria to meet some of the students. I leave you now in the capable hands of Professors Grenzen and Glaube.' As everyone rose to depart for the coffee bar, Nicholas followed Professors Grenzen and Glaube into the corridor.

'Philomena Bodkin is a phenomenon,' observed Professor Grenzen, as they walked. 'The style is sweet but the content bitter.'

'And to be taken,' added Professor Glaube, 'with a pinch of salt.'

'What is the Body of Gender?' asked Nicholas.

'It's an institution that was set up at the time of the Settlement to promote women's causes and protect their interests,' replied Professor Grenzen. 'Doesn't do much these

days except bring charges of sexual harassment. The women who run it can't agree about what it should be doing – or about much else.'

'There are four different factions,' explained Professor Glaube. 'There are the militant feminists who claim we treat women badly and are at odds with practically all our communities, religious and ethnic. But they can't criticize us openly because that would be to break the law. They're opposed by the relativists who say that every community's way of treating women is right in its own way. They spend their time attacking anyone who dares to criticize the traditions of any particular community, such as the Vilipendians, who practise female circumcision. Then there are the particularists. They say that a specific community has the answer to how women should be treated, but they don't agree on which that is: some say the Mellifluans, others the Indigens, and so on. And finally, there are the separatists who say that women should form a community of their own. They haven't got very far with that idea. As Grenzen says, all the various factions can agree on is to consider charges of sexual harassment brought to them. The Body of Gender conducts pre-trial hearings and, when they feel convinced there is a case, they press charges in the courts. They have a lot of success too, because all of our communities claim to respect women.'

They had reached the cafeteria which was full of people, some standing at the coffee bar, others seated at tables. Professors Grenzen and Glaube took Nicholas over to a table at which half a dozen students were waiting expectantly. They had, it seemed, been designated to talk to Nicholas and were delighted when he joined them.

'So what's it like being a student here?' he asked them.

This question elicited a litany of complacencies, a veritable unison in praise of diversity. Two of the students were Bees and vigorously disavowed 'Beecentrism' and aspirations for 'hegemony'; the curriculum, they claimed, was thoroughly 'de-Beeified' and 'polycentric'. The rest were combative and

self-assertive. No longer 'marginal' and 'subordinate', they had been 'empowered'. 'We all,' one insisted, 'have our Tolstoys and we all read them.'

'Are there no conflicts or frictions?' Nicholas asked. 'Does no-one ever give offence?'

'Ah,' replied one of the students, 'we have a speech code to prevent that.'

'How does that work?' Nicholas asked.

'If anyone is overheard making a derogatory statement about any community, he or she can be charged and brought before the Unidiversity's High Council. The punishments range from a warning to permanent expulsion. If professors do it, they can be jailed.'

'What sort of statements do you mean?' Nicholas persisted.

'Oh, we can't give examples. That would be dangerous,' said another student.

Nicholas pressed them. 'Please do,' he said, 'just one.'

'Well,' said one of them, looking round furtively and lowering her voice, 'you could be suspended for a month if you said "as busy as an Emmet".'

Nicholas began to feel oppressed himself. At that moment, to his relief, he saw the slim figure of Philomena Bodkin rising to leave a nearby table. Excusing himself, he went over to speak to her.

'I would,' he said, 'very much like to try to convince you that your view of the Enlightenment is disputable.'

'You can always try,' she said.

'Perhaps we could discuss it over a meal sometime?'

'Perhaps we could,' she replied. Was this an encouragement? He was not sure.

'How about this evening for dinner?' he suggested.

'No good. I'm on duty as Warden of a student residence.'

'What about lunch here tomorrow, then? At one o'clock?'

She agreed, bade him farewell and departed without a backward glance.

He was reluctant to rejoin his student interlocutors. They

seemed surprisingly conformist and uncritical of the state of their society. He thought with pride of his own children's independence of spirit and wondered, with anguish, how they were faring. As he stood there hesitating, he felt a tug at his sleeve. Just behind him stood two young-looking students. The boy was scrawny, dark-haired and wore a leather jacket; the girl was a fresh-faced blonde dressed in jeans and a red sweater. They looked anxious, intense and secretive.

'We very much want to speak to you, Professor Caritat,' said the young man, urgently, 'but not here and not now. Will you meet us this evening?'

'Yes, of course,' he said.

'We'll meet you here at six,' said the young man and they left quickly.

At that moment, Professor Grenzen breezed up to him and took him by the arm.

'We must take you to your office and your secretary,' he said, 'now that you are to be one of us.'

·21·

Malcontents

His Communitarian office was much like his Utilitarian one – featureless and functional, containing bare white walls, a simple chair, a desk and empty grey bookshelves. But perhaps such working environments were appropriate to his new, travelling, unsituated self. Both offices were a far cry from his Militarian inner sanctum, for which he mourned wistfully. And yet, as he reflected on the warmth of that sanctum and the comforts and consolations of his earlier self, he pondered to what extent they had been built on the cold cruelties of the regime.

The secretary assigned him showed him around the Departments and the Library. After lunch with Grenzen and Glaube, at which they made their morning's speeches to him all over again, he browsed in the Library and telephoned Goddington to explain that he might be late coming home. Just before six o'clock, he walked over to the cafeteria to keep his appointment.

The young couple were waiting for him at the entrance. They introduced themselves as Benjamin and Constance.

'Will you come with us to my room here in the Unidiversity?' Benjamin asked. 'We would like to offer you some wine and a light supper.'

Nicholas accepted and followed them out of the building and across the campus. He noticed that they seemed anxious not to be observed.

'It's very good of you to be willing to see us,' said Benjamin. 'We've heard about your mission, and we've managed to get hold of some of your writings which we find intensely interesting. We're worried that you are being given a very one-sided picture of life here. We have formed a group, a secret club . . .'

'It's a secret *revolutionary* club,' added Constance, excitedly.

' . . . to discuss alternative ideas. We would like to discuss these with you. But what we're doing is dangerous and certainly illegal. Are you still willing to come with us?'

'Yes,' said Nicholas firmly.

They walked past several buildings and came eventually to a series of tower blocks which were evidently student residences. They entered one of these, taking the elevator to the fifth floor, walked along a corridor and entered Benjamin's room. It was a small study-room with a bedroom adjoining. Papers and books were piled high on a desk by the window. In the middle of the room was a low round table around which sat eight young people, some cross-legged on the floor, some on chairs. Benjamin offered Nicholas an empty low-slung armchair. He and Constance joined the others around the table on which were several bottles of Mellifluan wine, an array of glasses and some sandwiches. Nicholas accepted a glass of wine from Constance while Benjamin introduced his fellow students by name.

'I've explained to Professor Caritat why we want to see him . . . ' Benjamin began.

'Please,' said Nicholas, 'call me Nicholas.' This invitation to informality obviously went down very well.

'You see,' Benjamin continued, turning to Nicholas, 'things here are not quite as they may seem to you. Our Professors and student representatives have given you the official story.'

'What,' Nicholas asked, 'is the real story?'

'Where shall we begin?' Benjamin asked.

'Let's begin with ourselves,' suggested Constance. 'I am a Bee and Benjie's an Indigen and we want to get married. But there's a huge social pressure in Communitaria against mixed marriages. They're not illegal, but they're very much discouraged by virtually all the communities. And any children of such marriages have to be brought up according to the father's religion and ethnic identity. My parents don't know about Benjie or his about me.'

'What would they do if they did?' asked Nicholas.

'Probably cut us off: disinherit us and have nothing more to do with us.'

'We have to meet secretly,' said Benjamin. 'Only our friends know. On the campus we'd be ostracized.'

'Is this a common problem?' Nicholas asked.

There was a ripple of laughter around the table. 'Impossible to know,' said Constance. 'So few people dare to step out of line. There are a few mixed marriages, but no-one knows how many secret *liaisons dangereuses* there are.'

'Illicit liaisons aren't the only thing that's dangerous,' commented a young man with black curly hair. 'There are lots of other ways of stepping out of line.'

'Such as?' Nicholas prompted, pouring himself a second glass of wine.

'Rejecting your ethnic or religious community, or pretending you don't belong to it, or that you belong to another one, or – worst of all – rejecting the whole idea of collective identities,' replied the young man.

A dark-haired girl next to him emphatically agreed. 'Just try to say you don't belong where you should and you're in real trouble.'

Another added, 'And just try saying you don't believe in belonging. See what happens to you then!'

A rather melancholy-looking boy next to Nicholas nodded his agreement. 'People who dare to say such things, or who are thought to believe them, are ostracized and find it difficult to

get good jobs. My Dad's been unemployed for years for just this reason. He just isn't chosen for the quota.'

'But worst of all,' said another, 'is when you want to belong to a community – whether ethnic or religious – that isn't officially recognized. You recognize yourself but the authorities don't recognize you. Such unrecognized communities are perceived as a real threat by those on the list.'

'In short,' said Benjamin, 'people who don't fit into the official story are given a bad time. People say that they're not true Communitarians. Sometimes they are called "rootless cosmopolitans".'

Nicholas found what they were saying of absorbing interest. He also found their company extremely congenial and was moved by their friendliness, intensity and obvious sincerity. They told many stories from their own experiences and the cumulative effect was quite devastating. As time passed, Constance kept plying him with glasses of the highly agreeable Mellifluan wine. He began to feel a little light-headed and ate some sandwiches to try to counter its effects.

'Nicholas!' said Benjamin suddenly. 'You must help us. We know about your work and we've even read some of it. But we need to know how to defend and protect ourselves and, above all, how to convince others that they need to be defended and protected.'

'Against what?' Nicholas asked.

'Against belonging,' said Benjamin.

'And against longing for belonging,' said Constance.

'I suppose my lectures on the Enlightenment will be about such matters,' said Nicholas, 'I shall certainly talk about the rights of man and of citizens . . . '

'Your lectures will be carefully framed and confronted with refutations by all the other Professors,' said Benjamin. 'They want to use you as a provider of object lessons in what not to think.'

A thought occurred to Nicholas. 'But what about Professor Bodkin?' he asked. 'Isn't she an ally?'

There was a stir around the table. There was clearly some disagreement on this point. 'She's alright,' said Constance. 'She's certainly against the prevailing orthodoxy. The trouble is that she only dissents because the Settlement left out women. She's obsessed with identity, like everyone else, and is only interested in you if you think of yourself first as a woman. She only cares about women, not about people.'

'Doesn't she care about men?' asked Nicholas.

'Definitely not!' said Constance. 'She hates them.'

Nicholas felt depressed.

'We want to ask you to be a member of our club,' said Benjamin, 'to advise us and supply us with texts that we can use as propaganda in our struggle for human rights.'

'Let's drink to that!' said the curly-haired student.

Constance filled Nicholas's glass once more.

'I agree to your proposal,' he said recklessly, downing a sixth (or was it a seventh?) glass of delicious Mellifluan wine. The faces around him seemed suffused with a delightful amiability. He had lost all sense of time but knew that it must be getting late. He also felt an urgent need to answer the call of nature. 'Where,' he asked Benjamin, 'is the nearest toilet?'

'Along the corridor to the left,' said Benjamin.

Nicholas left them and made his way unsteadily along the corridor. There were several doors with signs on them, but he had difficulty making them out. The signs were line drawings of human figures in ethnic costumes. The problem was that all the figures seemed to be wearing trousers, some baggy, some tight-fitting. Doubtless these were meant to indicate separate bathrooms for men and women but Nicholas could not discern which was which. For a while he went back and forth between them. Finally, under pressure of need, he opted at random for one and pushed open the door.

Inside was a tiled washroom with several sinks and at the far end a series of shower curtains. From behind one of them he could hear the sound of running water.

'Ah, there you are,' said an imperious voice. 'Quick! Hand me the soap.'

He looked around for soap but could see none.

'It's on the stool over there. For heaven's sake, do be quick!'

Nicholas did as he was told. He picked up the soap and went over to the shower curtain. Slowly, he pushed it aside, to reveal Philomena Bodkin in full frontal nakedness. Their eyes met.

'Get out!' she hissed.

He hesitated, proffering the soap.

'I'm sorry,' he said, trying to explain. 'It's my mistake. I . . .'

'Get out!' she screamed.

'I'm sorry you're indignant,' he said, 'but I hope that we can still have lunch tomorrow.'

'Get out!' she shrieked. He dropped the shower curtain and left, clutching the bar of soap. Back in the corridor he tried another of the hieroglyphic doors which was locked. Finally, he found what he was seeking and obtained physical, but not mental, relief.

He returned to the students in a state of high anxiety and told them what had happened. 'Oh dear!' said Constance. 'She mustn't find out that you have been visiting us. She doesn't know about the Club.'

The time had come to go home. 'Your support means a lot to us,' said Benjamin. 'We must continue to meet with you. But don't speak of our meeting with you this evening to anyone under any circumstances. We must preserve total secrecy.'

Nicholas promised to meet them again and to keep their secret. He took pleasure in their eagerness and energy and their critical spirit; in truth, they reminded him vividly of Marcus and Eliza. One of the students had a small car and offered to drive him home. His unexpected encounter with Philomena had been a distinctly sobering experience. The memory of it worried him all the way home.

At the house Goddington was waiting up for him and looked troubled.

'Jonny has disappeared.'

'Why?' he asked.

'Probably because of an anonymous letter I received today. It read: "Beware of your guest and let your guest beware". Jonny must have taken it as a signal to leave, although it could, of course, have been referring to you. What sort of a day have you had?'

Nicholas gave him a summary account of his visit to the Unidiversity, omitting the evening's events. Goddington seemed pleased.

'You are obviously going to make a success of it here,' he said cheerfully. 'You mustn't let this Cypselus business worry you too much, though we must be attentive to the dangers. Which of our institutions would you like to visit next? The Parliament? The Law Court?'

'How about the Body of Gender?' suggested Nicholas.

'Ah, you've heard about that. Excellent idea. I'll take you there myself the day after tomorrow. I have some mediating to do there. It'll give you an idea about how we deal with the Woman Question.'

Nicholas retired to bed and pondered his own woman question and how, in particular, he was going to explain to Philomena his presence in her bathroom without breaking his oath of secrecy to Benjamin, Constance and their friends. He consulted various Enlightenment thinkers but found none of them of any help.

·22·

The Body of Gender

*H*e slept badly and awoke next morning with a miserable hangover. He seemed to be accumulating sources of unease: the ominous threats of the Malvolians and Stalactites, the congealed and uncongenial consensus of his future colleagues and students and now the Philomena Problem. The last seemed quite intractable. How, without telling the truth, could he explain his presence late in the evening on the fifth floor of a students' Hall of Residence – the very Hall of Residence of which she was Warden, and the very floor on which she was taking a shower?

After breakfast Goddington drove him to the Unidiversity. Nicholas thought of asking the minister's advice but decided against it. He had, after all, promised Benjamin total secrecy. Nor could he ask Benjamin, Constance and the others to corroborate the truth to Philomena, since they plainly distrusted her. He wrestled with the problem for the rest of the morning without success. If Philomena should turn up for lunch, as he still half-hoped, he would simply have to say that he had worked late in the library, taken a night stroll on the campus, and got lost looking for a toilet. Perhaps this would be sufficiently implausible to be convincing.

His half-hope turned out to be forlorn. He sat alone in the

cafeteria from one o'clock until one-thirty but she did not appear. Gloomily he rose to leave as Professors Grenzen and Glaube arrived and invited him to join them. Nicholas accepted, but their conversation did not alleviate his despair. What, they asked, would he be lecturing on exactly? It was evident that they had a correct answer in mind. Benjamin had been right: their purpose was that he should give object lessons of erroneous thought. He was to be their pet poodle, a rationalist among believers, a Fall Guy-in-Residence.

How should a rationalist address believers? It was not an easy problem, especially since the plan was to use his rationalism as a foundation for strengthening their beliefs. The existence of Benjamin, Constance and their friends was an encouragement, but how many potential supporters did they have in Communitaria? The only solution to the problem was to lecture as convincingly as he could and hope that truth would prevail. Unhappily, the truth was unavailable for solving the Philomena Problem, which continued unavailingly to preoccupy him for the rest of the day. The only bright spot came at dinner when he told more of his adventures to Goddington's children.

Next morning, Goddington drove him to the Unidiversity at nine o'clock, promising to return at ten to take him to the Body of Gender. On entering the main building he saw a small newspaper kiosk at which a young man was selling the Unidiversity newspaper. He bought a copy and looked at the front page. The blood drained from his face.

The headline, in large, black bold capitals, read: 'VISITING PROFESSOR MOLESTS BARE BODKIN'. Below it was a large photograph of Philomena Bodkin smiling demurely. Horrified, he read the story that followed:

A shocking incident occurred this Wednesday evening at the Pinetop Hall of Residence. Philomena Bodkin, Professor of Gender Studies and Warden of Pinetop, was taking a shower at 10.30 in the evening, when a man entered unannounced, pulled aside her shower curtain and uttered an ethnic slur in violation of the Unidiversity's speech code.

The intruder, who pretended he was delivering a bar of soap, was none other than Professor Nicholas Caritat, newly appointed Visiting Professor in the Departments of Ethnic and Religious Studies. Professor Caritat, recently saved from a Bigotarian-sponsored kidnapping in Utilitaria by the Reverend Goddington Thwaite, had previously escaped from Militaria where resistance fighters had assigned him the mission of seeking the 'best possible world'.

'This episode gives a whole new sense to the phrase "Visiting Professor". As for his so-called "mission", it is only too clear what Professor Caritat is seeking!' was Professor Bodkin's comment on her distressing experience. Professors Grenzen and Glaube, Heads of the Departments of Ethnic and Religious Studies, were unavailable for comment today. The Unidiversity Administration has issued a warning to everyone to lock their bathroom doors when taking baths or showers.

Shaken and shaking, Nicholas rushed to his office to try and collect his thoughts. In his pigeonhole in the corridor were three envelopes addressed to him. One was marked 'PERSONAL'; the others were marked 'URGENT' and 'VERY URGENT'. He opened them in order of decreasing urgency.

The very urgent letter was a summons to appear at the Body of Gender. It read: 'You are required to attend on (that day's date followed) at 11 a.m. at the Body of Gender (there followed an address) at a Preliminary Hearing of the complaint of *Bodkin versus Caritat* to determine whether a charge or charges should be brought under the Statute against Sexual Harassment.'

The urgent letter was a note stating that the Rector wished to see him at the earliest possible opportunity.

The letter marked 'PERSONAL' was an anonymous letter which simply read: 'Cypselus is a danger to his enemies and to his friends. You have been warned.'

Nicholas went into his office and sat down. The public accusation of intrusion and molesting was bad enough. How

could he defend himself without betraying his friends? But what of the charge of uttering an 'ethnic slur'? What could that possibly mean?

Better, he thought, to face the Rector immediately. Perhaps he could try to avert any further impending disaster. He walked over to the Rector's office, knocked and was admitted.

The Rector was, as ever, elegantly affable. 'Now, what's all this about, Caritat,' he asked. 'I feel sure that there must be some innocent explanation.'

'There is, but I can't give it to you now,' said Nicholas truthfully. Perhaps he could find Benjamin and devise some convincing alibi? But how could that explain his appearance in Philomena's shower? The Rector looked disappointed.

'That's a pity,' he remarked. 'Professor Bodkin is not an easy person to deal with and when she's on the warpath it's best not to be in the way. For all our sakes, I hope your explanation is available soon.'

So do I, thought Nicholas.

He took his leave of the Rector, promising to be in touch as soon as possible, and returned to his office to think out his situation. This seemed ever more dire. Should he go in search of Benjamin? But where would he find him? And how could Benjamin really help him anyway?

The time came for his rendezvous with Goddington. He met the minister at the Unidiversity entrance. The news had clearly reached him. Goddington looked extremely upset.

'Nicholas! My dear Nicholas!' he exclaimed, placing his arm around Nicholas's shoulder. 'I'm sure there's been some ghastly mistake.'

'There has,' he agreed.

'Perhaps,' said Goddington hopefully, 'it's all a case of mistaken identity?'

'No,' replied Nicholas, uninformatively.

They got into Goddington's car. Nicholas showed him the summons from the Body of Gender.

'It seems obvious to me,' said Goddington, as they set off,

'that what is needed here is some professional mediation. I've had some experience in that domain, that field, that department – as you know. But, if I am to help, you'll have to take me fully into your confidence.'

Nicholas reflected. Could he trust Goddington with Benjamin and Constance's secret? Goddington was, after all, a man of the system, thoroughly committed to Communitarianism. There was no mistaking *his* identity. He would be bound to regard the revolutionary club as subversive and unpatriotic. And how would he view Nicholas's support of it? He decided to play for time.

'There is an explanation,' he said, 'but I can't give it to you yet.'

'A pity,' said Goddington, 'I would like to be present at your Hearing to represent your interests, but it will be difficult if you can't give me your side of the story. We must try to clear this business up as soon as we can. You're in enough trouble with the Malvolians and Stalactites for appearing to defend Cypselus.'

He told Goddington of the anonymous letter.

'I didn't want to worry you, but another one came to the house this morning,' said Goddington. Nicholas began to feel distinctly off colour.

They had reached the Body of Gender, yet another structure built in the local, nondescript style. Parked outside the building were some television vans. As they walked towards the main entrance, Goddington explained that he was to mediate later that day in a case of sexual harassment.

'It'll be the case after yours,' he said. 'They've obviously given yours priority. My case concerns a middle-aged male professor taking advantage of a female student. I'm going to try to persuade them to drop the case. These things only ruffle feelings and disturb community relations. I probably won't succeed, though. They're very militant on this issue here.'

They entered through the main doors, passed through a security check and found themselves at a reception desk

where they had to sign their names and receive identification badges with their names spelt out in large black letters. The main lobby was full of people milling about. There seemed to be a general air of expectancy, even excitement. Nicholas pinned his label to his lapel. There could now be no mistaking his identity.

He followed Goddington into an elevator which filled up with people. The door slid closed. As the elevator rose, so did the interest of its occupants in his person. As it murmured in its ascent, so did they. It reached the fifth floor, the door slid open and everyone moved out. As Nicholas stepped out, he was accosted by a young woman who had been standing next to him.

'Excuse me, Professor Caritat,' she said, whipping out a notebook. 'Do you mind if I ask you a couple of questions?'

'No.'

'Can you tell me: Is this your first time?'

'How do you mean?'

'I mean, have you had previous convictions for sexual molestation?'

'Certainly not,' said Nicholas indignantly.

'How about child abuse?' she asked, hopefully.

Goddington intervened. 'Your questions, young woman, are offensive and uncalled-for,' he said.

She closed her notebook. 'The behaviour we're going to hear about today is far more offensive than my questions,' she replied fiercely and marched off.

A crowd, largely composed of women, was gathered in the corridor and was slowly entering through a double door half-way down, past a uniformed official. On reaching the door, Goddington explained to the official who they were. He motioned them to an anteroom further along the corridor, where they were to wait until the Hearing began.

Goddington pressed him for more information. 'Are you sure you can't tell me more about what happened?' he asked.

'I'm sorry,' said Nicholas helplessly. 'The facts are that I

did not molest her, but I was in her shower, and I can't explain why – at least not for the time being.'

Goddington looked baffled but supportive. 'Well, we'll just have to act on the old principle that attack is the best form of defence,' he remarked.

They continued to wait for some time, during which Goddington told Nicholas of the range of penalties the courts could impose for sexual harassment, beginning with a month's imprisonment. Perhaps he should inspect Communitaria's prisons from the inside as part of his mission? He felt like a fly must feel in a spider's web. With every move, the threads seemed to tighten around him.

Eventually the official arrived to lead them to the Hearings Room. It was brightly lit with television lights and packed full of reporters, photographers and curious observers. The cameras were focused on the proceedings in the centre of the room where ten members of the examining Committee were seated around a large oval table. All but one were women. At one end sat Philomena Bodkin surrounded by advisers whispering in her ear and passing her papers. She looked cool and entirely collected, her eyes fixed in front of her. As Nicholas and Goddington entered she observed them without any sign of recognition. They sat down at the other end of the table on two empty chairs. Lights flashed. Cameras clicked.

A grey-haired and rather stout woman, evidently the President of the proceedings, spoke:

'I hereby open the Hearing of the Complaint of Bodkin versus Caritat and I call on Professor Bodkin to explain to us the nature of her complaint.'

'I do so with regret,' said Philomena, calmly and coldly, 'since Professor Caritat has been newly appointed as a colleague of mine. But from the very start his behaviour towards me gave cause for concern. At our very first meeting, he suggested meeting for dinner that very evening on the pretext of enlightening me about the Enlightenment.' There

was a titter around the room. The stout woman banged a gavel on the table. One of her colleagues leant forward.

'Did you accept?' she asked.

'I did not. In fact I made the mistake of explaining to Professor Caritat that I was on duty that evening as Warden of a students' Hall of Residence. He then suggested lunch the next day.'

'Did you accept that?' asked the Committee member.

'I did, reluctantly. I was already in some doubt about the purity of his motives but did not wish to seem uncollegial.'

'Was that wise?' asked the Committee member.

'It was not,' Philomena agreed.

'Tell us what happened next,' said the President.

'That evening I took a late shower at ten-fifteen. The door of the shower room opened. I assumed it was one of the female students and asked her for the soap. Suddenly, Professor Caritat appeared before me.'

'How did he look?' asked another Committee member.

'Unsteady,' replied Philomena. 'He may well have been drinking. He purported not to understand my request that he should leave forthwith.'

'Did he touch you?' asked the male member of the Committee.

'I didn't let him but I fully believe he intended to,' answered Philomena. 'On realizing, albeit dimly, that I was unamenable to his advances, he uttered an unforgivable ethnic insult, to which he added the injury of once more suggesting lunch the next day.'

'How did you manage to get rid of him?'

'By screaming,' said Philomena.

'Thank you, Professor Bodkin,' said the President. 'Does the accused or his representative have anything to say?'

'I do,' said Goddington, leaning forward. 'Professor Caritat has answers to all these unfounded accusations, but wishes to reserve his defence until the appropriate moment. In the meantime, I would like to know why the door of the shower

room was left open by Professor Bodkin. Is that not a little unusual? Could it not even be regarded as an invitation to interesting potential visitors of whatever sex?'

Howls of anger, catcalls and whistles broke out around the room. The President banged her gavel.

'I regard that suggestion as beneath contempt,' said Philomena without emotion.

Nicholas wondered whether, in making it, Goddington had aided his cause. He decided to ask a question himself.

'Excuse me,' he said, 'but there is something I don't understand. What is the ethnic insult I am supposed to have uttered?'

For the first time Philomena showed signs of anger. Her dark and beautiful eyes flashed and her voice rose.

'You said,' she said, her voice quivering with emotion, 'you said that you were sorry I was an Indigen,'

Nicholas racked his brains, searching his memory. 'What I surely said,' he protested, 'was that I was sorry you were *indignant*.'

Disbelieving laughter echoed round the room.

'The Indigen Council will be making an official complaint to the Unidiversity High Council about the matter. I am happy to leave it to them to decide which of us is telling the truth.'

'Does the accused have any further comments or questions?' asked the President.

Goddington leant over and whispered in his ear. 'Don't say any more. You've already admitted you were in her shower, which was a mistake.'

'No, thank you very much,' said Nicholas.

'Does the complainant have any further observations?'

'Yes, I do,' said Philomena. 'We are preparing a psychiatric report on the accused who, it appears, has a history of severely repressed sexual aggression. We have secured the cooperation of Professor Orville Globulus, the world authority on such disorders from Militaria. Dr Globulus has volunteered his services without charge and is in the process of preparing a detailed report on the accused, with whose case he is closely familiar.'

'Thank you Professor Bodkin. The Hearing is adjourned. The decision on whether to proceed to the courts will be taken this afternoon,' announced the President. 'Next case!'

'I shall have to stay,' whispered Goddington. 'I suggest you take a breather.'

Nicholas fled the Hearings Room pursued by a horde of reporters and ill-wishers. He ran down the back stairs and into the street. Some continued to follow him; several took photographs of his flight. He dodged into doorways and ran down side streets, without knowing where he was heading. Eventually, he seemed to have shaken free of the crowd. Before him was a large Communitarian building that he recognized as a railway station. He walked inside and studied a Departures Board listing various destinations of trains soon to depart to places unkown to him. One caught his attention: 'FREEDOM', leaving from Platform 3 at 13.30. He went up to the ticket counter.

'How much is a ticket to Freedom?' he asked.

He had enough to pay for one. With less than an hour before the scheduled departure, Nicholas grabbed a taxi to Goddington's. He asked the driver to wait while he went to his room and stuffed his few belongings and papers into his travelling bag. The taxi dropped him back at the station at 13.25.

Nicholas ran at full speed to Platform 3. The train was standing at the platform. It was a rather shabby, old-fashioned locomotive and largely empty. He climbed aboard, found a vacant compartment and collapsed exhausted on a red imitation-leather seat by the window. Outside the whistle blew.

·23·

Freedom Bound

The train pulled out of the station, gathering speed through long, dark tunnels. Eventually, it emerged into what looked like the suburban edge of the city. Soon they were in the countryside, surrounded by fields with rolling grassy hills stretching into the distance on both sides. There were cattle in the fields and sheep on the hills. They passed streams and ponds and occasional farmhouses. Silver clouds floated across the sky. The sun was shining.

Nicholas realized that he owed Justin another letter. He took paper and an envelope out of his travelling bag, set up the folding table in front of him and started to write:

Between Polygoplis, Communitaria and Freedom

Dear Justin,

I am sorry not to have written to you before now but my time in Communitaria was rather hectic and (he searched for the right word) *stressful*. I only hope that Freedom is less so.

I suppose that the main source of my anxiety while in this country was that I never felt at home. I was – and still am – looking for a home and most of the Communitarians were more than eager to offer me one. But did we mean the same thing? I see a home as a place full of familiar people and things, within which a person can move freely and from which one can

depart and freely return. They seem to see a home as both an origin and a destination, something of overwhelming importance that determines one's life-course, defining how one sees oneself and dictating all social and personal relations.

So, as you can see from the address above, I have decided not to settle in Communitaria. Frankly, I could not imagine living here; indeed, to live here I would have to cease imagining. Communitarians live lives (which they call 'identities') that are shaped externally and collectively, not individually and separately; and if they were to try to step outside them, they would find no place to stand. I met a few brave individuals who were trying to break free, but I believe their cause is doomed. Nor does it seem possible to pass from one identity to another, or to live several together, or to reject one without having to acquire another. Eliza would find even less of a toehold here for her human rights work than in Utilitaria. There the idea is unknown; here it is banned. Marcus would not be able to stand the omnipresence of compulsory religions, and the Communitarian view of truth would drive him mad. At least the Utilitarians believe that every question has a correct answer that can in principle be calculated. For Communitarians every question-and-answer comes with a point of view, and no point of view can be judged superior to any other, since there is no further point of view from which this can be done (though, oddly, they seem to have a point of view from which this, in turn, can be known to be true).

So how would I answer the embryo in search of a birthplace? That is more difficult. I would of course explain to it why we three children of the Enlightenment could not make our lives here. On the other hand, I do believe that some of Communitaria's communities are very adept at bringing up their young in ways that perfectly fit them for the lives they are required to lead without friction or resistance. And why should we welcome, let alone encourage, such resistance? On what grounds can we urge that without it their lives are poorer than they might be? Are we sure that a life led from within is always better than one shaped from without, or even that it is generally so? Why should the embryo choose freedom rather than identity? I hope to have an answer for you in my next letter.

Give Marcus and Eliza all my love and tell them of my hope that we will all be reunited soon.

Yours ever,
Pangloss

Nicholas folded the table away and put the letter in his pocket for posting on arrival in Freedom. He leant back in his seat, recalling his recent sense of entrapment, how he had felt like a fly in a spider's web. The gently rhythmic sound of the train's motion was most agreeably soporific and Nicholas gratefully succumbed to an overwhelming sense of release and relief. He heard a voice proceeding along the corridor outside his compartment and the ringing of a bell. It was evidently a first call for lunch. Hunger vied with tiredness. He struggled to keep his eyes open. Perhaps he would wait for the second call.

Suddenly, he noticed that the train had stopped at a very small country station. There was no sign of lunch, no fellow passengers. No-one was to be seen, in his carriage, or any-where else. No-one left and no-one came on the bare platform. All that could be heard was the twittering of birds and the mooing of cows in the distance. A blackbird sang close by. Nicholas got out of the train and walked along the deserted platform to the engine. There was no driver. He returned to his compartment, picked up his travelling bag and walked out of the unmanned station entrance.

Nicholas found himself on a country road surrounded by open fields, willows, willow-herb and grass. Along the roadside there grew crow-flowers, nettles, daisies and long purples. In the far distance he could see a wooded hill at the top of which stood what looked like a farmhouse. A footpath led towards it across the fields. He struck out along the path. Before long he came to a stile, jumped over it with his bag in his hand and continued on his way.

Up ahead, he could see the glistening of water in the bright sunshine. As he approached, he saw that it was a large, round

pond. Two men with fishing rods were sitting at the water's edge, deep in conversation. One was powerfully built, broad-shouldered and wide-chested. He was dark in complexion with a high forehead, thick, woolly jet-black hair and beard, and sharp, piercing eyes. He talked at length and with great intensity, and would occasionally smile sardonically, revealing a streak of vehement sarcasm. The other man was taller, slim, bony and boyishly youthful, with sharp-cut features, a fair moustache, long sandy whiskers and merry, twinkling eyes. His agile movements were quick and vigorous, his manner of speaking brief and decisive, and his bearing as erect as that of a soldier. They were both wearing riding costumes.

'Good afternoon, gentlemen,' said Nicholas.

They stopped talking and stared at him in amazement.

'I'm very sorry to disturb you,' Nicholas continued, 'but I wondered if you could tell me where I am.'

'You are at our fish pond,' said the man with the twinkling eyes.

'Yes,' said Nicholas, 'but in which place? You see, I'm afraid I'm rather lost. I'm on a journey, to find the best possible world, and I'm trying to find my bearings.'

'Ah,' said the other man, pressing a monocle to his right eye, 'I can see you are a utopian. You think that one can call up an ideal in one's imagination and then go and find or create a reality to match it. We know otherwise. We have attained the world you seek through the inexorable process of world-historical development and through the revolutionary struggle of the Proletariat. In short, the Workers of the World united as we told them to, and we now live in the New World made possible by their successful struggle.'

'What's the New World called?' asked Nicholas.

'It's called *Proletaria* after the class that brought it into being. Of course, that class has now withered away, like all other social classes,' said his tall companion. 'By the way, we haven't introduced ourselves. My name is Fred, and this is Karl.'

Nicholas shook their hands, introducing himself. He was consumed with curiosity. 'Why, if you don't mind my asking,' he said, 'are you both fishing in riding outfits?'

'Well,' said Karl, 'we went hunting this morning. Now we're fishing. This evening we're going to rear cattle and we're all set to criticize after dinner. But the really important thing to realize is that we aren't hunters or fishermen or farmers or critics. We do these things as we have a mind. No-one in Proletaria is confined to an exclusive sphere of activity.'

'I see,' said Nicholas. 'Are you good at hunting?'

The question caused both men great amusement. 'He is,' said Karl. 'I always used to chide him for it. He would go hunting with the local gentry and aristocracy – never failed to attend a meet. He replied that when the Revolution came, someone would have to lead the cavalry. He was always among the leaders in clearing ditches, hedges and other obstacles. I always feared that one day I would hear that he had had an accident.'

'As for him,' said Fred, 'he likes to pretend he can ride a horse. Says he learned to ride as a student, but he never got further than the third lesson! We caught some foxes this morning – at least I did. Not so lucky with the fishing this afternoon, though.'

'The essential point about fishing,' said Karl, 'is the opportunity it provides for a really good conversation. Why,' he asked Nicholas, handing him a spare fishing rod, 'don't you join us?' Gladly, Nicholas sat down beside them and extended his rod over the gently rippling water.

'You're obviously a travelling man,' said Fred. 'Tell us some of your traveller's tales.'

Nicholas started to tell of his adventures. His two companions were avid listeners, constantly interrupting him with exclamations and questions. First, he told them of his arrest and imprisonment in Militaria and the planning of his escape. Karl was very interested to hear about Justin and Nicholas's mission.

'Surely,' said Karl, 'your young friend Justin had heard of this place?'

'Yes, he had,' Nicholas replied, 'but I'm not sure that he any longer believed all he heard.'

'You must strengthen his belief,' said Karl firmly.

'Yes,' agreed Nicholas. Then he told of his escape to Utilitaria. Karl and Fred were both vastly amused by his account of life there.

'We always said Utilitarianism was based on an absurdity,' said Fred. 'The very idea that you can merge all the manifold relationships of people into the one relation of *usefulness*! Utility is just another name for commercial and monetary relations.'

'Typical of Bentham to have thought of it,' added Karl, smiling sardonically, 'that leather-tongued oracle of the bourgeoisie!'

Nicholas proceeded to tell them about his visits to the Parliament and the Court and about his kidnapping by the Bigotarians. Both Karl and Fred were surprisingly sympathetic to the latter.

'Victims of class oppression and blinkered by ideology,' declared Karl.

Both took the same view of the citizens of Communitaria.

'The Bees are obviously still running that place,' Fred commented, 'touching people's hearts but filling up their heads with idolatry and primitive illusions. Religion may be the heart of a heartless world but it is also the opium of the people. The essence of the matter is that those Bees are obviously very successful at extracting surplus value from the workers. What an immense difference between their civilization and ours! They are Bees; we are Architects, Architects of a City fit for human beings. Just compare the best Bee with the very worst of our Architects! And as for that Philomena of yours, why didn't she join the workers' struggle?'

'I don't think there was one,' said Nicholas. Karl and Fred both looked very sceptical.

'So now you've come to us in your quest,' said Karl. 'What would you like to know about Proletaria?'

'Well,' said Nicholas, 'for instance, what sort of state does it have?'

'That's easy: it doesn't have one,' said Karl. 'The state has withered away.'

'The government of men has been replaced by the administration of things,' Fred explained.

'What does that mean?' Nicholas asked.

'It means,' said Fred, 'that administrators decide where to put the fish ponds, but everyone is free to fish in them.'

'I see,' said Nicholas, though he was not sure he did. 'What about the law? What kind of legal system do you have?'

'Also withered away,' said Karl.

'But what about people's rights? What rights do people have?' asked Nicholas.

'We don't have rights,' Karl announced with pride. 'In fact, the very concept of rights has withered away. All that talk about "equal rights" and "justice" and "fairness" that people used to go in for in the Old World, it's all so much ideological nonsense and obsolete verbal rubbish. We don't need rights. People don't need protections or guarantees or rules to ensure justice here because their interests don't conflict. Why should they? After all, we've abolished scarcity and selfishness and irrationality and intolerance.'

'All withered away?' asked Nicholas.

'Exactly!' said Karl.

'But,' Nicholas asked in some perplexity, 'if all these things have withered away, what's left?'

Karl and Fred both roared with laughter.

'An excellent question!' remarked Fred. 'We know a brilliant young scholar who is writing a book with that title. What's left is the true realm of freedom – real, rather than merely formal, freedom for all – freedom that is creative and productive.'

'We have emancipated human beings from the wage slavery

of the past,' added Karl. 'Individuals are no longer sub-ordinated to the division of labour. The opposition between mental and physical labour has vanished. Labour has become not only a means of life but its central point. The productive forces have increased with the all-round development of the individual, and all the springs of cooperative wealth flow more abundantly. Everyone is now free to develop his or her gifts in all directions. Here in the true realm of freedom, the associated producers regulate their interchange with Nature rationally, bringing it under their common control instead of being ruled by it as by some blind power, under conditions that are proper and worthy of human beings.'

'I see,' said Nicholas once more.

'You *will* see,' said Fred. 'We'll show you our truly human society at work – and work is where we become truly human.' He looked at his watch. 'It's time to go and attend to our cattle. Would you like to come with us?'

Fishless but fulfilled, the trio trudged up the hill carrying their tackle in the direction of the farmhouse. As they approached the farm, they came upon a flock of sheep being rounded up by sheepdogs. Tending the sheep were several shepherds and shepherdesses. The former were playing flutes and the latter, dressed in pink and white frilly dresses, were carrying baskets of flowers and singing in harmony, some contraltos and others sopranos. The combined effect of the baaing of the sheep, the barking of the sheepdogs, and the flutes and the harmonious female voices was altogether delightful. Karl and Fred took flutes from their pockets, put them to their lips and joined the shepherds. Nicholas gazed in wonder on this bucolic scene.

Once the sheep were rounded up, Karl and Fred put away their flutes and led Nicholas on into the farmyard. Passing geese and hens in coops, and butter, yoghurt and cheese-making sections, they went into the cowshed, where the cows were being milked by a chorus of milkmaids singing, once more, in harmony. Karl and Fred joined them, milking and

singing: Karl in a rich baritone, Fred in a ringing tenor. Once again the combined effect was most pleasing to the ear.

Their milking done, Karl and Fred invited Nicholas to join them for dinner with various friends in the farmhouse and stay the night. As they walked towards the house, he asked them a question.

'How do you market the produce of the farm?'

'Market?' exclaimed Karl angrily. 'Markets have withered away too. No more buying and selling. No more commodities. No more cash nexus. No more money. Money deprived the whole world, both the human world and nature, of it's own proper value. Money transformed real human and natural faculties into mere abstract representations. Money was a disruptive power for the individual and for social bonds. Money changed fidelity into infidelity, love into hate, hate into love, virtue into vice, vice into virtue, servant into master, stupidity into intelligence and intelligence into stupidity.'

'I see,' said Nicholas. 'But what happens to the milk and the cheese and the butter and the eggs and the meat?'

'From each according to his ability. To each according to his needs,' replied Karl.

'I see,' said Nicholas.

Dinner was a most convivial occasion. The food was magnificent, lavish and fresh from the farm, and there was abundant wine. They ate pâté de foie gras and fat capons with roast potatoes and fresh peas, followed by strawberries and cream. Fred told a joke during dessert. A Communist had once foretold that after the Revolution everyone would have strawberries and cream. 'But I don't like strawberries and cream,' someone had objected. 'After the Revolution,' the Communist had replied, 'you will like strawberries and cream.' The joke was much appreciated.

The guests included old friends and former revolutionaries, his hosts explained, from their days in exile. Most had been either intellectuals, teachers, artists or writers; a few had been workers. All were delighted that they were now none of

these things because everyone was all of them. They talked freely of literature and history. At one point, Karl recited from memory a long passage from Dante's *Divine Comedy* and a scene from Shakespeare's *Macbeth*. Fred kept cracking jokes and seemed to speak an amazing number of languages.

After dinner they all fell to what they called 'criticizing'. Nicholas recognized this as being like a philosophical discussion, yet he noticed one striking fact. They all began with the same assumption: that they shared the unique stand-point of perfect rationality, possessed absolute, objective knowledge, and that their form of life embodied the highest stage of human fulfilment. At one point, Fred remarked, to general approval, 'True philosophy is the science of thinking. Everything else is of merely historical interest and has long been a kind of survival.' 'Criticizing' seemed to consist in examining examples of these survivals in order to show their one-sidedness and inadequacy in contrast to what Karl and Fred called 'historical and dialectical materialism', though Karl seemed more interested in the former and Fred in the latter.

When Nicholas told the party of his scholarly interest in the Enlightenment, his confession was met with a mixture of sympathy and puzzlement. 'So many of those thinkers were reactionary idealists,' remarked Fred, 'and even the material-ists only accepted materialism surreptitiously and denied it before the world. You should move on in your interests, Nicholas, and become more dialectical.'

Karl remarked that his own father had learnt much of Voltaire and Rousseau by heart. 'Important and progressive thinkers in many ways,' he observed, 'but prehistorical figures. We must give you some other texts to study.'

'Thank you very much,' said Nicholas.

Eventually, the criticizing came to an end and the guests took their leave. Karl and Fred showed Nicholas to his room. Nicholas felt sleepy and contented after the good food, the flowing wine and the stimulating conversation. 'Tomorrow,'

said Fred, 'we'll show you some more of Proletaria at work. We'll take you to one of our Musical Factories.'

Next morning, the three of them sat down to a hearty breakfast of tea, fresh farm eggs, milk and yoghurt.

'Have some tea,' said Karl in an encouraging tone.

Nicholas decided to question his two companions further about life in Proletaria.

'Tell me,' he began, 'what are the problems you still haven't overcome?'

'Such as?' demanded Fred.

'Well,' Nicholas ventured, 'I don't quite see how you are able to plan production to meet people's needs without markets to provide information through prices about costs.'

'Ah,' said Fred, 'it is easy to be informed about both production and consumption. Since we know how much a person needs on average, it is easy to calculate how much is needed by a given number of individuals. Since production is no longer in the hands of private producers but in those of the community and its administrative bodies, it is a trifling matter to regulate production according to needs.'

'But,' Nicholas persisted, 'how do you know what people want?'

'People want what they need,' said Karl.

'Which is to say that they need what they want,' added Fred.

'That's not the same thing a bit,' said Nicholas. 'Why, you might just as well say that "I see what I eat" is the same thing as "I eat what I see". Or that "I like what I get" is the same thing as "I get what I like". Or that "I breathe when I sleep" is the same thing as "I sleep when I breathe".'

'Ask us another question,' said Karl.

'Well, what about social problems such as crime, delinquency, the alienation of youth? Or cultural problems: How do people from different backgrounds and with different ways of life get along? And what about personal problems? Aren't there personal conflicts: when marriages break up, say, or between fathers and sons, or lovers, or colleagues?

'That's eight questions,' said Fred.

'The answer,' said Karl, 'is very clear. Communism is the definitive resolution of the antagonism between man and nature and between man and man. It is the true solution of the conflict between existence and essence, between objectification and self-affirmation, between freedom and necessity, between individual and species. It is the solution of the riddle of history and knows itself to be the solution.'

'I see,' said Nicholas, without conviction. The solution seemed even more puzzling than the riddle.

After breakfast, the three of them set off by foot down the hill in the opposite direction to the fish pond. On reaching the main road, they came to a railway station and took a train, though they did not seem to need to buy tickets. After a couple of stops, they alighted in a sort of industrial park containing a series of well-designed Victorian buildings set amidst well-kept lawns and flowerbeds, stretching as far as the eye could see. But the strangest thing was the sound of the place. From each building there emanated a softly surging wave of blended harmonies composed of many timbres. Each individual timbre could be heard distinctly, yet all these waves of sound contrived to merge into a whole that was somehow both restful and stimulating. Nicholas followed Karl and Fred into one of the buildings. 'This is where Fred works,' explained Karl. 'He used to work in his father's cotton mill. He's still in the rag trade. Here they make clothes, as you see.'

The interior of the factory was circular in shape, about the size of the British Museum Library, rising up into an enormous cupola of frosted glass through which sunlight streamed. The ground floor was divided into many sections separated by glass partitions. The spherical, gleaming white wall was also divided into a series of ascending balconies that ran along its entire circumference and between which glass elevators rose and fell. These balconies were also divided into sections separated by glass partitions. On the floor and on the balconies were, Nicholas guessed, maybe a thousand

workers sitting and standing at various machines, all in view of one another. In the very centre of the floor was a raised rostrum, where the chief manager stood, baton in hand, surveying the scene.

It was a scene of contrasts which seemed to combine high technology and individual craftsmanship, planning and improvisation, cooperation and spontaneity. In some of the sections there were designers creating clothes on computer screens. There were machines for weaving, dyeing and cutting different fabrics. There were machines producing belts and others buttons. The machine tenders were also seated at computer terminals. Then there was what looked like a clerical and accounting section, on the second platform, to which Fred had ascended, staffed by workers also seated before computer screens. Yet Nicholas could also see sections of seamstresses and tailors, rhythmically snipping, cutting and stitching to designs on computer screens. Nicholas noticed that from time to time workers would rise and go from one position to another: a seamstress would join the design section, a machine tender would become a craftsman, an accountant would take up snipping, and so on.

On the highest platform, tall, lithe, elegant, stunningly attractive young women and tanned, muscular and athletic-looking young men walked slowly and sensuously back and forth modelling the clothes made that day. A thousand eyes were continually raised to observe them. In this way, Karl explained to Nicholas, alienation from the product of one's labour was overcome: the workers could, simply by gazing heavenwards, see at any moment the final product of their collective labour.

But the strangest thing of all was the music. Each worker's activity produced a distinctive sound. As they tended their machines, tapped at their keyboards, stitched and snipped, they made music. And each made his or her own music yet all cohered into a Symphony of a Thousand, with the manager on the rostrum conducting.

The music was compulsive and hypnotic. Its richly inter-weaving melodies were deeply soothing, yet its rhythms were unrelentingly repetitive, like the motion of a train's wheels on the rails.

·24·

Freedom Unbound

here was a sharp tap on his right knee. Nicholas shook his head and rubbed his eyes. The insistent rhythm of the music had ceased. All was silence. The train had stopped.

'Passport, please. Passport and ticket!' He was being addressed by a uniformed customs official.

His first, groggy reaction was one of considerable annoyance – annoyance that he could not after all send Justin a letter from the best possible world with the message 'MISSION COMPLETE'. He produced his Pangloss passport from his inside pocket with his ticket.

The customs official inspected them both and handed them back.

'Thank you,' he said. 'I see you are a Professor. On holiday, I suppose?'

Nicholas said he supposed so too.

'Funny name, Pangloss,' remarked the official.

'Yes, it is unusual,' said Nicholas expansively. 'It comes from a character invented by Voltaire who believed that this is the best of all possible worlds.'

'Can't have lived here then,' said the official drily.

'Forgive my asking,' said Nicholas, 'but where is here? What country are we in?'

'Don't you know where you're going?' said the official in surprise. 'This is Libertaria and your ticket is for Freedom, the capital city.'

'What's so bad about living here?' asked Nicholas.

'It's not a place to be unlucky, or unemployed, or,' the official added glumly, 'to work for the state. It's alright for some though. Well, enjoy your holiday, Professor Pangloss. I'm sure *you'll* have a good time in Freedom.' He slid the door closed and went off.

Nicholas looked out of the window. It was getting dark. All he could see was a number of platforms and railway sidings at which various trains were standing. It was raining.

He heard footsteps in the corridor and his compartment door slid open again. It was another official.

'Ticket please,' said the official. Nicholas handed over his ticket once more.

The official inspected it and asked for a sum of money.

'I don't understand,' Nicholas protested. 'I already bought this ticket.'

'Of course you did,' said the ticket inspector. 'But now you're in Libertaria. You only bought the *journey*. You've got to pay a seat supplement. Your seat is part owned by Fare's Fair Enterprises. They have a time-share in it and you have to pay for occupying one of their seats while in Libertaria.'

'But is that really fair?' Nicholas protested.

'Please yourself,' said the inspector. 'You could always shop around and try to find a cheaper seat.'

'What if I stand?' Nicholas asked.

'Then you'll have to pay a floor supplement. It would,' he admitted, 'be cheaper. Then there's the track supplement.'

'What's that?' Nicholas asked.

'Use of the track. Fast Track Enterprises – which, as a matter of fact, I also represent – own the track, you see. Maintaining it costs money.' The inspector named another not inconsiderable sum of money.

'Of course, if you don't want to pay,' said the inspector, 'you

could always get off here.' Nicholas looked out of the window again at the pouring rain. He examined the contents of his wallet. He did not have a lot of money left and, in any case, it was in Communitarian currency. He explained the problem to the inspector.

'You can always change your money in the station,' said the inspector, 'but you haven't got a lot of time. The train leaves in half an hour and there isn't another one today. Of course,' he added, 'if you get off the train, you'll have to pay a platform fee to the Platform Services Company – which owns the platform and which I also represent.' He named another sum.

'What if I don't pay all this?' Nicholas asked with growing defiance.

'Well,' said the inspector, 'if you don't pay the seat or floor and track supplements, I'll have to ask you to leave the train.'

'And if I don't pay the platform fee?'

'In that case,' said the inspector triumphantly, 'I can't allow you to leave the train. It's your choice. Freedom of choice! That's what we believe in here in Libertaria.'

Nicholas left his bag on his seat, promising to return with the various fees, and walked rapidly along the platform into the station. He could see two currency exchange offices on either side of the main hall. He made for the one on the left which seemed to be the more official-looking office, advertising its rates of exchange for various currencies on a screen in the window. Behind the window a middle-aged blonde woman sat painting her nails. Alongside the window stood a queue of some eight miserable-looking persons. He asked one of them if there was a problem.

'Run out of money, so we've got to wait.'

'How long?' he asked.

'Who knows?' came the reply.

He ran over to the other office, a makeshift kiosk with a sign that read 'FASTCASH ENTERPRISES' and a placard outside advertising rates of exchange much less favourable to the prospective buyer of Libertarian currency. If you cashed

less than a certain sum, the rate was even more unfavourable. Here people were being served quickly and there was no queue. Nicholas realized that the choice was his, changed a small sum at the worst rate and rushed back to his train. The inspector was waiting for him. He paid him and received three receipts as the train resumed its journey.

As the train gathered speed, Nicholas's anxieties started to mount. Until now he had focused exclusively on his escape to Freedom. It was now time to consider what it was he was escaping to and how he was to survive in a country of which he knew nothing except its encouraging name. He had little money left, a few clothes in his travelling bag including his fur-lined cloak, and a passport in the name of Dr Pangloss. Although he thought hard, he could not recall the name of a single colleague or fellow scholar from Libertaria to whom he might appeal for help.

The train passed through various stations at high speed. After about an hour and a half it approached the outskirts of a metropolis. Where, Nicholas wondered, would he stay the night? How would he live? His future seemed wholly opaque.

The intercom crackled and a voice loudly announced that they were approaching Freedom. Nicholas took down his travelling bag. The train came to a halt. He descended onto an almost deserted platform and walked into the main station, which was full of the familiar denizens of urban nightlife: hot dog vendors, a few drunks, sleepy travellers sprawled on benches, groups of raucous adolescent boys disinclined to go home. Nicholas also noticed a surprising number of sleeping figures huddled under blankets in doorways and dark corners. He made his way past them out of the station into the street outside. It was raining and cold. At some distance he could see a neon sign that read 'HOTEL'. He crossed the road and walked towards it.

As he came near, he saw the hotel had a distinctly pleasing name: 'PILGRIM'S REST'. He *was* a pilgrim, he thought – rather than a traveller or migrant or visitor – but a pilgrim

whose journey had no preassigned destination. Was the Pilgrim's Rest, he wondered, a final resting place or only another station on the way?

He entered the hotel lobby. It seemed modest and clean and slightly dilapidated. A grumpy elderly man was on duty at the reception desk, exhibiting the indifference of those who work in places of innumerable transitory encounters. Nicholas asked tentatively for a single room for the night at the cheapest rate.

'Room five hundred and one,' said the old man, without looking up. 'No extras. No bath. No breakfast. No animals. You'll have to leave by noon tomorrow.' He demanded Nicholas's passport for the night before handing him a key. 'Take the lift to the fourth floor and walk up a flight.'

Clutching his travelling bag, he did as instructed and found himself in a small, bare, boxlike attic room with a downward-sloping ceiling and tiny window. He undressed and immediately fell into a deep but troubled sleep.

·25·

Money

Nicholas awoke early the next morning, dressed quickly and descended to the hotel lobby. At the reception desk sat a sad young man in rimless glasses with curly brown hair, wearing an open shirt and corduroy jacket and reading a newspaper. Nicholas put his key on the desk top. The young man returned him his passport without looking up from his newspaper.

'Professor are you?' asked the young man sourly.

'That's right,' Nicholas answered in a friendly tone.

The young man scowled.

Nicholas cleared his throat. 'I was wondering,' he ventured, 'whether I might stay a little longer here. Is my room available for a few more days?'

'How many days?' muttered the young man, opening the hotel register.

Nicholas made a rapid calculation. If he spent minimally on food and other necessities, his money might just last a month, but he'd better not ask for too much.

'Let's say – seven?'

The young man looked up. 'Alright,' he said, with the first faint show of interest. Nicholas responded, 'You see, I don't know anyone here and I'm hoping to find some work . . . '

The young man emitted a hollow laugh: 'Who isn't?'

'Is it so difficult?' Nicholas asked.

'I wouldn't say that it was difficult,' said the young man, 'just bloody near impossible. I certainly wouldn't be doing this job if I could get a better one – was lucky even to get this one.'

'What sort of job would you prefer?' Nicholas asked.

The young man shrugged his shoulders. 'Anything – management, accountancy, clerical work. You see, Professor (he uttered the word with some bitterness), I've got a university degree. Economics. I've got what they call a qualification. Trouble is I'm overqualified. That's what they always tell me when I apply for jobs. You won't want to stay at this job, they say, you'll soon be moving on to something better. I've made two hundred applications in the last six months.'

'That's terrible!' said Nicholas sympathetically.

'It is terrible,' agreed the young man. 'But you mustn't let the Depression depress you. What's your line of business, then?'

'I'm a scholar of the Enlightenment,' said Nicholas.

'Oh Lord!' the young man said. 'Another producer of useless graduates!'

Nicholas felt despondent.

'I'll tell you what you should do,' the young man said in a fleeting burst of generosity. 'Go to the University and see whether they've got any vacancies – in the Enlightenment field or in anything else that might suit you. Go to the Administration – they'll give you a list of what's on offer. But while you're there, go and hear a lecture by my old professor, Professor Tipster. He's always good for a laugh and full of free advice about how to make money. Maybe he'll give you an idea or two, and then perhaps you can pass the good tips along to me. My name's Leon, by the way. The number eight bus near the station will take you to the University.'

Nicholas thanked Leon warmly and set off. The shopping area around the station consisted mainly, it seemed, of sex

shops, betting shops, video clubs specializing in 'adult' films, cheque cashing and currency exchange offices (including, he noticed, 'Fastcash Enterprises'), all-night groceries and derelict cafés. People wrapped in blankets huddled in doorways asking anyone who passed for the price of a cup of coffee. He changed some more money, drank a coffee in one of the cafés and made for the number eight bus stop.

The bus stop was on a road near the railway station in which there were office buildings fronted by gardens and a low wall. As he walked towards the stop, he noticed a middle-aged man sitting on the wall with a small suitcase beside him. He was clean-shaven and well dressed in a suit and tie and looked like a businessman or civil servant waiting, presumably, for the bus. The number eight came and Nicholas boarded it. The man remained on the wall, observing him closely.

The University was a large modern campus whose massive buildings were all marked with large blue and white signs. He walked towards 'ADMINISTRATION', a largely windowless building in the centre of the campus. On reaching the main entrance, he found himself before a reception desk manned by a porter.

'Where can I find out about posts that might be available?' he asked.

The porter directed him to the Personnel Office on the second floor. As he walked up the stone staircase, Nicholas reflected that it was hardly normal to seek an academic post in this way. But what else could he do? At least he could obtain a list of the Departments and Faculty members. Perhaps he might find a name he recognized. And perhaps there might be some non-academic position for which he might apply – in the University library, say. Or perhaps he could help to cultivate its garden?

In PERSONNEL there was a series of glass-fronted booths at which various people were being attended to. He went up to the one labelled 'EMPLOYMENT VACANCIES'. It was closed.

He knocked on the glass. No-one came. He knocked again.

A grim-faced woman in horn-rimmed spectacles of indeterminate age appeared before him.

'What do you want?' she asked aggressively.

'I was wondering,' he said, 'whether there might be any chance of employment in the University.'

'There are no vacancies,' she said. 'That,' she added patiently, 'is why this section's closed.'

She exhibited the indifference to which he was becoming accustomed. He decided to test it with one further question.

'Might there not be some future possibility? I'm a scholar from abroad and I'm interested in working here . . . in any capacity that might seem suitable.'

She looked at him with neither interest nor sympathy. He was yet another asker of tedious questions.

'You can leave your name and qualifications and we'll put you on a list,' she said blandly and thrust a piece of paper at him – a list, he conjectured, of other tedious questioners. Still, Nicholas thought, he might as well leave his name. But which name? It was probably better to use Pangloss in view of his passport, yet how would anyone who knew anything about the Enlightenment take seriously the application of a Dr Pangloss? It was a risk he'd have to take. For 'qualifications' he put down his degrees and under 'specialization' wrote 'Enlightenment'. There was a column titled 'Employment Sought' and below it he wrote: 'Anything suitable – e.g. teaching or research or position in library or garden.'

'One last thing,' he said to the grim lady. 'Could I please have a list of the Departments and Faculty members?' She went away and came back with a University list.

'Oh, and one very last thing,' he said. 'Where might Professor Tipster be lecturing?'

'If you're not a student here, you'll have to pay a fee,' she said, naming a sum. He paid her, took a receipt and went off in the direction she indicated towards ECONOMICS.

There was a noticeboard at the Department of Economics announcing various lectures. In an hour's time Professor

Tipster was due to lecture on 'The Theory and Practice of Money'. Nicholas took a stroll around the campus and made his way to the theatre in time to secure a seat in the back row.

Professor Tipster was a stocky man with grey-black hair, a square face, moustache and extremely bushy and expressively mobile eyebrows. He spoke forcefully, meticulously articulating every syllable in a thin, high-pitched voice and thumping the rostrum with his hand at moments of emphasis. A few of his utterances contained words but most consisted in equations expressed in mathematical and algebraic symbols rendered visible to all in transparencies projected onto a screen by an overhead projector. For the first fifty minutes most of what he said was opaque to Nicholas, who passed the time watching the students taking careful notes. Then, suddenly, the Professor changed gear.

'That,' he said, 'is enough theory for today. Let us now turn to practice.'

To his surprise, Nicholas noticed that all the students immediately closed their notebooks and seemed to lose interest.

'Money,' continued Professor Tipster, 'is something I have observed no-one ever wants to have less of. The art of making more of it at the least possible cost is an accomplishment to which all aspire but few achieve. As an acknowledged master of that art, ever willing to impart its mysteries to the wider world (titters went round the audience), I conclude today's lecture with a word or two of advice. Invest, my friends, in the National Library of Libertaria! They are privatizing it and selling shares at a grossly undervalued figure. Buy National Library shares and make a quick killing. I guarantee that if you follow my advice, you'll have trebled, even quadrupled your money.' He projected a transparency onto the screen which read: '$X \times 3 = 3X$ and $X \times 4 = 4X$'. The audience tittered once more. 'There is a simple reason for my certainty about this, which I shall not divulge before the event. But take my word for it, National Library shares are where the money is today. Enrich yourselves!'

With these final words, the students broke into half-hearted and somewhat sarcastic applause. Nicholas decided to ask a fresh-faced young man to his right why his peers were less impressed by the Professor's practical wisdom than by his theoretical knowledge.

'We're all very interested in money,' explained the student. 'We just don't have any. It's all very well telling us to invest but most of us can't even buy textbooks on our meagre student loans! We can't risk following his advice.'

Professor Tipster remained on the lecture platform talking to students. The last few minutes of his lecture had impressed Nicholas who found himself taken with Tipster's apparent authority and conviction. Nicholas decided to approach him.

'Excuse me, Professor Tipster,' he said, 'I am a visitor from abroad. I very much enjoyed your lecture and I wish to ask you a question.'

'By all means!' said Tipster expansively, his eyebrows raised. 'Always delighted to meet visitors from abroad – especially mature students such as yourself – who've come to see the economics of freedom at work. You've come here at the right time. Under our new government everything is being privatized. Soon we won't even know what the word "public" means! This flotation of the National Library shares is only the beginning. Once that's done, the public libraries will go private and then the museums, art galleries, opera houses and monuments, and then the public parks and beaches will be sold off in the form of time-shares. It's a wonderful explosion of freedom – the freedom to buy and sell and above all *own*. Wonderful! Wonderful, don't you agree?'

'I don't know enough about it yet,' said Nicholas cautiously. 'It sounds very exciting. But could you please tell me one thing? How would I go about buying these National Library shares and how would I sell them?'

'Easiest thing in the world,' said Tipster. 'Go to the Post Office and apply for your Library shares. Everyone's entitled to a thousand each. When you receive them, go to my broker

(he opened his wallet and handed Nicholas a business card).
He'll sell them for you. Just mention my name.' Tipster held
out his hand. 'Delighted to meet you. What did you say your
name was?'

'Pangloss,' said Nicholas.

'How very appropriate,' Tipster quipped as he rushed away.

Nicholas looked at the business card of 'Osgood Mickle-
thrust, Stockbroker'. He put it in his pocket and walked
through the campus towards the main entrance. On the way
out, a large notice caught his eye. It read: 'LIBERTARIAN
ASSOCIATION OF PSYCHIATRISTS: ANNUAL MEETING'. The
meeting was to start that afternoon at four p.m. with a recep-
tion in one of the University buildings. A thought occurred
to Nicholas, one that he turned over in his mind, again and
again, as he made his way out of the University to the nearest
Post Office.

·26·

Psychiatrists

There was a jostling crowd in the Post Office at the counter marked 'SHARE SALES'. People of various ages and varying degrees of apparent prosperity were united in a single wish: to get to the counter and buy. Nicholas picked up an application form at the entrance, filled it out and joined the rest of the crowd, waving his completed form in the air and shouting along with everyone else. The teller tried to control the mob but his efforts were in vain. Nicholas gradually edged his way forward. He was about to stake almost all he had at the advice of someone he scarcely knew on a venture about which he knew even less. After buying a thousand shares at the price offered he would have at most three days' subsistence left, without even paying his hotel bill. Yet the risk of what he was about to undertake gave him a thrilling and utterly unfamiliar sensation of freedom. He would soon veer upwards like a bird or downwards like a diver – either way he was heading freely into the unknown. He had discovered something utterly new and unsuspected about his self: that it harboured the cravings of a gambler. His only fear was that it might be too late to satisfy them.

Finally he reached the front and handed over his application form made out in the name of Dr Pangloss at the Pilgrim's

Rest Guest Hotel, Freedom. Nicholas asked the teller how long it would take to receive his shares.

'Some time,' she replied.

'How much time?' he persisted.

'Some time,' was the unhelpful reply. The teller was not telling. She then asked for the price of the shares plus a large and unexpected commission fee, thereby reducing his subsistence money to one day. Nicholas felt even freer; it was now a case of all or almost nothing. Both his pocket and his head felt lighter as he left the Post Office to return to the hotel.

Whistling to himself, he went up to his room and undressed. From his travelling bag he took out a green velvet suit, bright yellow shirt and red-spotted bow tie and put them on. He then left his room, still whistling, walked down to the lift, descended to the ground floor, left the hotel and walked to the number eight bus stop. The smartly dressed man with the suitcase whom he had seen there that morning was, he noticed, still sitting on the wall. Nicholas nodded vaguely at him, but he did not respond. Nicholas took the bus to the University. It was nearly four o'clock.

He made straight for the Psychiatrists' Congress which was being held on the first floor in one of the main buildings. He entered the building and made a quick dash for the men's toilet and washroom. Luckily, it was empty. From the suit pocket he fished out the beard tinged with grey and carefully smoothed it onto his face. He checked his appearance in the large mirror and, well satisfied, left the washroom and walked upstairs.

The psychiatrists were all greeting and meeting each other over cups of tea and coffee and plates of dainty biscuits set out on a long table. The room seemed to be full of people whom Nicholas felt he almost knew. He walked confidently up to the table and armed himself with a cup of coffee and, a supply of biscuits. A hand landed on his left shoulder.

'Globulus, my dear fellow,' said an unfamiliar voice that belonged to a rotund, red-cheeked man in a tweed jacket on

which was pinned a label that identified him as Dr Julius Stuffington, 'How splendid to see you here. My goodness, it's been a long time. A lot of water's passed under the bridge here in Libertaria since we last met. Where was it, I wonder?'

'Can't remember myself,' said Nicholas. 'But tell me, what's new? What's been happening here?'

'It's been an extraordinary time,' said Dr Stuffington. 'The state has truly been withering away here. (Am I still dreaming? Nicholas wondered.) A mass of controls and regulations have gone, everything that was once public has been privatized – railways, buses, the telephones, water, gas, the Post Office, the Law Courts, parks, beaches, prisons, the police, even the National Library.'

'Yes,' said Nicholas, 'I've heard about that.'

'The new government's done away with progressive taxation – the more money you make the less taxes you have to pay. It's all happened with breathtaking speed! I suppose you'll be coming to hear the Prime Minister tomorrow?'

'Where is that?' Nicholas asked.

'Here at the University hospital. She's coming tomorrow morning to deliver an important policy statement about private health care. We'll all be going to hear her. Then the conference resumes in the afternoon.'

'I'll be there,' said Nicholas. Another hand landed on his shoulder.

'Globulus! Welcome to Libertaria! What an honour that you should have come! We so much admire your work, you know.' Nicholas turned in the direction of the rather nasal voice and saw a storklike man with a pale, pinched face and gold-rimmed glasses. His name tag identified him as Professor Cyril Syndrome. 'How long will you be here?'

'Oh, some while, I expect,' replied Nicholas vaguely.

'Really,' exclaimed Professor Syndrome, 'that's wonderful news. Is it conceivable that we could induce you to act as a visiting consultant here at the University hospital during your stay?'

'I should be honoured,' said Nicholas without hesitation. He did, after all, badly need a job.

'No, the honour will be ours. Can you come to the psychiatric wing tomorrow morning – at half-past nine, say? We'll set you up with an office and secretary and so on. Then we can go and hear the Prime Minister together.'

Several more hands landed on his shoulders, belonging to colleagues expressing similar friendly sentiments. It was, Nicholas reflected, an agreeable feeling to be so highly esteemed by one's fellow professionals.

The reception came to an end and the psychiatrists settled down for their annual business meeting in the course of which Dr Globulus's presence was duly remarked upon by the Chairman. At this point, a young woman psychiatrist asked permission to speak. In a quavering, impassioned voice, she reminded her colleagues of the academic boycott against Militaria and went on to detail Dr Globulus's total complicity with the Junta, whose brutalities she started to list. Nicholas was struck by the accuracy of her account and he warmed to the fierce strength of her passion. She sounded exactly like Eliza challenging policemen for information about the disappeared or chiding newspaper editors for their cowardly self-censorship. He wanted to embrace the young psychiatrist and cheer her on, yet her words might put him in an awkward spot. Would he now have to speak in defence of Globulus and his masters?

He need not have worried. After two minutes or so of the young woman's speech, the Chairman interrupted her to deplore what he called her discourteous intervention. He then asked for a show of hands on the question of whether their honoured guest was indeed welcome. So far as Nicholas could see, Globulus and the rulers of Militaria were virtually unanimously *personae gratae* among the psychiatrists of Libertaria.

After the business meeting, they all adjourned for dinner in the dining room, during which everyone he encountered

apologized for their colleague's unpardonable discourtesy. Nicholas imparted bits of news about the recent past in Militaria, carefully omitting anything discreditable to the regime, and gleaned more about Libertaria's lurch towards freedom and the rosy outlook it promised for private medicine and psychiatry in particular. After dinner there was a lecture by his future colleague and host intriguingly entitled 'The Syndrome Syndrome'. Nicholas sat in the front row in the lecture theatre and listened attentively. Professor Syndrome had, it appeared, discovered a new disorder which he jocularly described as 'the case of Buridan's ass in the super-market'. Buridan's ass, the Professor reminded his audience, had starved to death because it could not choose between two identical piles of hay equidistant from its nose. The Syndrome syndrome, he explained, was a distinctive form of mental paralysis that resulted from an excess of insignificant choices and occasionally resulted in suicide. It was, apparently, a growing problem in Libertaria. The lecture generated a lively discussion during which various forms of therapy were discussed, all of them intensive – and clearly expensive. Nicholas enjoyed the evening greatly and returned to his hotel stimulated and instructed. He had regained his professional status, if in the wrong profession. Things were decidedly looking up.

He rose early next morning, donned his Globulus attire and, after taking a coffee in one of the sleazy bars, headed straight for the number eight bus stop. The middle-aged man with the brown suitcase was sitting on the low wall. He had obviously been there all night. He looked unshaven and his tie was askew. He noticed Nicholas noticing him and looked away. Nicholas took the bus and went straight to the hospital's psychiatric wing. Professor Syndrome was waiting for him at the main entrance.

'Fascinating lecture last night,' said Nicholas.

'Thank you, thank you,' said Syndrome, appreciating the appreciation. 'It's true that life here can bring its own

problems. Ah, the burdens of freedom! The art is to solve them without reducing it.'

'Quite so,' Nicholas agreed.

Syndrome took him to his new office, which was carpeted and tastefully decorated with a long leather couch and easy chairs. He introduced Nicholas to the smartly dressed secretary who would be working for him. Like everyone else, she seemed in awe of his fame. 'Of course we'll pay you a very handsome retainer for your services here but, needless to say, you are free to charge whatever the market will bear. I think you'll find it'll bear quite a lot!' Syndrome chortled.

His short-term professional future established, Nicholas felt buoyant, as though he were floating on a sea of goodwill. All he needed to do was to keep afloat by saying the minimum and conforming to people's expectations. It was as if he was playing a part in a play which was evolving naturally.

'Perhaps,' suggested Syndrome, 'you would care to come and visit the ward? We have a little time before the Prime Minister's visit and she's speaking right here in our new theatre.'

Nicholas followed Professor Syndrome along the corridor into the psychiatric ward. Syndrome opened the locked door by pressing a secret code and they entered a common area. A few patients were watching television with intense concentration. On the screen was a test-card accompanied by light, jingly music. The patients sat motionless and mesmerized.

The two professors walked into the ward. Nicholas noticed a strange sight to his left: a bed piled high with shiny pots and pans, old books, tattered clothes, a feather duster and covered with notices that read 'KEEP OUT' and 'TRESPASSERS WILL BE PROSECUTED'. Sitting in the middle of this heap of bric-a-brac was a short, stout woman in late middle age with a grey bun, frightened eyes and pursed lips.

'This woman suffers from a severe case of kleptophobia, or an obsessive concern with private property,' Syndrome explained. 'The patient is called Mia. She won't let go of what

she calls her "holdings" – thinks the whole world is out to steal them.'

'Hello, Mia,' said Nicholas. She eyed him distrustfully and clutched a frying pan. He stepped back to reassure her, but she did not look reassured.

They walked on, past other patients. A short, shrivelled man in his mid thirties, with little round spectacles, a fierce expression and a prominent scar on his left cheek, leapt from his bed and accosted Nicholas.

'What do you want?' he hissed.

Nicholas fumbled for an answer: 'I want . . . '

'*That's* your problem!' said the man. 'I've diagnosed it. If you would only stop *wanting*, you wouldn't be in here. You must control your insatiable appetites. Get a hold of yourself!' He was growing more and more agitated and started to shout. 'Overcome your passions! Then you'll become free. They're all trying to stop you getting what you want, right? Well, get your own back and stop wanting! What can they do then?'

'Thank you,' said Nicholas. Syndrome motioned to a nurse and she gently guided the patient to his bed.

'An interesting case,' explained the doctor, 'of Orexiphobia: the fear of desire. We call him Seneca. He's our resident Stoic philosopher. Has to be watched carefully, though, as he keeps losing control of himself. But, now, there's another patient I'd very much like you to see.' They walked towards a bed at the far end of the ward on which there sat a large, swarthy man in a silk dressing gown and cravat with a hooked nose and a black patch over his left eye. 'We call this patient Aristotle.'

'Is he a philosopher too?' Nicholas asked.

'No, he's a ship owner,' said Syndrome, 'or thinks he is. He suffered an injury to his head several years ago: hence the eye patch. Aristotle thinks he's immensely wealthy and that all his documents and money are locked away in a Swiss bank account the combination of which he can't remember. Fascinating case of plutomanic amnesia.'

Syndrome introduced Nicholas to Aristotle, who rose from his bed and shook them both warmly by the hand.

'I'm working on the five thousands,' he confided to Syndrome. 'Perhaps,' he asked Nicholas, 'you have a suggestion?'

'Five thousand nine hundred and eighty-two?' Nicholas volunteered. Aristotle looked doubtful. 'You must come and visit me on my yacht.'

'With pleasure,' said Nicholas.

'Though it'll need some renovation after all these years.'

'Quite so,' Nicholas replied.

'It's about time to go and hear the Prime Minister,' said Syndrome. 'Shall we?' They took their leave of Aristotle and Nicholas followed Syndrome back through the ward and out of the main door.

In the corridor there had gathered a crowd of nurses, cleaners and other persons, including patients in pyjamas and dressing gowns, hoping to catch a glimpse of the official party. The meeting was to take place behind a door marked 'THEATRE'. Nicholas wondered whether it was of the lecturing or operating variety. It turned out to be the former and contained a large audience of senior doctors and consultants, including all the psychiatrists, invited for the occasion and seated together in a block near the front. There were television cameramen, reporters and security guards hanging about the aisles and a large podium at the front with a long table covered by a blue cloth. Nicholas joined Syndrome in the front row alongside various hospital dignitaries. At exactly 10.59 the official party entered and mounted the podium, led by the Prime Minister.

On seeing her, Nicholas suffered a sudden shock of quasi-recognition. She was dressed in a tight-fitting, dark blue suit and her hair was in perfect and elegant trim, her eyes were steely, her expression firm and steady.

'Ladies and Gentlemen,' said the silver-haired chairman, the Director, Syndrome informed him, of the hospital, 'we are honoured today by the presence of the Prime Minister, Mrs.

Jugula Hildebrand. She has come to deliver an important policy statement before us which we are, of course, most eager to hear. The Prime Minister!'

She rose to her feet and addressed the audience in sharp, ringing tones.

'Friends,' she began, 'I feel that I am among friends – we have embarked upon an exciting and ennobling adventure. With each day that passes under our Government, individual freedom has grown wider and deeper and the so-called social doctrines and policies that used to threaten it have been exorcised. I am glad to say that the very word "social" has been expunged from our vocabulary. No more social this and social that! No more social justice or social welfare or social policy or social problems or social services or social safety nets! No more social class! No more social engineering! As I have often said, there is no such thing as society. Only individual persons exist, and their freedom grows daily.

'Today it is to grow some more. Another nail is to be hammered into the coffin of *social*ism with its spendthrift and misdirected social conscience. Today I am glad to announce yet another measure that will make individuals free – individuals who have up to now been living very close to where you are all sitting.' An excited and puzzled murmur went around the audience.

'I refer,' she continued, 'to the mental patients of our hospitals. From today they will go free. Into the community. They will be decarcerated. The psychiatric wards will be made available for other, far more important uses. This hospital, for instance, will now offer cosmetic plastic surgery, which will certainly be much more profitable and yield a far bigger turnover. Meanwhile the former occupants will have to find their feet and become self-reliant and responsible citizens. Families and friends will be called upon to exercise their personal responsibilities in helping their previously incarcerated loved ones to learn to enjoy the fruits of their newly won freedom. This,' she concluded, 'is a great day for mental health.'

As she resumed her seat there was loud applause and some cheering. Nicholas turned round to observe the reactions of the psychiatrists. Some looked pleased but most seemed puzzled and unsure of how enthusiastically to respond. Professor Syndrome looked crestfallen.

'This is a disaster!' he whispered to Nicholas. 'My life's work destroyed in one speech. Me and all my colleagues thrown onto the scrapheap. I'm afraid we'll have to cancel our agreement, Globulus. What a disaster!'

Nicholas wondered just who had been thrown onto the scrapheap. He bade a mental farewell to his office and secretary and his handsome consultancy fee. The Prime Minister and her party were descending from the platform and the Hospital Director brought her over to meet Syndrome.

'This,' he announced, 'is Professor Syndrome, our Professor of Psychiatry.'

Syndrome shook her hand, smiling wanly. 'Soon to be erstwhile Professor, I fear,' he said.

'Come now, Professor,' said the Prime Minister, 'you can still profess, and practise, your trade privately.'

Syndrome seemed lost for words and so introduced Nicholas: 'Allow me to introduce Dr Globulus, the celebrated psychiatrist from Militaria.'

She turned her gaze on Nicholas. 'Militaria!' she remarked. 'An admirable place in only one respect. You have order without freedom. We have both. Gentlemen,' she continued briskly, 'I suggest you come with us to the ceremony.' She swept forward out of the theatre with the Director and her officials in tow. Syndrome and Nicholas followed.

In the corridor outside the theatre, the mob of eager watchers was held back by security men as the Prime Minister's party proceeded towards the psychiatric wing. The main doors were open and the party entered. In the front area, the television had been switched off and the nurses and doctors stood in a row to attention as Jugula Hildebrand marched purposefully into the ward, the Director at her side.

The ward was bright from television lights and cameramen were filming from various vantage points. The patients were sitting or lying on their beds; some looked amazed, others bewildered, others utterly indifferent. A few slept. Syndrome and Nicholas stood along the wall between the beds. The hospital staff entered their ward to observe a scene which was evidently being broadcast live to the world at large.

'Ladies and Gentlemen,' declared the Director, 'we are honoured today by the visit of the Prime Minister, who has come to this very ward to make an announcement that will change your lives – that will, if I may put it so, transform you from patients into agents. The Prime Minister!'

Her officials clapped loudly and a few of the patients joined in the applause. She began to speak, in harsh, ringing tones.

'We have come here today with a single, simple message: You are to be free. You will no longer be victims of *social* concern and the so-called helping professions. You will help *yourselves*. You will no longer be incarcerated in this ward. No more wardens for you! Today you will walk free into the community. From being burdens on your community, you will become members of it. From being dependents on the State, you will become fully fledged citizens and consumers. And all we ask of you in return is your support at the next election. My government has already made Libertaria into the freest of all possible worlds. What we want . . . '

'Aha!' a familiar voice interrupted her loudly from one of the beds. 'There's your problem. That's why you're here. All this wanting.' It was Seneca.

'We all want freedom,' said Jugula Hildebrand.

'The more we want it, the less we have. We must eliminate our wants and control ourselves,' he shouted, beginning to tremble. Two nurses rushed to him to administer a sedative.

'I want the world to see your liberation today,' said the Prime Minister. 'The nurses will now give each one of you your belongings, a week's maintenance money to ease the transition to freedom and a piece of paper on which to write

your new address. Ambulances are waiting outside to take you there. It's up to you to choose where to go – to your loved ones, your family, your friends. If you fail to give an address, you will be deposited at the Central Bus Station. I wish you all well in your future lives. May you flourish in freedom!'

As she finished speaking, the nurses went round the ward prodding those patients still in pyjamas and nightdresses to get dressed. Nicholas noticed Mia militantly refusing to move from amidst her pots and pans. Aristotle, near whose bed he stood, had donned a once elegant but now shabby suit, white shirt and pink tie and was sidling up to the Prime Minister.

'So you're a Prime Minister, are you,' Aristotle said to her. 'I've met a good number of Prime Ministers in my time. Entertained quite a few on my yacht. We've even had a fair number in here. They're terribly boring. All they ever want to talk about is themselves – and contributions to their party funds. How are your party's finances, by the way?'

'They're fine, thank you,' she replied coldly.

'Do call me Aristotle,' he urged. 'You'll be very welcome aboard – when I find my number – although she will need a lot of renovation.'

Suddenly, a bell rang and a team of hospital porters entered, to lead the departing patients from the ward. Most proceeded obediently to the street below but several still in their night-clothes, including Mia, refused to leave their beds. Three of the resisters, two elderly men and a young woman, were attached to drips. After consulting with the Director, the matron ordered the porters to wheel their beds out of the ward after the departing column.

Professor Syndrome observed the entire scene with a look of helpless resignation. Jugula Hildebrand noticed his miserable expression as she swept out of the ward. 'Don't worry, Professor,' she said. 'The world's mad enough to keep you in business.'

Nicholas and Syndrome followed her to the street. At the hospital entrance, the patients clambered into waiting

ambulances, clutching their bags and handing their pieces of paper to the drivers. A large, curious crowd had gathered around the scene which the television cameras were filming. Nicholas saw Seneca and Aristotle entering one of the ambulances. Porters emerged from the building pushing the beds on which the remaining patients still sat or lay: Mia surrounded by her bric-a-brac, several others in nightclothes and the three patients still attached to their drips. The Director, the drivers and the porters conferred. Then the drivers slammed closed the back doors of their vehicles and drove off, blowing their horns in farewell, while the porters set off along the road, pushing the beds and drips in the direction, Nicholas surmised, of the Central Bus Station. The last in line to leave was Mia, her pots and pans gleaming in the sunlight, her eyes narrowed and her lips pursed.

'No position for you here, Globulus,' said Syndrome. 'Perhaps you can find one for me in Militaria! Let's go and have lunch.'

They joined their fellow psychiatrists at the conference lunch. Everyone asked Nicholas for his thoughts on what he had just witnessed. Imagining what Globulus might have said in such a circumstance, he declared himself thoroughly in favour of the Hildebrand policy on mental health and urged his colleagues to think of ways of adapting to and profiting from it.

After lunch and coffee the psychiatrists stood about in the building's courtyard anxiously discussing their futures. Nicholas consulted the list of lectures scheduled for the afternoon. One in particular caught his eye. There was to be a 'workshop' on 'The Ambiguities of Schizophrenia' in the main lecture hall at three p.m. He decided to take a solitary walk and return in time to attend it.

He enjoyed his walk and arrived at the lecture hall at 3.15. The first talk had already begun. Nicholas opened the door very, very slowly, so as not to attract attention. There was something disturbing about the speaker's voice.

' . . . and my research into the schizophrenic mind has shown that it can under certain circumstances attain an extraordinary degree of vividness. A split personality can, so to speak, encounter itself and endow that encounter with a remarkable sense of reality. Sometimes this can happen in a very public way: these symptoms are not confined to private, incommunicable fantasies . . . '

Nicholas had opened the door sufficiently wide to enter the hall. To his utter astonishment, he beheld Orville Globulus, dressed in green velvet suit, yellow shirt and red-spotted tie, his beard tinged with grey, his hands gesticulating, and his eyes gleaming evilly behind his glinting glasses, addressing a rapt and respectful audience that filled the large lecture hall.

'Sometimes the schizophrenic can be absolutely certain that he sees himself, embodied as in a doppelgänger, which, as you know, was experienced as a real presence, portending death . . . '

At that moment, Globulus's eyes fell upon Nicholas. His mouth fell open and he froze. In the ensuing silence all eyes were fixed upon the speaker, the audience awaiting some dramatic conclusion to his argument. Nicholas too was transfixed. Globulus raised his arm and pointed an unsteady forefinger towards him as if confronting a ghost.

Nicholas fled down the stairs, out of the building, across the campus, and to the bus stop, tearing off his beard and bow tie as he ran. The number eight bus took a nerve-racking five minutes to arrive. Back at the Pilgrim's Rest he found Leon sitting at the reception desk. Nicholas greeted him with a nod, rushed to his room and discarded his disguise.

·27·

Porter

S itting on his bed, Nicholas reflected that it was time to reflect. His career as a psychiatrist was over. His available funds were almost at zero and he had no idea when the windfall he hoped for might materialize. He already owed the hotel for three nights and they would no doubt ask for payment soon. He had no-one to turn to in Libertaria for help – except Leon. He dressed and went downstairs.

'Any luck with the job hunting, Professor?' Leon asked.

'Not yet,' answered Nicholas. 'Look, could we possibly have a private chat?'

'Sure,' said Leon. 'I finish here at eight. Pick me up then and we'll go and have supper.' Feeling relieved, Nicholas went off for a walk in the streets around the hotel, past the sex shops, video clubs, all-night supermarkets and the many bodies that lined the pavements. He could now face their tired and timid requests for money with a clean conscience, for he was probably poorer than they were.

At eight, they were ready to leave and went out together to a small restaurant, two blocks away, which was a favourite of Leon's. 'Sam's Place' was a comfortably down-at-heel establishment: bulbs were missing from the ceiling lamps, the dark

green carpet was worn and pictures of boats in harbours hung incongruously on green and yellow flowery wallpaper. Only three tables were occupied, by customers in shirtsleeves with loud voices. Sam, also in shirtsleeves, was behind the bar at the back.

As they sat down, Nicholas explained his financial difficulty. With an expansive gesture, Leon declared his intention to pay for the meal.

'You can invite me out,' he said, 'when you hit the jackpot. Did you go and hear Tipster?'

Nicholas told him about Tipster's tip and his purchase of the National Library shares.

'Wow!' exclaimed Leon. The young man seemed impressed by his boldness – or was it his credulity? After placing their orders with Sam, Nicholas proceeded to tell Leon his story, from his arrest in Militaria onwards, leaving out only his most recent adventure among the psychiatrists: Leon might, after all, have psychiatric connections. As he told his tale, Nicholas was struck by how sad it all sounded; it seemed to him to be an unbroken tale of woes. Leon's response was one of both sympathy and pity: sympathy for a fellow victim of adversity; pity for the victim of an illusion – the illusion that his was a mission worthy of consideration, let alone pursuit.

'The question is not one of finding the best possible world,' Leon observed, 'but of avoiding the worst – and settling in the least worst. From all you've told me, that might just be Libertaria.'

'Do you really think that no better society than this one can be attained?' Nicholas asked.

Leon smiled. 'People here used to imagine that there was a place called "Egalitaria" where all were treated as equals. A paradise where all were supposed to have equal rights. These were supposed to be real, not fictitious as they are here – realities, not false promises. Everyone would have a real basic income, a real job, a real home, go to a decent school, have proper medical care. Ordinary people would be inter-

ested in politics because they thought they could make a difference. Imagine! No sleeping or begging or squalor or vandalism in the streets, no humiliation of people just because of their origins or their beliefs or because they didn't conform. A place in which everyone was equally free to live by their own lights and not only by the rules of the market. A place where you could breathe freely, no matter who you were. In short, the sort of place you and I might rather enjoy living in.'

'Where was it supposed to be?' asked Nicholas.

'Beyond our northern frontier,' said Leon. 'Trouble is: it didn't exist. It was a utopia – which, I seem to recall, means "nowhere" – a figment, a fable, a fairy story – in which that weird guy Justin still apparently believes – or wants to.'

'Why did people stop believing it existed?'

'Well, lots of people went exploring, but it just wasn't there. They got discouraged. And with the arrival of this new government, it became embarrassing even to talk about it. At the beginning, there was still quite a bit of protest – over all the privatization plans and everything. People marching against closing hospitals or schools or to defend their houses against property developers and so on. They still had some notion in their heads that things were better in the north and so could be better here. But that's all over.'

'No protesters left?' asked Nicholas.

'None. Honestly, I'd advise you to make the best of things here. For money, you could always steal. The police are privatized now and they've stopped paying overtime and so the cops no longer arrest people for petty crimes. Saves money on trials too. If you're caught, you'll only get a caution. Provided you move about a bit and don't commit too much violence, you could do quite well.'

Nicholas looked doubtful. 'Otherwise,' Leon continued, 'you could go on looking for work. You could even end up as a professor again if you work at it – or driving a taxi. You could do a lot worse.'

'But what about the hotel?' asked Nicholas.

'Maybe stay for a few days more while we see if anything turns up,' suggested Leon. He got up and went to the back to settle the bill. After a while he returned.

'Sam says he might be able to find you a job as a waiter and that you should go and see him in a few days' time. But he points out that it's very badly paid. In fact, it's hardly paid at all.'

'Thanks,' said Nicholas, 'and thanks for the meal.'

Next morning, Nicholas got up early. Leon's suggestion of a mobile life of petty crime did not really appeal to him. Perhaps he might be able to drive a taxi or find work as a waiter? At the reception desk in the hotel lobby was the grumpy old man he had first encountered.

'How much longer are you staying,' he asked.

'Another week,' Nicholas suggested. The suggestion seemed acceptable.

'Here!' said the old man, 'these are for you.' He handed him two letters in brown, official-looking envelopes. They were both addressed to Professor Pangloss at the Pilgrim's Rest. Nicholas opened them eagerly.

The first was a job advertisement sent from the University Personnel Office. It was for an electrician specializing in lighting. Nicholas was puzzled. Then it occurred to him that this must be in response to his putting 'Enlightenment' down among his qualifications. He considered the possibility but rejected it. He could have been a psychiatrist for a while: Who knows how long he might have gone on undetected? But electrical light fittings were decidedly beyond his powers. He opened the second envelope. It was also from the Personnel Office and contained an advertisement for a job as hospital porter. That looked distinctly more promising. The advertisement indicated that prospective applicants should present themselves forthwith to the Head Porter at the hospital. Foregoing his morning coffee, he rushed to the number eight bus stop.

The middle-aged man was sitting limply on the ground against the wall with his suitcase at his feet. He looked

dishevelled, unwashed and unshaven. As Nicholas's gaze fell upon him, the man sat up and straightened his tie in an effort to regain a semblance of respectability. Nicholas boarded the bus for the university.

As they approached the hospital, Nicholas remembered the sad scene of the departing mental patients, and of Mia disappearing along the road with her pots and pans. How different it looked today. Purposeful people were coming in and out; a car park attendant was busily preventing visitors from parking in the numerous empty spaces. Nicholas entered the building and, as instructed, presented himself to the Head Porter.

'Come round the back,' said the latter in a gruff voice, 'and we'll have a look at you.' Nicholas followed the bald giant into a small office. The Head Porter sat stiffly behind a desk like a military commander and motioned Nicholas to sit down on a chair in front of him.

'So you're a professor who wants to be a porter,' he began. 'Isn't that a bit odd?'

Nicholas agreed that it was. 'But you see,' he responded rather piously, proffering an explanation that might convince his interlocutor, 'I've spent enough time studying abstract ideas. I want to do something concrete that will help improve the quality of real people's lives.'

The Head Porter was unimpressed. 'Have you seen the wage scale?' he asked, handing him a sheet of paper. 'You'll be at the bottom end, since you've never done the job before. You're also a foreign citizen – aren't you? – and therefore a guest worker. Right at the bottom. Still interested?'

'Yes,' said Nicholas firmly.

The Head Porter seemed to take a liking to him, perhaps because he came so cheap.

'O.K. You're hired. You can start this morning.' He handed Nicholas a document, stamped and signed. 'Sort out all the paperwork in the Personnel Office, then come back at noon and I'll assign you your clothes.'

'Thank you,' Nicholas replied, 'but may I ask just one thing? Please don't tell anyone else that I am a professor. It could be awkward.'

'Don't worry, Professor,' said the Head Porter loudly, winking complicitly, 'I'll keep your guilty secret.'

At the Personnel Office once again he found himself facing the grim-faced woman with horn-rimmed spectacles. She gave no sign of recognition as he handed her the document from the Head Porter. To be hired as a porter, he had to become an employee of 'We Help the Ill Portering Services' (WHIPS for short) to whom the hospital's portering work was contracted. As he later discovered, all the hospital's services – nursing, catering, cleaning and clerical – were similarly contracted out to profit-making companies, while the doctors worked for themselves, charging fees to the patients or their insurance companies. WHIPS took ten percent of its employees' wages. As a guest worker, Nicholas learnt that he had no pension rights (and of course no voting rights) but heavy tax liabilities. He was to be hired on a probationary basis for three months and would thus be liable to instant dismissal by WHIPS for 'inadequate performance' of his duties.

On returning to the Head Porter, he discovered what these were. He was to deliver medicines from the dispensary and to be on the lookout for unauthorized persons on the wards, usually people trying to get themselves treated without having been admitted as patients. To be admitted one had to pay hospital and consultants' fees in advance. Scores of indigent or feckless persons were, the Head Porter explained, endlessly trying on all sorts of ruses and pretending that they were real patients.

'Just demand to see their admission papers,' he advised. 'If they can't produce them, they're out on their necks. You may use all reasonable force.'

'Who decides how much force is reasonable?' Nicholas asked.

'I do,' said the Head Porter. 'This hospital is a free hospital:

free for those who pay to be treated here and free from those who don't. Remember that, Professor. That'll be all.'

His induction was over. Nicholas had not appreciated the Head Porter's sarcastic attitude to his previous profession but he soon learnt that this was not an atypical response. Over lunch in the Staff Canteen with other porters, he discovered that the boss had been nicknamed 'Napoleon' by his underlings. The common view was that, although large in height and girth, the man was a petty emperor with aggrandizing ambitions. He was a true believer, apparently, in the Jugula Hildebrand shock therapy of privatization and it was widely believed that he had been a strong and influential advocate of the decarceration of the mental patients, on the ground that they were a menace to the good order of the hospital.

Nicholas's fellow porters divided into two categories. On the one hand, there were guest workers like himself, though for the most part they were much younger and had families to support. Although grateful for their jobs, they felt like aliens in Libertaria and talked, rather unconvincingly, about eventually going 'home'. On the other hand, there were older porters, survivors really, who had worked in the hospital before privatization but, in the course of the latter, had lost most of their pension rights and paid holidays and suffered a considerable reduction in wages. They all seemed to nurse a sullen but resigned sense of grievance at their reduced condition and at the complete collapse of what they called the hospital's 'morale'. Porters, nurses, cleaners and caterers still performed their shifts but, these older porters told Nicholas rather wistfully, they no longer worked together in teams. Now, hardly anyone knew anyone else and no-one knew the patients.

All the porters, however, agreed that Napoleon was bad news. Yet obeying him to the letter was the price of one's job and, Nicholas discovered, everyone seemed to agree with Napoleon's policy of using all reasonable force to eject non-paying would-be patients. No-one had any sympathy for those

even less well-off than themselves, namely those who were needy but destitute or uninsured.

Nicholas had been assigned a locker and a light blue uniform. After lunch, he donned the latter and started work, carrying medicines from the Dispensary to the wards. It was hard, tiring work pushing a trolley along innumerable corridors and into and out of elevators. The corridors and wards had different tempos, all of which required some getting used to. Around the Emergency and Accidents Ward, events occurred in fast, sporadic spurts. In other areas, such as the Outpatient Ward, the atmosphere was one of total stasis: patients sat with varying degrees of patience on long wooden benches for long hours, waiting for consultations. Wherever Nicholas's work took him in the bright sterile building, he would pass by unattended patients, preoccupied consultants, frantic nurses, exhausted cleaners and lost-looking visitors. He noticed that no member of any of these groups ever noticed any member of the others.

He quickly learnt three interesting lessons. First, that wearing a porter's uniform immediately renders you invisible to all persons of superior status unless they need you urgently. Second, that the hospital seemed to contain a surprising number of empty beds, doubtless awaiting lucrative occupants. And third, that several patients he saw had recovered but were willing to continue paying for the attention, the conveniences and perhaps the company the hospital provided. He even felt inclined to advise members of the latter group against taking the medicines he was delivering for fear that they might damage their obvious good health.

His shift over, Nicholas changed back into his own clothes and returned to the hotel where he found Leon at the reception desk. He told him the news of his job. Leon was impressed. 'Good luck to you,' he said. 'Who knows? Perhaps they'll promote you and you'll end up as a consultant!' Little did Leon know that only yesterday he had all but been one.

The next morning Nicholas once more passed the man with

the suitcase slouched against the low wall by the bus stop. Once again he responded, though with less alacrity, to Nicholas's presence. His stubble had grown and he looked grimy and despondent. Yet it seemed that he wanted to keep up the appearance of a fast-disappearing respectability.

Nicholas had passed his first shift learning the job and the lay-out of the hospital. On his second day on the job, he started to notice other features of hospital life. The older porters were right. There was an atmosphere of total anonymity. Few of the staff seemed on personal terms and everyone ignored the patients. The nurses, employees of a private agency, worked irregular shifts, spending the rest of their time in more lucrative employments elsewhere. The catering staff delivered prepackaged meals to the patients. There had once been a hospital kitchen but it had been closed; now all meals arrived at the hospital frozen, to be heated up in on-site microwave ovens.

He also became aware of the would-be patients hanging about individually or in small groups. When challenged they would immediately invent brothers-in-law or aged aunts in one or another ward whom they claimed to be visiting. They looked pleadingly into the eyes of his fellow porters, who never needed to use force to eject them. Sometimes they were bold enough to beg for special consideration on account of their ailments, pointing out that there were beds available and insisting that they would be no trouble. Nicholas felt sorry for them and made great efforts to avoid their pleading eyes.

On the third day, the man with the suitcase was still sitting against the wall by the bus stop. For the first time, Nicholas nodded to him in greeting. He barely noticed and Nicholas walked on and took the bus for the hospital. Nicholas arrived at his locker to find an envelope pinned to it addressed to 'Professor Pangloss'. It contained a typed letter from Dr Julius Stuffington, Senior Registrar in Professor Syndrome's Department of Psychiatry. Evidently Napoleon had not kept his promise of secrecy. The letter read as follows:

Dear Professor Pangloss,

It has come to our attention that you are working as a porter in this hospital. We understand that you are a distinguished philosopher from abroad and we wish to make a proposal to you that we hope you will consider.

I am conducting research into the effects of culture shock on immigrants to Libertaria and, in particular, into their varying (and, it would appear, not always favourable) reactions to the realities of the free market. Professor Syndrome has authorized me to say that we would be very pleased if you felt inclined to collaborate with us on this research and I would be glad if you would pay me a visit to discuss such a possibility.

I should however make it plain that we will not be able to offer you any financial rewards for such collaboration, only intellectual ones. As you may know, the Psychiatric Ward in the hospital has just been closed down and our research funds are being cut off. But we intend to continue with our research and hope that you will find it possible to cooperate with us.

Yours sincerely,
Julius Stuffington.

Stuffington! Stuffington's was the first hand that had landed on his shoulder at the psychiatrists' reception. Visiting him now, as Pangloss rather than Globulus, might be risky. Either Stuffington or Syndrome might recognize him. On the other hand, the offer (or rather request, as it was not exactly an offer) sounded interesting. Nicholas resolved to go and find Stuffington at the end of the day's shift.

He set to work delivering medicines. Midway through the morning, he noticed a striking sight in the Visitors' Cafeteria. Seated at a table were three familiar figures, miserably sipping cups of tea: Aristotle, with his hooked nose and eye patch; Seneca, with his scar; and Mia, with her narrow, frightened eyes. They were looking around furtively as if in search of something or someone. Nicholas entered, ordered a cup of

tea and sat down at the table next to them. Aristotle caught his eye and, after a few minutes, addressed him.

'Good day!' he said.

Nicholas nodded.

'You are, if I am not mistaken, a new porter,' Aristotle continued.

Nicholas agreed.

Aristotle moved his chair closer to Nicholas and spoke more confidentially. 'I wonder if I might presume to raise a problem with you? You see, we are in difficulties. We were living here. This was, in a manner of speaking, our home. I was on the way to solving a problem, and my friends here were getting on very well. And then suddenly, without any warning, this dreadful woman came and threw us all out.'

'Where have you been living since?' asked Nicholas.

'In Freedom,' Aristotle answered. 'But we'd like to come back here, even for a night or two. It would make all the difference.'

All three of them looked imploringly at him.

'I'll do what I can, but I can't promise anything,' he said. 'Why don't you come back here tomorrow morning at the same time?'

At these words Seneca started to tremble with excitement and the other two quickly hustled him out of the Cafeteria. Nicholas saw, as they left, that Mia was carrying five or six plastic bags under her shabby black coat.

That afternoon there occurred the kind of coincidence that tempts even the sceptical to believe in miracles. On arriving at the Dispensary after lunch, Nicholas was told that he should go to the hospital storeroom to pick up some supplies for the Accounts Department, the place where patients had to register. At the storeroom he was handed a package containing the forms to be signed by those seeking admittance to the hospital as patients. As he arrived at the door of the Accounts Department, Nicholas stealthily removed three of the forms and placed them in the inside pocket of his uniform. He

entered the office. The secretary was busy dealing with an aspirant patient through a glass partition and no-one else was around. Nicholas noticed a hospital stamp on a table just behind the secretary. He deftly pocketed it just as she finished with the patient and turned to receive the forms with the usual indifference reserved for uniformed inferiors.

His delivery completed, he returned to the Dispensary and continued with his afternoon's work, in the course of which he ascertained that the old Psychiatric Ward, now dedicated to plastic surgery, was by no means full. There were at least ten beds still available: demand had evidently not yet matched supply.

At the end of the day, he went in search of Dr Stuffington. He wore his uniform to reduce the chances of recognition. Stuffington's office was still in the hospital; presumably it would soon be removed, now the psychiatrists were no longer practising and could only preach and teach. He knocked at the psychiatrist's door and a jovial voice called out to him to enter.

Stuffington shook him warmly by both hands.

'Marvellous you should be working here!' he exclaimed. 'Marvellous for us! You must be a true missionary.'

It seemed a useful line of thought to encourage. 'One tries to do what little good one can in this world,' said Nicholas piously.

Stuffington seemed to wince slightly. 'Well, Professor Pangloss, let me come to the point. You see, we are conducting research into what some people call "culture shock" – a term we use literally to describe the various symptoms of people who come here from abroad, immigrants and such, who can't cope with the demands of our Libertarian way of life. We thought, as such an immigrant yourself, who is obviously highly intelligent but also working rather closely with such immigrants among the hospital staff, that you might find it interesting to do some participant observation to help our research along.'

'What is the nature of this so-called culture shock?' Nicholas asked.

'Ah! As I might have expected – a highly probing question!' Stuffington seemed delighted he had asked it. He whispered, 'We haven't any idea. It's all Professor Syndrome's idea. He's always looking for syndromes. In practice, we've found that the diagnosis of culture shock seems to depend on the personal views of the individual making it rather than on generally accepted criteria. The label alone doesn't indicate what signs and symptoms those who are held to suffer from it display. The only common ground for diagnosis that we psychiatrists can detect is that the patients seem ill.'

'Perhaps they aren't,' suggested Nicholas.

'But there does seem to be a pathology exhibited by newly arrived immigrants to Libertaria,' Stuffington insisted.

'Perhaps,' suggested Nicholas, 'what is pathological is the life they have to lead?'

Stuffington's eyes narrowed. 'I see, Professor Pangloss, that you are something of a social critic.'

Evidently, Nicholas had put a foot wrong. Dr Stuffington suddenly seemed inclined to bring the conversation to an end.

'I'll tell you what, Professor Pangloss,' he said. 'Let us both turn the matter over in our minds. You can reflect on our offer, and we can reflect on your suitability. So nice to meet you!'

Nicholas shook his hand and left without looking back. In the corridor outside, two figures were approaching. Both looked familiar. As they drew near, he saw to his alarm that Professor Syndrome and Orville Globulus were bearing down upon him. They were deep in conversation, discussing, it appeared, the prospects of a post for Syndrome in Militaria. As they passed, Globulus's eyes fell upon Nicholas and gazed for a second or two on his face. Nicholas walked on purposefully and did not look back. It was strange, he thought, how, ever since their encounter in the Militarian prison, Globulus had followed him. Whichever country he found himself in, his

malevolent, threatening double was there, ready to offer his services to some prevailing orthodoxy. Why was Globulus pursuing him? Would he ever find a world where he no longer had influence?

On the way back to the hotel, he planned how he would help Aristotle, Seneca and Mia. He would fill up their forms as best he could overnight and make them official with the hospital stamp. But he lacked a crucial element: ink. He was relieved to see Leon at the hotel.

'How's the portering, Professor,' Leon asked.

'Very hard work,' he answered truthfully. 'Not used to pushing heavy trolleys along corridors. But,' he asked confidentially, speaking in a lower voice, 'could I possibly ask a small favour? Could I borrow your inkpad for ten minutes?'

'O.K.' said Leon jocularly, 'I won't charge you for it.'

Nicholas took it to his room and filled out the forms as best he could, leaving the personal details for the 'patients' to complete. He specified that all three were to be admitted to the Plastic Surgery Ward. Under 'TREATMENT REQUIRED', he wrote 'straightening of nose' for Aristotle, 'removal of scar' for Seneca and 'face lift' for Mia. He invented a suitably high fee for each operation and stamped each form with the hospital stamp, adding an indecipherable squiggle for the secretary underneath. His work done, Nicholas returned the ink pad to Leon and went off to bed.

The next morning Nicholas passed the man with the suitcase on his way to work. His formerly smart suit was utterly crumpled. He had evidently neither washed nor shaved and was, it seemed, no longer interested in how he appeared to Nicholas or anyone else. The man seemed to be in a kind of daze, no longer aware of his immediate surroundings, of the bustle of the street he had made his home. Nicholas tried but failed to attract his attention.

Back at work, Nicholas kept looking in at the Visitors' Cafeteria. Eventually he saw his three charges sipping tea and looking around with hopeful expressions. He sat down at

the next table, leant over to Aristotle and passed him the forms under the table.

'Fill these in,' he said, 'and hand them in at your old ward. It's changed its name, by the way, and function.'

Aristotle nodded and the three made a rapid exit, Mia dragging her plastic bags behind her.

Halfway through the afternoon, Nicholas called in at the Plastic Surgery Ward with a supply of medicines. The three former residents were back in their old beds. Mia had set up her pots and pans and other bric-a-brac as before, and the notices against trespassing were back in place. She sat motionless and scarcely acknowledged him as he walked by. Seneca was sitting upright, observing him intently. One of the medicines he had brought, a sedative, was, it appeared, intended for him. Aristotle, at the end of the ward, was busy writing numbers on a large piece of paper. He looked up as Nicholas walked up to his bed. Nicholas, wanting to be neither intrusive nor obtrusive, engaged him in a brief conversation.

'Everything O.K.?' he asked.

'All is well, thank you,' said Aristotle. 'They have been giving us what they call "pre-op" tests. They are speaking about operating on Seneca this evening. We are very grateful to be back here. I hope very soon to repay you for your kindness. I shall invite you for a cruise on my yacht.'

Nicholas nodded. Seneca's and Mia's eyes followed him out of the ward.

When Nicholas arrived at his locker the next morning, he found a note from one of his fellow porters. It read: 'NAPOLEON'S ON THE WARPATH. HE WANTS TO SEE YOU.' Nicholas put on his uniform and went to the Head Porter's Office at the hospital entrance. He knocked and entered. As he did so, Napoleon stood erect. He ordered Nicholas to sit down at the table and, continuing to stand, towered above him.

'Nice of you to come, Professor,' he began, with what sounded distinctly like a sneer. 'I have only four things to say to you.

'First, you are suspected of theft of hospital property: to wit, three application forms plus one hospital stamp. Have, you anything to say?'

There seemed no point in prevaricating. 'As for the forms,' said Nicholas, 'they have, so far as I am aware, been returned. As for the stamp (he took it from his pocket and placed it on the table), I hereby return it. It wasn't stolen, only borrowed.'

Napoleon, unimpressed, pressed on. 'Second, in violation of my orders, you helped procure through illegal means the admission of three unauthorized persons into this hospital as patients.'

Nicholas said nothing.

'Third, you sought to bring about their serious disfigurement – an outcome that was only avoided because one of them revealed the whole sorry story just as the surgeon was about to operate.'

Strange, Nicholas thought, how if you paid for your treatment, it was a surgical improvement, but if you did not, it was a serious disfigurement.

'And fourth,' concluded Napoleon, 'you are fired forthwith.'

He handed him a document, signed and stamped. 'Take this to the Personnel Office to pick up your severance pay, such as it is.'

It turned out to be very little indeed, after tax and a fine for the three crimes of which he stood accused. The grim-faced woman with horn-rimmed spectacles handed him his wages and closed her counter with evident relief.

He returned to his locker to change back into his clothes. Some of the younger porters were gathered around and expressed some sympathy for him, though not for what he had done. They told him what had happened. Apparently, Seneca had refused all anaesthetics and insisted on mirrors being placed in the operating theatre so that he could watch what was happening. As the surgeon had approached his face with his scalpel, Seneca had cracked and explained that he and his two friends were there on false pretences. Under questioning,

he had revealed the whole story. Although it was late in the evening, the three of them were immediately bundled off the hospital premises and had not been seen again.

Nicholas left the hospital and made straight for the number eight bus. He had been accused of crimes. Perhaps the hospital would seek his arrest. They knew his address at the hotel. Maybe it would be better to move? He boarded the bus and continued to think. Now he had to find another source of livelihood. Perhaps he might try the restaurant. Of course, there was always the hoped-for windfall from the National Library shares, but he had no idea when to expect the payoff from them. Deep in thought, he missed his stop and found himself getting off the bus with the remainder of its occupants at the Central Bus Station.

It was a grimy, noisy building, smelling of oil and petrol fumes and full of people milling about waiting for buses. The pavements outside were bustling with private enterprise: trinket sellers, sock salesmen, aspirant bag carriers, un-licensed cab drivers, hustlers and thieves. Everyone was on the make – except, that is, for those seated or lying on rugs in door-ways and against walls. These inert and listless figures were trying hard not to be noticed.

Suddenly, Nicholas caught sight of Aristotle, Seneca and Mia. He noticed Mia first, surrounded by her plastic bags, sitting at the bottom of the steps leading to some office. Next to her against the wall were her two companions with bags and rolled-up mattresses at their feet. He went over to them.

'Hello,' he said.

All three looked at him with what was clearly alarm, though he could not tell whether this was due to fear or guilt.

'I didn't mean any harm,' said Seneca.

'It was only a temporary visit, anyway,' said Aristotle philo-sophically.

Where, Nicholas asked, were they planning to spend the night?

'Ah!' replied Aristotle, 'we're thinking of moving.'

'Where to?' Nicholas asked.

Aristotle pointed to a railway arch along the street, under which the street ran. 'We've found three excellent boxes at the supermarket. We'll be picking them up and we'll probably move this evening.'

'Could you possibly get a fourth?' Nicholas asked.

Aristotle nodded without emotion. 'O.K.' he said. 'You helped us. We'll help you.'

Nicholas walked back to his hotel, still deep in thought. If he were to pay his bill, he would have no cash left. Was he, as Kant might have said, under a categorical obligation to pay what he owed? Or did his existential predicament at least qualify its absolute force?

The old man was on duty at the reception desk. Taking his key, Nicholas went up to his room. Carefully, he packed all of his few belongings, including his fur-lined cloak and the woollen blanket on his bed, into his travelling bag. Whistling softly to himself, he opened the small window and dropped the bag into the garden below. Then he left the room, locking the door behind him, went down the stairs and left the hotel. Once outside, he doubled back and into the garden, picked up his bag, closed the gate noiselessly behind him and walked off, still whistling, in the direction of the Central Bus Station.

·28·

On the Street

ristotle, Seneca and Mia were still sitting where he had left them. He put his bag down on the pavement. 'May I join you?' he asked.

'Make yourself at home,' said Aristotle, making space for him against the wall. Further along there sat a group of teenagers playing guitars who, to judge by the sight and the sound of them, could well have been drug addicts.

Aristotle told him that the three of them regarded themselves as fortunate when compared with the others evicted from the ward by Jugula Hildebrand. Most of those who had given addresses to be taken to had been thrown out by the people they had named. The community, it seemed, had not welcomed them. One had committed suicide and others had been arrested for violent crime.

'At least we've got a home,' said Aristotle. 'But it's nearly lunchtime. We'd better get our lunch and the boxes. I'll go with Mia to the supermarket. It's where she used to work.' He spoke more confidentially to Nicholas. 'We have to keep Seneca away from supermarkets. You can keep him company, look after our stuff and keep our places.' Nicholas agreed and sat down next to Seneca.

How, he wondered, had Seneca become a Stoic unable to

control his turbulent passions? Seneca was still evidently embarrassed at his capitulation before the advancing scalpel. Nicholas sought to relieve the tension by asking him about his life.

Seneca, he discovered, had once worked for an advertising agency as a jingle composer, writing ditties to sell all kinds of products, from shampoos to dog biscuits. He had loved the job. He was wonderfully inventive. His head was permanently full of ideas, never short of a suitable jingle. But the inspiration and commitment did not last. The jingles, as he explained to Nicholas, began to drive him sane. He came to see the admen as madmen. 'They are,' he said with a fierce passion, 'destroyers of people's freedom.'

'But surely,' Nicholas objected, 'freedom is choosing to live as you want. How do the admen destroy that?'

Seneca snapped back: 'Do you imagine that people want to want what they want? Where do you think their wants come from? I'll tell you! From the jingles!'

'But what,' Nicholas asked Seneca, 'do *you* want?'

Seneca looked at him with an earnest intensity. 'I want,' he said, 'I want people to be free from want and I want them only to want what they want to want. And for that they must control themselves and stop wanting what they want. Then they'll be free.' His eyes roamed across the street scene around them. 'It's not easy,' he admitted.

Nicholas wondered how Seneca had got his scar. He had, it seemed, once he left his job, started a one-man campaign which he called 'War against Wants' and had been beaten up by some skinheads out for trouble outside a supermarket.

Aristotle and Mia returned with four large folded cardboard boxes under their arms and a bag of groceries. They opened the bag and handed out some yoghurts and sausages, all past their consume-by dates. 'We have to eat them all now, you see, because we don't yet have a refrigerator,' Aristotle explained. When they had finished, he suggested moving. 'It's easier,' he said, 'to find places earlier in the day.'

As the four of them walked towards the railway arch carrying the boxes and their belongings, Nicholas asked Aristotle how Mia had come to be the provider of their sustenance and their accommodation. She had, he explained, once worked as a cashier in a supermarket. Unfortunately for her, she had both an attraction and a weakness for indigent friends – unmarried mothers, lost teenagers and the like. One of them persuaded her to check out only every fourth item when they went shopping at the supermarket, and they were all caught red-handed. When the case came to court, her friends testified against her, claiming it had been Mia's idea. As it happened, she was by this time an unmarried mother-to-be herself. The judge before whom they appeared decided that Mia had contrived her pregnancy in order to evade the prison term she clearly deserved and so sent her down for six months as an example to others. Her baby, when born, was taken from her and placed in care on the basis that she was unfit to be a mother. From this sequence of experiences Mia derived the unshakeable belief that the whole world was involved in pilfering and that, in particular, it was out to steal from her all that she held precious: her self-respect, her means of livelihood and her child. But some of her co-workers at the supermarket remained loyal friends and, when she was unable to find work after her prison sentence, provided her with regular supplies of packaged foods that had exceeded their sell-by date and cardboard boxes. Hence her role as supplier of food and shelter.

They reached the railway arch and staked their claim to an as yet unoccupied patch halfway along on the right-hand side that was sheltered from the wind and rain. Every hour a train passed overhead making an incredible racket. The four of them placed their boxes on the ground. There they would sit until evening with their belongings at their feet. Nicholas sat next to Aristotle.

Aristotle's life-story seemed the most inaccessible. Perhaps, Nicholas reflected, it might even be true that he had once been a wealthy ship owner who had lost his fortune because he had

lost his number. Certainly the other two were not disposed to express any doubts on the matter. For the entire afternoon, Aristotle sat writing down numbers and consulting Nicholas about their plausibility. It was an activity that utterly absorbed him. It did not take Nicholas long to conclude that Aristotle's mental world, peopled by an infinite series of numbers offering ever-renewable hope, was not a world he could enter.

Nicholas began to realize that he was not well prepared for life on the street. Apart from his hotel blanket, he had nothing to protect him from the physical elements. Nor did he have any weapon to protect him from unwelcome human elements. Nor were his inner resources in much better shape. He tried to summon up his eighteenth-century interlocutors of former days, but they resolutely refused to appear. He had nothing to read but this was probably for the best. Reading would certainly draw unwelcome attention from the local residents who had started to take an interest in the new arrivals. Their neighbours were a varied lot: a couple of ageing drunks who seemed to be drinking methylated spirits; a sad, pale-faced youth, who had written a long and incoherent hard-luck story on the pavement; three rather menacing young men in their twenties in dark glasses and leather jackets who seemed to be playing with razor blades; and a middle-aged woman who was viciously scolding herself – for what Nicholas could not tell.

As darkness fell, Mia distributed some salami and some more yoghurts. The others sat silently eating and looking vacantly across the street. Nicholas began to feel a little chilly and took his fur-lined cloak out of his travelling bag. He put it on, turned up the fur collar to keep himself warm, got up to stretch his legs, and took a walk along the pavement and out of the far end of the arch. The street beyond the archway was deserted and badly lit. Suddenly, Nicholas was grabbed from behind. A hand clasped his face over his eyes and he felt his cloak being ripped off his back .

He struggled free and found himself facing two middle-

aged, rather well-dressed, respectable-looking persons, a man and a woman, wearing armbands.

'You,' said the man accusingly, 'are a criminal.'

'We represent the Freedom section of the S.O.S.,' explained the woman.

She thrust her armband before his eyes. It showed a picture of a sad-eyed cow and calf within a circle around which was the logo: 'Save Our Skins'.

'And you,' she continued, 'represent genocide.'

The man lifted Nicholas's cloak in the air and declaimed, as though addressing a large crowd: 'This animal skin has been liberated from human ownership. It is now no-one's property.'

'That's good news!' shouted a voice from behind them, where there was a sudden commotion. 'That means we're not stealing it then.' It was one of the three razor-blade fondlers, who must have followed him out of the arch. The three of them pushed Nicholas to the ground and grabbed the cloak from the man. The woman began to scream.

'Shut up, you old cow!' one of them shouted at her. The intended insult seemed misdirected. The three ran off down a side street with the cloak.

'Sorry about that,' said the man to Nicholas, rather sheepishly. The woman was sobbing. At least, Nicholas reflected, they had saved their own skins.

He left them and returned to his trio of companions. They had begun to assemble their boxes for the night and Nicholas followed suit. On its side, his was just large enough to sleep in lying with his knees tucked into his chest. Covered by his blanket, clutching his travelling bag in front of him as a barrier between himself and the outside world, he settled down to sleep.

Nicholas slept very little. Every hour a train, whistle hooting, rattled over the arch. Unfamiliar street noises, whose significance he could not judge, punctuated the uneasy silence of the night. For the first time in all his travels, fear gripped his

insides and hope began to slip away. Try as he might, he could not slough off his despondency.

As dawn broke, he fell into a deep sleep and had a dream in which he was in a dark tunnel at the end of which there was a light. But the light was inexorably advancing towards him. As he lay on the track, a train kept repeatedly bearing down on him, its whistle hooting. In the last of these episodes, he was lying on the track, feebly raising his hands to stop the oncoming engine. It was about to crush him when he woke up with a violent headache.

Mia, Seneca and Aristotle were sitting on their folded boxes playing cards. Nicholas climbed out of his box, wished them good morning and told them he was going off for a walk. They nodded and told him they would look after his things. He went to the public toilet at the Central Bus Station where he washed and shaved. Then he had breakfast in the dingy self-service cafeteria. It was mid morning.

Perhaps Sam might still have a job for him as a waiter? He walked to the restaurant, taking care not to pass by the Pilgrim's Rest Hotel. It was a sunny day and his spirits lifted a little at the prospect of work.

Sam was busy laying out the tables. He was friendly but cautious.

'You come with good credentials,' he said, 'but no experience at the job.'

Nicholas could only agree.

'However,' Sam continued, 'I do need some help here, though I can't pay you much.' He made it clear that the financial arrangements would have to be 'informal' and that Nicholas would have to rely mainly on tips.

'When can I start?' asked Nicholas, seizing his chance.

'How about now?' suggested Sam. 'You can finish setting out these tables.'

Within an hour the restaurant opened for lunch. Sam's only other employee seemed to be his wife, the cook, who was rather bad-tempered and worked in the steamy kitchen in the

back. The menu was basic but the food, as Nicholas recalled, was rather tasty. Over the next three hours, several customers arrived and Nicholas took their orders on a small notepad, which he relayed to Sam's wife through a hatch at the back, next to the bar. He managed to deliver their meals and drinks without mishap. The customers who were regulars asked Sam who he was.

'Friend of Leon's,' said Sam. 'Good fellow!'

None of them, however, left him a tip.

He finished work at three-thirty and returned to the railway arch. Aristotle was still busy with his numbers. Seneca was asleep and Mia sat, as ever, silently observing her surroundings. Nicholas told Aristotle about his job.

'I had six waiters on my yacht, all in white uniforms with gold braid,' said Aristotle. 'What do you think of the thirteen thousands?'

Nicholas helped Aristotle with his numbers for the next couple of hours and returned to resume work at Sam's Place for the evening. Business was slow and Sam was in a mood to chat. Leon had, it seemed, told him that Nicholas had been a professor of philosophy.

'Can't be much of a thing to be,' he said, 'if you end up working for me!'

Nicholas urged the restaurant owner not to undervalue the services of someone working for him. Sam did not, however, seem inclined to increase his wages.

'The value of everything is fixed by what people are prepared to pay for it,' said Sam. 'That's what I learned at school. So your philosophy can't be of much value.'

At that moment Leon entered the restaurant. He greeted Sam warmly and then saw Nicholas.

'Good Heavens!' he exclaimed, sitting down at a table as Sam went off, 'I am glad to see you are still among the living.'

Nicholas gave him a brief account of what had happened at the hospital and why and how he had left the hotel. He felt like a naughty child who had been found out.

'Don't worry, Professor,' Leon reassured him. 'I guessed something like that must have happened, so I told the management that you had been beaten to death in a dark alley near the hotel and that I had been along to the morgue to identify your corpse.'

'Thank you,' said Nicholas with feeling.

'The only thing is: don't go near the hotel,' Leon warned. 'Oh! there is another thing.' He pulled an envelope out of his inside pocket. This came for you at the hotel. I was keeping it just in case.' He handed it to Nicholas, who opened it at once. It contained his thousand National Library shares.

'You really are in luck,' said Leon. 'Those shares have done very well. I'd sell them quickly if I were you. What nobody thought of was that, once privatized, the books could all be sold off. There are lots of foreign dealers who've been bidding for the most valuable ones at astronomical prices. Tipster was right.' Thanking him profusely, Nicholas put the envelope in his pocket.

'Glad to see Sam gave you a job,' said Leon. 'I'll have a beer and steak and chips, medium rare.' Nicholas, feeling rather elated, took Leon's order and shouted it through the hatch to Sam's wife. When Leon finished and paid, he left Nicholas a generous tip. It was the only tip of the evening.

At midnight Nicholas returned to the arch and found his companions asleep in their boxes. He put up his own and clambered inside. He placed the envelope containing his shares inside his shirt next to his body, covered himself with his blanket, folded up his knees against his chest and fell into an uneasy sleep.

He awoke next morning early, took a clean shirt to the bus station and, spending his last remaining coins, washed, shaved and breakfasted, and returned to the trio to tell them that he was off to do some business. Out of his wallet he retrieved the business card that Professor Tipster had given him, in the name of Osgood Micklethrust, Stockbroker. Now totally penniless, he set off walking, making straight for the broker's office.

Micklethrust was luminiferous, smooth-faced and ruddy with a large, flamboyant moustache, irradiating confidence. His hair was glossy and perfectly groomed and he wore a phosphorescent pink tie, shiny grey suit and extra large initialled gold cufflinks. He clearly had very little time to spare.

Nicholas explained his simple desire to sell his thousand shares, bought on the advice of Professor Tipster. Micklethrust smiled expansively. 'Tipster's given you some *very* good advice, my friend,' he said. 'Tell me, how is the old fraud? Haven't seen him for yonks.'

Fortunately Micklethrust was too busy to wait for an answer. 'Look,' he said, 'I've got to go and do some dealing right now. Always willing to oblige a friend of Tipster. If you like, you can come with me and we can sell your shares on the spot. I've got lots of others to sell. It's quite a bonanza!'

Nicholas agreed and followed him into the back seat of his chauffeur-driven Mercedes.

'The truth about old Tipster,' said Micklethrust, 'is that he's far too smart to be a professor.' Nicholas enthusiastically agreed.

'What's your line of business, then, my friend?' Micklethrust asked.

'Oh, I'm a colleague of his – visiting from abroad,' said Nicholas vaguely.

'Don't take offence at my view of the academic world,' said Micklethrust. 'What you professors don't see is the *value* of knowledge. That's what Tipster understands. What is the point of knowledge unless someone profits from it?'

'Not all knowledge,' Nicholas protested mildly, 'is directly useful.'

'Exactly!' exclaimed Micklethrust. 'Precisely! Think of all that knowledge in all those old books being sold off. It's not their authors or readers but people like you and me and Tipster who are profiting from it.'

The journey was a very short one. They had arrived at the skyscraper housing the Stock Exchange. Nicholas followed

Micklethrust through the huge glass doors into the crowded entrance hall, past a reception desk, where Micklethrust presented his identity badge and secured Nicholas a day pass, and then up to the tenth floor where he secured him another pass for the Commodities Exchange.

'No point your observing the heart of Libertarian life from the visitor's balcony,' he said, 'through a glass darkly. You have to experience it, my friend, at close hand, in the raw!'

As they approached the doorway, Nicholas could hear a wild cacophony of loud, rough male and sharp, piercing female voices. The sound was disturbing, like a ward of violent mental patients out of control.

But his eyes contradicted what his ears had predicted. The floor was carefully organized into different sections, each for a different commodity, within which stood groups of furiously energetic youngish men and women yelling and gesticulating at each other and stepping back every now and then to yell something down a telephone or check something on a nearby computer terminal. Many of the sections were in full cry, but some appeared to be in the pause mode, presumably gearing themselves up for the next yelling session.

Picking their way across the floor, taking care not to disturb either the yellers or the pausers, and avoiding the tangles of telephone and computer wires, Micklethrust led Nicholas to the 'LIBRARIES' section. This was stopped temporarily, and Micklethrust took the opportunity to ask colleagues standing around some urgent questions. He introduced Nicholas to them.

'A friend of Tipster,' he announced, Professor . . . er . . . '

'Pangloss,' said Nicholas.

The dealers nodded towards him and resumed their rapid consultations.

'What did you say you were a professor of?' asked Micklethrust.

'Philosophy, actually,' said Nicholas.

Micklethrust seemed interested. 'D'you want to know my philosophy? I'm an idealist. The world, my friend, is ruled by ideas. Look around you! This is the *Commodities* Exchange, but what are people really exchanging? What are they all shouting about? Expectations! Futures! Derivatives – whatever in the world they are! (He gave Nicholas a wink.) What are they all doing? *Speculating*!

Nicholas overcame the temptation to discuss philosophy with his host and broker. A practical question preoccupied him. 'That is really very interesting,' he said, 'but how have my shares been doing?'

'You are in real luck, my friend,' said Micklethrust, pointing at a screen above them full of figures in rapid movement. 'The Library shares have already quintupled in value. Are you sure you don't want to wait a bit?'

'Quite sure,' said Nicholas.

The pause was over and the yelling began. Micklethrust, he could see, was an accomplished yeller. For all his lambent elegance, he could have been a football coach or a sergeant major. The odd thing was that the yellers seemed to hear and respond to one another, despite the overwhelming din. Micklethrust hastily scribbled something down on a notepad and then resumed his yelling.

When a pause finally came, he turned to Nicholas and slapped him on the back.

'Well, you're on the way to being a rich man, my friend. Just sold thousands – of thousands, that is. Yours included. How and when do you want to be paid?'

'How about in cash and today?' asked Nicholas boldly.

'Why not?' exclaimed Micklethrust, writing him a note to present at his office.

Nicholas thanked him profusely. 'Always willing to oblige a pal of old Tipster's,' said Micklethrust in farewell. 'Don't forget to pay him his commission.'

Nicholas considered this suggestion as he walked back to the broker's office, but decided to reject it. Tipster's tip, he

decided, had been an act of philanthropy of which he would not be the sole beneficiary.

On arrival, he thrust Micklethrust's note into the hands of the cashier, asking to be paid straight away in cash. The cashier indicated that a hefty commission would, of course, be charged. Nicholas asked that the money be divided equally into four small packets.

On returning to his new home, he found that Mia and Aristotle had gone off to get more provisions from the supermarket. Nicholas sat down next to Seneca and addressed him slowly and carefully.

'Now, I know you're against materialism and consumerism,' he said, 'but I want to make you a gift of something you despise. I've just come into some money (Seneca cringed) and I'm proposing to divide it equally between the four of us. After all,' he added, 'it might always come in useful and you've done a lot for me.'

Turning his back to the street, and coming close to Seneca he handed him one of the envelopes. Seneca took it instantly and hid it from view. At that moment, Mia and Aristotle returned laden with provisions.

'I've something for you both,' said Nicholas, handing them the envelopes. 'Seneca will explain.' And so saying, he picked up his travelling bag, now lighter after the theft of his cloak, and walked out of the arch towards the bus station.

He went to a public telephone and telephoned Sam.

'This is Professor Pangloss,' he said, 'I'm so sorry. I won't be able to make it today, or ever.' He thanked Sam for his help and asked him to convey a message to Leon. 'Tell him,' he said, 'that he's given me an idea for the pursuit of my mission. He'll understand.' He hung up.

Next Nicholas went to the information office in the Bus Station and, when it came to his turn, asked which bus went to the northern border of Libertaria.

'You want the number three hundred and sixty to Minerva,' said the information clerk. 'Leaves at midday. Long distance.'

Nicholas went to the ticket office and bought a ticket to Minerva. Then he bought some sandwiches for what was going to be a long journey. The 360 bus stop was set apart from the others at the far end of the station. It was nearly midday. The orange, single-decker bus was waiting, almost empty. Nicholas boarded, stamped his ticket, settled down in his seat and the bus departed.

The landscape became more desolate as they drove northwards. In the distance, Nicholas could see blackened hillsides ruined by opencast coalmining, abandoned pit villages, disused steel mills. They passed towns that had been centres of manufacturing and local civic pride but were now run down and dilapidated and surrounded by an unregulated suburban sprawl. He saw miserable-looking housing estates, grey tenement blocks with shattered windows built around narrow streets in which apparently unemployed youths were roaming. All along the motorway there were glossy advertisements, but they did not seem to be addressed to the inhabitants of this once industrialized landscape.

·29·

On the Road

It was early evening when they arrived in Minerva. The bus pulled up in the central town square – a large desolate area surrounded by darkened shop fronts, a hotel, a church, the town hall and a café called 'THE HEGEL CAFE'. Sunset was late in coming. It had evidently been a hot sunny day and the air was heavy and sultry. In the middle of the square was a large fountain surmounted by a statue of a goddesslike figure wearing a helmet but there was no water. The statue's pedestal and the large, low, round bowl of the fountain were long encrusted with the greens, yellows and greys of moss and lichen. The square was empty save for a stray black cat walking slowly and purposefully across it. The shops were closed and there was no-one about. Nicholas walked across to the café and sat down at a table, putting his travelling bag on the seat beside him. The café was empty except for two elderly men, drinking and chatting at a table next to the window, who were observing him with mild interest.

The waitress, a plump platinum blonde wearing a frilly apron, approached.

'What do you have to eat?' he asked

'Would you like an omelette?' she suggested.

An omelette! When poor, exhausted Condorcet was on the

run, condemned to death by the Jacobin Dictatorship of Virtue after being denied refuge by his old friends the Suards out of fear for themselves, he had entered an inn at Clamart and asked for an omelette. 'How many eggs?' the innkeeper had asked. After some hesitation, Condorcet had replied, 'A dozen', thereby confirming the innkeeper's suspicion that – despite the strange tattered clothes, the grizzly stubble and bandaged leg – this vagabond was an aristocrat. Two men lunching at the inn had immediately denounced him to the local committee of surveillance who interrogated him in the local church. Within two days he was dead, lying on the ground, his arms alongside his body, in the small dingy municipal prison for thieves and beggars, before he could even be transported to Paris to be guillotined. While in hiding, he had just completed his *Sketch for a Historical Picture of the Progress of the Human Mind*, the Enlightenment's most optimistic work. Nicholas called to mind its concluding sentence. The contemplation of the future, Condorcet had written, was a consolation to the philosopher:

> That contemplation is for him a refuge, where the memory of his persecutors cannot pursue him: where, living in thought with human beings restored to their rights and the dignity of their nature, he forgets human beings as they are, tormented and corrupted by greed, fear and envy; it is there that he truly exists together with his fellow beings, in an Elysium that his reason has been able to create and that his love for humanity embellishes with the purest joys.

'Alright,' he said, 'I'll have an omelette.'

He opened his bag, took out some notepaper and started to write:

The Town Square, Minerva, Libertaria

Dear Justin,

I am writing you this from the northern frontier of Libertaria on the eve of yet another journey into the unknown. My life in Freedom here was not a happy experience and I definitely

wouldn't want to make this country my home, or try to convince Marcus and Eliza to come and live here.

I do not want to mislead you. Life in Freedom was undoubtedly free in several very important ways. I wasn't arrested or informed upon or harassed by policemen or soldiers and I wasn't imprisoned. I was free from the results of the calculations of benevolent experts and planners and I was free from the pressure of other people's ideas about how one should live. I was, to put it bluntly, left alone. So was pretty well everyone else I encountered in Freedom.

But were we really free? Nicholas asked himself. Karl and Fred would have laughed heartily at the very suggestion, but he decided not to mention this to Justin who, he was sure, did not want to hear about them or about his dreams. We weren't, he reflected, *unfree*, even under the railway arch: no-one was ordered or compelled or forced to go and live there. But were we free?

What, after all (he continued his letter to Justin in professorial style), is it to be free? Is it just to be left alone: not to be ordered or compelled or forced or bullied or harassed or bothered or interfered with by others? Or is it all these because of something more basic? Isn't what is basic to be allowed to live the life one chooses and finds worth living? But if that's the basis of freedom, then being left alone can't be all there is to it. At the very least, there must *be* choices – choices worth choosing.

As the waitress brought him his omelette, Nicholas thought of his fellow porters and of his fellow dwellers under the railway arch, of Leon and of the man with the suitcase by the bus stop. Judging by what Leon had told him, that man had little chance of finding anything but the most menial job at the lowest possible pay, and little chance of that. He was of course free to choose which wall to sit on, or whether to sit or stand or lie down, or whether to beg or not. A Libertarian would say that he was as free as Osgood Micklethrust.

You remember that I am concerned to give sound advice to a wise and discriminating but ignorant embryo who doesn't know at which place in the social order it will emerge (or indeed what its sex or colour or creed will be). It will want to know where its chances of being able to choose a life worth living are best. The society in which it decides to be born will have to reassure it on several points. First, there will have to be a social framework: of order, civil peace, mutual predictability, the rule of law. Second, there must be social provision: at least the security of a guaranteed basic minimum of basic resources on which it can rely and at best a just system of rewards that ensures that the least well off are as well off as they can be. And third, there will need to be a rich and varied social context of different practices and traditions valued for their own sakes, providing alternative forms of fulfilment, not just alternative ways of making and spending money. I'm afraid that I would have to tell the embryo that in respect of all three points Libertaria is a disaster area.

So it's time to move on again. But where to? Where do we – the embryo and I – have the best prospects? Actually, it occurs to me that our points of view are converging, the embryo's and mine, for who knows where I shall end up? I've heard of somewhere that is supposed to be near here, though no-one seems quite sure. I hope to have more to tell you before too long.

Love, as always, to my two children whom I think of often.

Yours ever,
Pangloss

Nicholas folded up the letter and put it in an envelope for future posting. He finished eating his omelette and, summoning the waitress, paid his bill. Then he took up his bag and approached the two men by the window. One of them was reading a newspaper, Nicholas noticed the head-line: 'OUR WILD LIFE GOES FREE! LIBERTARIAS'S FORESTS PRIVATIZED'. Underneath was a picture of an exultant Jugula Hildebrand.

'Excuse me, I'm sorry to interrupt you,' he said, 'but would you be kind enough to tell me which road I take for the border?'

One of the men pointed to the opposite right-hand corner of the square.

'You take the road there,' he said. 'On foot are you?'

Nicholas nodded. The man looked surprised.

'Well, if you want to *walk* there, it's quite a way from here. What are you proposing to do when you get there?'

'I'm on a walking tour,' Nicholas answered.

'Off to Egalitaria are you' said the other man in what sounded like a mocking tone.

Nicholas thanked them and left the restaurant.

'Have a good trip!' shouted the second man. It seemed to him that the two of them were laughing.

He crossed the square, passing the black cat, dropped the letter in a letter box and started to walk along the road. He seemed to have reached the town's limits and was soon in open country, descending a hill with a wood at the bottom. There were fields and trees on either side and blue-grey hills in the distance. His bag, though lighter, started to weigh him down like a burden. It had travelling straps and he attached it to his back.

As he approached the bottom of the hill, he suddenly heard a loud fluttering near his head. He looked up and around him but could see nothing. Then, looking down, he saw a large, beautiful white snowy owl walking along the road beside him. But the strangest thing was that it was walking forwards with its head swivelled backwards, looking over its shoulder with its round, glistening, wide-open eyes firmly set in the direction from which he had come.

The sun was beginning to set. It lent a golden sheen to the blue-grey hills in the distance.

Then, out of the silence, a thin, rasping voice said: 'You've come a long way, Professor Caritat.'

Nicholas stopped and looked around. The owl also stopped.

There was no-one to be seen. Oh dear! he thought, I am start-ing to hear voices.

Then he heard the voice again. 'It is supposed to be polite,' it said 'to respond when one is spoken to.'

He looked around once more. He was quite alone. Then he noticed that the owl was looking at him, as if expectantly, its head cocked on one side.

'I'm sorry,' he said.

The owl started to walk, still looking backwards, its eyes directed at Nicholas. Nicholas followed. They were heading for the wood directly in front of them. As they entered it, the golden sunlight vanished and the lonely silence of the road was shattered by a plangent hubbub of birdsong all around them, a polyphonic din of chirruping, clacking, crowing, cooing, peeping, hooting and twittering that seemed relentless and inescapable. The wood was dark and the straight path on which they had been travelling was lost. Nicholas felt fearful. The wood seemed threatening and oppressive, savage, harsh and dense, but he kept his eye on the sure-footed owl marching straight in front of him through the towering trees.

Suddenly, Nicholas noticed something else; the unmis-takable sound of human voices, shouting nearby, calling to one another, some of them singing. In the darkness there was no-one to be seen. Then he looked upwards and saw an astonishing sight. There were scores of young people high up in the trees. Some were sitting on branches, others lying in hammocks slung across them, others looking out of makeshift tree-houses high above his head. Others moved precariously along multiple thick branches that bridged the tree-houses, like the medieval inhabitants of high tower-houses defending their aerial city. Young men and women dressed in slacks and sweaters who were full of good humour but also, it seemed, agitated and even angry about something.

'Can you tell me what they are all doing?' he asked the owl.

'They are occupying our branches,' said the owl rather crossly. 'On the other hand, they are trying to save our trees.'

'From whom?' Nicholas asked.

'Listen!' said the owl.

Nicholas strained his ears and heard a low rumbling roar in the distance.

'Bulldozers,' said the owl. 'Property developers. Our home is to be "developed".'

'Can they help save it?' Nicholas asked the owl, but the owl remained silent. So Leon had been wrong: protest still survived in Libertaria. Peering through the trees as they walked, he could just make out a large orange bulldozer manned by two men in yellow helmets. It was slowly approaching the wood. The young people above him had started to sing in unison. One of them called down to him to come up and join them. He considered the idea but, seriously doubting his ability to shin up the tree, he waved and, shouting a word of encouragement, continued to follow the owl which was proceeding towards a source of light. It was the edge of the wood, from which they soon emerged.

They were now walking westwards into the setting sun.

'Don't those bluish hills in front of us look beautiful against the reddish-gold of the sky!' Nicholas remarked.

The owl went on walking forwards and looking backwards. 'I couldn't say,' said the owl. As it spoke, its hooked beak snapped open and shut, revealing an inverted acute triangle of bright pink tongue. 'I have limited vision. Not only do I see in one direction only; I am also colour-blind. I see only grey on grey.'

'Isn't that rather inconvenient?' asked Nicholas.

'Not at all,' said the owl. 'It helps concentrate the mind on what is really important.'

'What's that?' Nicholas asked.

'Grasping the meaning of things past,' replied the owl.

Nicholas wanted to ask the owl to interpret the meaning of his recent past, but the owl spoke again before he could pose the question.

'It is, in fact, humans who have truly limited vision,' it remarked.

'How so?' asked Nicholas.

'You are unable to see more than one thing at a time and you find the greatest difficulty in seeing the interconnections between things. You fail to see that nature has linked human ideals together in an indissoluble chain.'

'How do you mean?' Nicholas asked the owl.

'Consider the countries you have visited, all of which you have left behind. Each was devoted to the pursuit of a worthy objective: one to ensuring order and security, another to maximizing welfare and happiness, another to securing stable identities where people feel at home with others of their kind, another to the delirious vision of real individual freedom in harmony with all others, another to the protecting of individuals and their property from interference to live as they choose. Yet each pursued its favoured goal to the exclusion of the others and in the process sacrificed countless individual humans at the altar of its abstract ideal. How many human lives have been ruined and destroyed in the name of such ideals? What human folly!'

'What,' Nicholas asked, 'is the alternative?'

'Only connect!' replied the owl. 'The alternative is to see that none of these ideals is worth anything without the others. Only then will you create a world fit for humans, and also,' he added as if as an afterthought, 'for owls.'

They walked on. Nicholas pondered the owl's remarks. Surely the owl was badly mistaken? How could all these ideals be jointly realized in the same society? Pursuing one excludes pursuing others. Everything is what it is and not another thing. Not all good things come together. Wasn't it the supreme human folly to suppose that they do: to aim at perfection and try to bring into being a harmonious world in which all human goals are realized together? Surely that hope was the most dangerous illusion of our time?

Nicholas wanted to discuss these points with the owl, but the owl seemed to be in a hurry and disinclined to engage in debate.

'What I really want to know,' he asked the owl, 'is whether the world fit for humans – and owls – of which you speak, is possible. Is it called Egalitaria? Does it lie ahead of us?'

Dusk was falling. At Nicholas's words, the owl became aroused, winked an eye, spread its wings, let forth a piercing scream and soared upwards into the darkening sky.

Nicholas walked on. The night was drawing in and the burden on his back was getting heavier. After a while, in the distance, he saw a solitary building. As he drew near, he saw that it was a customs post. No-one, however, was to be seen: the placed looked deserted, although there was a light on. As he came up, he noticed that someone had scrawled a message on the wall below the light which read: 'HANG ON TO HOPE ALL YE WHO EXIT HERE'.

He sat down on the ground by the wall, opened his travelling bag and pulled out his remaining notepaper and wrote another letter:

Northern border, Libertaria

Dear Justin, Marcus and Eliza,

Two rather odd events have just occurred. First, I met a bird with which I had a conversation. Then I saw some people living in trees. On reading this, you will probably conclude that I have become deranged, but I beg you to read on since each of these events has taught me something that might be of interest to you.

First the bird. It was an owl, the owl of Minerva, and it was certainly wise, as owls are generally supposed to be. It knew all about my travels and interpreted the meaning of them up to now, by quoting Condorcet's observation that human ideals are linked together in an indissoluble chain. But it gave a meaning to that observation that I had never thought of before. I had always thought of it as expressing what was excessive, even dangerous about the optimism of the Enlightenment: the dream of perfection, in which truth, happiness and virtue would all coincide and there would be no more conflicts between values, no more moral dilemmas, no more clashes between right and

right, no more tragedy. The dream of a world in which political equality and economic growth and efficient organization and social justice are all compatible with one another and with universal individual liberty; in which universalism no longer conflicts with particularity, or solidarity with individuality, or public with private loyalties. A world in which pursuing one worthy human ideal no longer means sacrificing others. Did not the pursuit of such all-embracing, all-reconciling perfection here on earth lead to the Dictatorship of Virtue which killed Condorcet himself? For how much death and destruction has it been responsible ever since, above all in this terrible century? Has the dream not turned into a nightmare?

And yet, one must ask, does this hope really have such deadly power – more deadly than the otherwordly and atavistic faiths against which it was pitched? Isn't fanaticism a human trait that will seize on whatever ideas are at hand in pursuit of its victims?

But the meaning the owl gave to the indissoluble chain was altogether different: the simple idea that, whenever we pursue one ideal, it is disastrous to lose sight of all the others. Doing *that* is fanaticism. All the countries I have so far visited are run by fanatics with tunnel vision, fanatics obsessed with a single overriding, all-consuming conception of what gives value to life. They all *know* why the best possible world must be theirs. They and their fellow citizens are all victims of the same illusion. Even the few dissenters I came across seemed to have difficulty in thinking for themselves and seeing through it.

Which brings me to the people in the trees. I saw them as I came through a dark wood with the owl, living in hammocks and tree-houses and singing. They are resisting fanaticism, not just by thinking for themselves but by acting. They are defending the trees against bulldozers. But they are also defending a space for freedom against private property fanatics and thereby contradicting the Libertarian view of what freedom is. They are defending themselves and their futures and the owl and its future. They are also acting together, resisting together, in a state which discourages collective action. They asked me to join them and I must tell you I was very tempted but climbing up a tree was beyond me.

In the course of my travels, I have thought about all three of you a great deal. I did so again while in the wood. I am quite sure that if you had been living here in Libertaria, you would have been up those trees. So would many, many more people of your generation, if only they understood how people's lives get narrowed and distorted by fanatics. YOU ARE OUR ONLY HOPE!

When will we see one another again? I don't know. As Justin will be the first to point out, I have a mission to accomplish. But how will I know when I have done so? I think I am now a little bit clearer about that. One thing I have learnt is that whenever people assure me that my mission is over, I know my journey must continue. Another thing I have noticed is that almost everyone I have so far met seems to have stopped learning. They seem as if trapped in their language and their world and quite closed to one another's. Without meaning to, they have taught me to think again about how to recognize the enemies of an open society.

I am sure you remember the fable of the peasant who on his death-bed tells his sons there is a treasure buried in the garden. The old man dies and the sons dig everywhere but do not find it. There is no treasure, but their labour improves the soil and secures their well-being. In cultivating their garden, they tend its existing roots and attend to the flourishing of its luxuriant vegetation. But can it all flourish equally? An unweeded garden grows to seed; yet since the Enlightenment we know that there is no basis in reason or in nature for treating some plants as weeds.

<div align="center">

Love and best wishes,
Nicholas

</div>

He looked into the distance, where the hills were disappearing into the night sky. The road along which he was walking led onwards to a crossroads from which several roads extended – but how far they extended he could not see. Some seemed to peter out, others to wind and weave uncertainly forward but then disappear, others to double back. It was quite unclear which he should take. The light was fading fast.

Peering hard, he thought he could see twinkling lights ahead in the middle distance. Perhaps it was an inn or a hostelry at which he could put down his burden and rest for the night, before continuing on his way.